# NATIONS OF THE MODERN WORLD

ARGENTINA
    H. S. Ferns
    *Professor of Political Science,*
    *University of Birmingham*

AUSTRALIA
    O. H. K. Spate
    *Director, Research School of Pacific Studies,*
    *Australian National University, Canberra*

AUSTRIA
    Karl R. Stadler
    *Professor of Modern and Contemporary History,*
    *University of Linz*

BELGIUM
    Vernon Mallinson
    *Professor of Comparative Education,*
    *University of Reading*

BURMA
    F. S. V. Donnison
    *Formerly Chief Secretary to the Government of Burma*
    *Historian, Cabinet Office, Historical Section 1949–66*

CEYLON
    S. A. Pakeman
    *Formerly Professor of Modern History*
    *Ceylon University College*
    *—Appointed Member, House of Representatives,*
    *Ceylon, 1947–52*

CYPRUS
    H. D. Purcell
    *Professor of English,*
    *University of Libya, Benghazi*

DENMARK
    W. Glyn Jones
    *Reader in Danish, University College London*

MODERN EGYPT
    Tom Little
    *Former Managing Director and General Manager of*
    *Regional News Services (Middle East), Ltd, London*

EL SALVADOR
    Alastair White
    *Lecturer in Sociology,*
    *University of Stirling*

| | |
|---|---|
| ENGLAND<br>A Portrait | John Bowle<br>*Formerly Professor of Political Theory, Collège d'Europe,*<br>*Bruges 1950–67* |
| FINLAND | W. R. Mead<br>*Professor of Geography, University College London* |
| EAST<br>  GERMANY | David Childs<br>*Lecturer in Politics, University of Nottingham* |
| WEST<br>  GERMANY | Michael Balfour<br>*Professor of European History, University of East Anglia* |
| MODERN<br>  GREECE | John Campbell<br>*Fellow of St Antony's College, Oxford* |
| | Philip Sherrard<br>*Lecturer in the History of the Orthodox Church,*<br>*King's College, London* |
| HUNGARY | Paul Ignotus<br>*Formerly Hungarian Press Counsellor, London, 1947–49, and*<br>*Member, Presidential Board, Hungarian Writers' Association* |
| MODERN INDIA | Sir Percival Griffiths<br>*President India, Pakistan and Burma Association* |
| ITALY | Muriel Grindrod<br>*Formerly Editor of* International Affairs *and*<br>The World Today<br>*Assistant Editor* The Annual Register |
| JAPAN | Sir Esler Dening<br>*H. M. Ambassador to Japan, 1952–57* |
| KENYA | A. Marshall MacPhee<br>*Formerly Managing Editor with*<br>*the* East African Standard *Group* |
| LIBYA | John Wright<br>*Formerly of the* Sunday Ghibli, *Tripoli* |
| MALAYSIA | J. M. Gullick<br>*Formerly of the Malayan Civil Service* |
| MEXICO | Peter Calvert<br>*Lecturer in Politics,*<br>*University of Southampton* |

| | |
|---|---|
| MOROCCO | Mark I. Cohen<br>*Director of Taxation, American Express*<br><br>Lorna Hahn<br>*Professor of African Studies, American University* |
| NORWAY | Ronald G. Popperwell<br>*Fellow of Clare Hall and Lecturer in Norwegian,*<br>*Cambridge* |
| PAKISTAN | Ian Stephens<br>*Formerly Editor of* The Statesman,<br>*Calcutta and Delhi, 1942–51*<br>*Fellow, King's College, Cambridge, 1952–58* |
| PERU | Sir Robert Marett<br>*H.M. Ambassador in Lima 1963–67* |
| POLAND | Václav L. Beneš<br>*Professor of Political Science,*<br>*Indiana University*<br><br>Norman J. G. Pounds<br>*Professor of History and Geography,*<br>*Indiana University* |
| SOUTH AFRICA | John Cope<br>*Formerly Editor-in-Chief of* The Forum *and South*<br>*Africa Correspondent of* The Guardian |
| THE SOVIET<br>UNION | Elisabeth Koutaissoff<br>*Professor of Russian,*<br>*Victoria University, Wellington* |
| SPAIN | George Hills<br>*Formerly Correspondent and Spanish Programme Organizer,*<br>*British Broadcasting Corporation* |
| SWEDEN | Irene Scobbie<br>*Senior Lecturer in Swedish,*<br>*University of Aberdeen* |
| SYRIA | Tabitha Petran |
| TURKEY | Geoffrey Lewis<br>*Senior Lecturer in Islamic Studies, Oxford* |
| YUGOSLAVIA | Stevan K. Pavlowitch<br>*Lecturer in Balkan History, University of*<br>*Southampton* |

# EL SALVADOR

# EL SALVADOR

*By*
ALASTAIR WHITE

PRAEGER PUBLISHERS
New York · Washington

BOOKS THAT MATTER

Published in the United States of America in 1973
by Praeger Publishers, Inc.
111 Fourth Avenue, New York, N.Y. 10003

Library of Congress Cataloging in Publication Data

White, Alastair.
  El Salvador. *see slip*

  (Nations of the modern world)
  1.  Salvador.  I.  Title.
F1483.W47   972.84   72-93302

Printed in Great Britain

*La princesa está triste . . . ¿Qué tendrá la princesa?*
RUBÉN DARÍO


# TO THE POOR PEOPLE OF EL SALVADOR


*Con los pobres de la tierra*
*Quiero yo mi suerte echar.*

JOSÉ MARTÍ

# Foreword

FOR MAKING POSSIBLE three periods of residence in El Salvador (June–September 1965, February 1966–January 1967, and October 1970–January 1971) I am indebted to a number of institutions, including the Universities of Cambridge, Texas, and Stirling, the Nuffield Foundation, and the Carnegie Trust for the Universities of Scotland.

I owe a great debt to several hundred people in El Salvador who have answered my questions, and to several dozen who have done more; it would be impracticable to name all, even of these. My thanks to individuals go particularly to Sra Francisca Valle de Hernández and her husband Sr Pablo Hernández; to Sr Anthony Gregg and to his father Mr Robert Gregg; to Srta Cristina Palacios; to Sr Uriel Valencia; to Dr Rafael Menjívar; to Dr David Luna de Sola; to Sr Julio César Castro Belloso; and to Compañero Roque Dalton.

I also owe a great deal to my wife Ljiljana, who has contributed to the formation of the ideas contained herein, who accompanied me on the two earlier visits to El Salvador, helping in the collection of information, and who has shown great forbearance over the claim on my time which this book has entailed in its preparation; and to my father, H. Stanley White, who has helped with archival research in London.

*Stirling*                                                           A.T.W.
*January 1973*

# Contents

# List of Illustrations

# Maps

# Acknowledgements

ACKNOWLEDGEMENT for kind permission to reproduce illustrations is made to the following, to whom the copyright of the illustrations belongs:

Casa Presidencial, San Salvador: 7, 8, 11, 12
*El Independiente*, San Salvador: 15
Instituto Salvadoreño de Turismo: 14, 23, 25, 26
*La Prensa Gráfica*, San Salvador: 2, 3, 4, 5, 6
Percy F. Martin, *Salvador of the Twentieth Century* (London, 1911): 1
Ministry of Foreign Affairs, San Salvador: 16, 29
Nos. 9, 10, 13, 17, 18, 19, 20, 21, 22, 24, 27, 28, 30, 31, and 32 are from the author's own collection

# Historical Background: Spanish Colony

EL SALVADOR IS SIMILAR both in size and in population to Wales.[1] But that is where the similarity stops, for the high density of population in El Salvador is due to the fertility of the soil and the lack of high mountains, not to the development of mining or industry on a large scale in any region. The dense population is spread fairly evenly throughout the territory.

El Salvador is the smallest country on the mainland of the American continent at 8,259 square miles; the most densely populated (estimated to reach 4 million in 1975); the only country north of Ecuador which lacks an Atlantic coast; and finally, it is also exceptional in that all its Indians are virtually completely assimilated and there are no ethnic or racial minorities. One would have to go as far as Uruguay to find another country as homogeneous racially and culturally.

The high population is a result of geography. The country covers only the foothills of the Central American mountain chain on the Pacific side: the higher slopes, and the continental divide, fall entirely to the north, in Honduras. On the other hand, only a small part of Salvadorean territory, less than a fifth, is hot coastal plain, which was prone to malaria particularly before recent medical advances. This compares with a much higher proportion of such unhealthy areas in neighbouring countries with their low, humid Atlantic coastal plains. Most of El Salvador is relatively comfortably situated neither at sea level nor on the unproductive uplands of the mountain chain. A dense population can be supported on maize, which has been the staple crop of the whole region since agriculture began there more than two thousand years ago. Maize may, in fact, have been first developed in this area, independent of any other centre of agriculture.

Geography has also played an important part in the assimilation of all Indian tribes into the Spanish American culture: there were no regions so remote or so unpleasant to live in as to discourage the Spaniards from going there.

The country is situated along a fault in the Earth's crust, where according to the now generally accepted 'plate theory', two plates of the crust meet, and where the western, East Pacific, plate is shifting slowly but inexorably south-east and is being overridden by the Southern Caribbean plate. The conjunction of these two enormous pieces of crust here is doubtless the cause of the very existence of the isthmus of Central America connecting North to South America, and hence of the territory of El Salvador. But to the inhabitants it appears as a curse, for it means frequent violent earthquakes as well as volcanic activity. All is well where the crusts can shift sideways relative to one another smoothly and gradually along the fault, but wherever there is a hindrance and movement is held back for a few years or decades, then when the force does eventually become great enough to overcome the obstacle, it produces the kind of earthquake that ruined San Francisco (on an extension of the same fault line) in 1905 and hit San Salvador in 1575, 1594, 1671, 1719, 1798, 1806, 1815, 1839, 1854, 1873, 1917, and most recently on 3 May 1965. It also gave El Salvador one of the world's newest mountains, the volcano of Izalco, in the eighteenth century.[2]

Just as El Salvador's position is literally peripheral to two plates of the Earth's crust, historically it has also proved somewhat peripheral, first to the great pre-Columban civilizations and then to the Spanish Empire. Except within the narrow context of Central America, the country could still be said to occupy this periphery.

## Pre-Columban Civilization

In the western part of El Salvador's territory there are monumental pyramids dating from the flowering of Maya civilization, from fifteen to five centuries before the arrival of the Spaniards. But they are small relative to the centres of that civilization, which were in highland Guatemala and just across the present boundary in Honduran territory. The centre of Maya culture later shifted further away to the north, the Yucatán peninsula, and before the arrival of the Spaniards the Maya were almost entirely replaced in the western part of El Salvador by Náhuatl-speaking – 'Aztec' – people from the Mexican highlands beyond Guatemala. These, whose local name is Pipil, were the Indians whom the Spanish conquerors encountered in the western part of the territory, and who are best remembered today. They possessed urban centres of considerable size, perhaps up to 10,000 population, of which one, Cuscatlán, was located near to or overlapping with the present capital. They resisted the Spanish invasion, and the reputed leader of this resistance, Atlacatl, is now accorded more honour than the Spanish leader Pedro de Alvarado, in the same way but not to the same degree that in Mexico Cuauhtémoc is preferred to Cortés. The place-name Cuscatlán still designates, as Antiguo Cuscatlán, a small village now standing on part of the former city, perhaps its centre; but it is also used as the official name for one of the fourteen departments, the administrative divisions of the country, and as an affectionate name for the country as a whole: and Salvadoreans refer to themselves also as *cuscatlecos*. The Indian heritage is in general appreciated and emphasized, particularly in schools; but not insisted upon fanatically.

The Pipil branch of Aztec civilization did not, however, extend throughout the territory of what is now El Salvador, but only about as far to the east as the Lempa River, the country's biggest river. Beyond this river the main language group was the Lenca, related to the Maya but without their advanced civilization or monuments. It appears that while the Pipil centre at Cuscatlán held sway over a fairly wide area, the Lenca had no such mini-states, but were composed of a large number of autonomous local groups. The same is probably true of four other Indian groups who occupied parts of what is now Salvadorean territory, although their main areas of settlement were in Guatemala, Honduras, or Nicaragua: these were the Jinca, Pokomam, Chortí, and Matagalpa.

All these Indians lived principally by agriculture based on maize, which could support a dense population without such technological advances as the plough, the wheel, or draught animals. Other plants domesticated in the area included beans, chili peppers, and squashes; cocoa; tobacco; and cotton; while honey and wax were produced. There was a system of markets using the cocoa bean as currency.[3]

It is not known for certain to what extent authority was centralized among the Pipil. They certainly had a hierarchy of religious officials who exercised considerable influence which they reinforced by presiding over ceremonies involving human sacrifice.[4] This, at any rate, is asserted and described by the Spanish official García del Palacio, writing to King Philip II in 1576. He may perhaps be suspected of sharing a Spanish bias against the pagan priests. There were also secular chiefs and 'captains'. These were presumably more than simply war-leaders, voluntarily obeyed at time of crisis, since García del Palacio says that 'those who were not suitable for war cultivated the lands of the chief and of the priests', and that the chiefs, on their death, were succeeded by a son or a daughter, or failing them, a brother or another relative. We can assume that families were grouped in clans, *calpulli*, though how significant these were in urban centres, and indeed whether there were many people in these centres who were not engaged in agriculture on the surrounding land, we do not know. The *calpulli* had its headman, but his authority presumably rested on voluntary acceptance and not force, as was probably also true of the headmen of the Lenca and other tribes.

Like other Indians of the North American continent, they made

pottery without the aid of the potter's wheel, and wove cloth, but it
seems likely that these were tasks for the cultivator or his womenfolk
in the periods when agricultural work was not needed, rather than
specialist occupations. The Pipil may have had specialist merchants
as well as specialist priests, assistants to priests, and probably a
retinue of semi-permanent soldiers around the ruler. To what extent
there were gradations of commoner, serf, slave, and so on, as in the
Aztec civilization proper, is unclear: there was probably just one
position to which a man could fall, below that of clan member with
full rights. Even the latter had to contribute to the upkeep of soldiers
from the produce of their own gardens as well as working together
on the lands of the chiefs and priests. When García del Palacio
mentions a feast given by the chief, he says that the captains and
priests were invited but does not mention the commoners, so evidently
the chiefs and priests were to some degree privileged.

It seems that the Pipil were divided politically into two or three
mini-states and some smaller units. The larger territories were those
of Cuscatlán and Los Izalcos, each of about 700 or 800 square miles,
and Los Nonualcos, perhaps more loosely held together, of about
400 square miles. The smaller units covered from one to three villages
each, with areas not exceeding 50 square miles.[5] Los Izalcos was
expanding to the north near the present border with Guatemala and
displacing or absorbing Pokomam-speaking (Maya) groups. Other
Pipil were expanding to the east across the Lempa River, and had
conquered Chinameca, which is 15 miles beyond that river into
Lenca territory.[6] This means that the Pipil were in control of about
three-quarters of the territory of the present republic, a position akin
to that of their Aztec cousins in Mexico, though on a far smaller
scale. The fact that El Salvador shares with Mexico a similar heritage
of cultures, on the indigenous as well as on the Spanish side, is
remembered at least in El Salvador and is sometimes thought to
produce a special feeling of kinship between the two countries not
shared by Guatemala with its overwhelmingly Maya origins. One
must say at once, though, that this putative kinship is overshadowed
by the rhetoric of Central American unity, which excludes Mexico.

The Pipil are supposed to have come from Mexico to found Los
Izalcos and Cuscatlán in the year 1054, led by a Toltec prince after
his defeat in a bloody dispute over dynastic succession. Whatever the
historical status of the date and the story,[7] a migration in the
eleventh century does seem likely. The Maya groups whom they
must have conquered may or may not have been the direct descendants of those who built the pyramids there, but they no longer had
the strong central authority which their ancestors or predecessors
must have had to have built the pyramids.

Warfare was frequent between the various tribes and mini-states before the Spanish Conquest: it was carried on with bows and arrows, spears, and thick bands of cotton to protect the body.[8] Presumably the good land was already somewhat scarce in terms of the slash-and-burn agriculture they practised, in which each piece of land used for one or two years has then to be left for six to ten years to recover its fertility.[9] The whole territory of El Salvador was inhabited by cultivators, except for relatively small areas of mangrove swamp, some other very low-lying districts, and higher mountain slopes. The densest concentration, as today, was in the network of valleys which form, roughly, a band across the middle of the country parallel to the sea coast but higher than the coastal plain and separated from it by hills.[10] To the north of this belt, the country tends to become more broken by hills, and less fertile, as the border with Honduras is approached.

## Spanish Conquest

The first Spaniards to see Salvadorean territory, in 1522, were a group who sailed from the Pacific coast of Panamá with the intention of going to the Spice Islands: it was one of the Spanish aims ever since Columbus's first voyage to break the Portuguese monopoly on trade with these Indonesian islands by sailing straight there, but it seems they did not realize how far it was. The group in question found their ships were damaged and gave up the attempt, exploring the southern coast of Central America instead, in search of gold, and reaching as far as the Bay of Fonseca which separates El Salvador from Nicaragua. They gave the name Fonseca to the Bay after Bishop Fonseca, President of the Council of the Indies in Madrid and protector of the leader of this expedition.[11] No attempt was made by this expedition to conquer the Indians around the bay: they had already run into difficulties trying to subdue a tribe further east.

The next Spaniards to arrive came overland from the other direction, Mexico and Guatemala, in 1524, and with the full intention of adding the region to their conquests. This was only seven years since Francisco Hernández de Córdoba's first expedition to the Mexican coast in 1517, five years since Hernán Cortés first set foot on Mexican soil, and three years since he completed the overthrow of the Aztec Empire. The speed was in part due to the search for a possible channel through to the Pacific, which could only be shown not to exist by travelling overland all the way through the Central American Isthmus; and to competition between the *conquistadores* based in Mexico, led by Cortés, and those based in Panamá, led by Pedrarias Dávila.[12] Here again, El Salvador proved to be on the periphery, for before Pedro de Alvarado and his men from Mexico, sent by Cortés, could consolidate their conquest of Pipil territory west of the Lempa, an overland expedition under Martín de Estete, from the Pedrarias camp, became the first to win the part of El Salvador east of the Lempa, the province which became known as Chaparrastique, where the Lenca predominated. The encounter between the two groups was not friendly.

Thus, the arrival of the Spaniards led straight away to two parallel struggles: one, which lasted fifteen to twenty-five years, between the Spaniards and the Indians who resisted them, and another lasting six years, between the two rival parties of Spaniards. The first was fought out with arms, the Spaniards enjoying the advantages of vastly superior weaponry – horses, guns – and of having made allies of defeated tribes in Mexico and Guatemala, so that there was no occasion when they did not have numbers of Indians on their side as well as against them. The advantages held by the Indians of El Salvador were numerical superiority and knowledge of the terrain; and they could expect to be able to win over at least some of the Spaniards' allies, especially if ever their cause should appear likely to succeed. They too made use of alliances, though these were always made more difficult by old enmities, and probably also by poor communications and perhaps by the basic ethnic division between the Indians of the Mayan and Náhuatl language groups. One more effective alliance was reached in Guatemala, and this aided the Indians of El Salvador by forcing the Spaniards to withdraw all their forces in 1526; but they did not suffer total defeat in Guatemala, and were able after two years to return to El Salvador. Another more effective alliance was formed rather later, in 1537–39, under the leadership of Chief Lempira in Higueras, part of what is now Honduras. This facilitated a revolt in the province of Chaparrastique, which for a time reduced the Spaniards to their one stronghold at San Miguel, and almost succeeded in wiping that out.[13]

In the first phase of the conquest of Salvadorean territory, the Pipil Indians offered open battle on the plain, and were twice thoroughly defeated – killed in large numbers. But this phase lasted only a week, and thereafter their tactics, and those of the Lenca too, were better adapted to their circumstances, and bore some of the characteristics of guerrilla war. Thus after their two victories, near Acajutla and near Sonsonate, Pedro de Alvarado and his party of about a hundred horsemen, 150 Spanish foot-soldiers, and five or six thousand Indian allies, were allowed to proceed to the capital of Cuzcatlán without meeting any further open resistance, but the Pipil soldiers retreated to high ground.[14] The Spaniards stayed seventeen days in Cuzcatlán; then Alvarado decided to return for the time being to Guatemala, and to come back in the dry season which was less favourable to the kind of guerrilla warfare the Indians had now taken up. Years later, Alvarado was accused of having provoked opposition unnecessarily by cruelty and destruction and by taking as slaves even those Indians who had received him in peace. His reply was that he only used methods that were just and necessary to bring the territory under the Spanish crown. He implies that the only men enslaved were those who could be caught after they had retreated to higher ground and so become rebels.[15]

The 1524 expedition did not, however, succeed in putting Los Izalcos and Cuzcatlán under Spanish rule. The following year Pedro de Alvarado sent another expedition, probably under one of his five brothers or cousins who were with him, Gonzalo de Alvarado, who was the first to establish a Spanish settlement on Salvadorean territory, called San Salvador. No account of this expedition has survived, and it is not known exactly when it set out, what opposition it met, or precisely where the settlement was made. Perhaps the Indians merely avoided contact with the intruders, or perhaps they were pacified. Whichever way it was, Pedro de Alvarado was able to make a journey right through El Salvador in 1526 to Choluteca, Honduras, without meeting opposition. On his return, however, he found the Indians up in arms and had to fight several times. This resistance was encouraged by the rebellion led by the Cakchiquel Indians in Guatemala. It led to a withdrawal of all Spaniards from San Salvador and their retrenchment in their Guatemalan base.

The third and ultimately successful attempt to colonize Cuzcatlán from Guatemala came in the early months of 1528 and was apparently led by Diego de Alvarado. After the re-establishment of San Salvador, villages of Indians were assigned to the individual Spanish soldiers if they could pacify them. At first there were no constraints on what they could do in these villages. The pacification appears to have been carried out by the individual Spaniards with the aid of parties of the Indian allies who had been brought from Mexico. At any one time thereafter, it seems that about half the Spanish strength was concentrated in San Salvador – the same was true of San Miguel in its province – while the other half was dispersed over the country. The pattern of resistance, then, was obvious. The Pipil or Lenca would suddenly fall upon an individual Spaniard and his Indian allies – or those who remained loyal to him – in his village; and if these attacks could be concerted and by surprise, then the whole province could rise up simultaneously and attack the Spanish garrison town. This is exactly what happened in San Miguel in 1537; but on other occasions it was not so neat. Soon after the re-establishment of San Salvador in 1528, just one Spaniard was killed as a prelude to an attack on San Salvador, which was beaten

off. Then, as on other occasions, the Indians retreated to the fortified
hill villages which had served them well in inter-tribal warfare.
They could fend off attacks by shooting down arrows and rolling
rocks and boulders. But the *peñoles*, as these villages were called,
could not hold out against Spanish arms, although the account of
what happened on the occasion in question shows that the differences between the antagonists in military effectiveness were not so
very great under these conditions. A number of the Indians who had
been beaten off in their attack on San Salvador took refuge in the
*peñol* of Cinacantlán, which the Spaniards proceeded to attack and
besiege. At first its defenders were successful in repelling the attack;
until, on the inspiration of a Spanish soldier, a movable tower of
wood was constructed which protected the Spanish archers against
the arrows of their enemies and allowed them to shoot at about level
height. This so scared the Indians that they proposed peace talks.
A Spanish leader then negotiated with an Indian leader, with the
result that he and five other Spanish soldiers were allowed to climb
the *peñol* unarmed for further truce talks. But these six Spaniards
carried up concealed weapons and when they got to the top attacked
the Indians on a plan prepared in advance, so that their companions
could quickly follow up in pursuit. Thus victory was achieved by
deceit. They claimed later that the Indians were contemplating
treachery and intended to kill them.[16]

The Indians apparently lacked the co-ordination necessary for
true guerrilla warfare, and there seems to have been no continual
policy of harassment of the Spaniards, although there is a legend that
Atlacatl led an uninterrupted resistance from the mountains for
eight years.[17] However this may be, it seems that the threat of severe
punitive reprisal kept most of the Indians docile most of the time,
and brought the Spaniards fairly quickly after 1528 a position of
good day-by-day security, last interrupted by the major revolt
centred in Higueras in 1537–39. The fact that resistance continued
longer in the areas where the Indians were rather less advanced is
understandable: it was relatively easy for the Spaniards to take over
control of a more sedentary agricultural population, already used to
rule from outside the village.

In the separate struggle between the two groups of *conquistadores*
there was never a battle, but the greater numerical and therefore
military strength of the 'Panamanian' group gave it the upper hand
for a time. The dispute over Salvadorean territory was only a minor
part of a bigger contest over Honduras, which with Higueras was
reckoned a major prize. When in 1523 Hernán Cortés got news in
Mexico that Pedrarias was sending an expedition to Honduras, he
himself decided to send two: one, under Cristóbal de Olid, by sea,

and the other, under Pedro de Alvarado, by land. It was this expedition of Pedro de Alvarado which found itself over-extended in Cuzcatlán in 1524 and returned to Guatemala. Meanwhile, Olid arrived on the north coast of Honduras, but once there declared himself independent of Cortés. To punish him, Cortés first sent another expedition by sea; but, thinking mistakenly that it had failed when he heard it had been shipwrecked on the coast, he then decided to go himself, overland, by a new northern route which turned out to be marshy and very difficult. He arrived after a march lasting over a year, and prepared to conquer Honduras, but soon after his arrival he received news of a rebellion against his authority, encouraged by a rumour that he had perished, in Mexico City itself. Before returning to Mexico to quell the revolt, he sent a letter to Alvarado in Guatemala requiring him to come to meet him on the north coast of Honduras before his departure. This was the reason for Alvarado's march through El Salvador in 1526. When he reached Choluteca in southern Honduras, he found there two groups of Spaniards: the larger one was from Cortés's camp, which told Alvarado that Cortés had already embarked for Mexico; while the smaller was from Pedrarias. There was negotiation over spheres of authority, and according to Bernal Díaz del Castillo, one of Cortés's men present on the occasion who in his old age wrote a history of the Conquest, there was even mention of a marital alliance, presumably between the families of Alvarado and Pedrarias.[18]

Nothing could be resolved, however, and the two groups of Cortés's men marched back together to Guatemala, leaving southern Honduras for the moment in the *de facto* sphere of Panamá. New authorities then entered the scene of contention, in the form of a new governor of Honduras sent from Santo Domingo, and a new governor of Panamá, direct from Spain. Cortés and Alvarado, too, were having serious difficulties in Mexico, as the crown sought to exercise more direct control.

However, for the time being Pedrarias emerged as governor of Nicaragua, while Alvarado was able to return as governor to Guatemala. *Conquistadores* of their kind were still needed, since these territories had not yet been fully pacified. At the end of 1529 or beginning of 1530, before Alvarado was re-established in Guatemala, Pedrarias sent his captain Martín de Estete to San Salvador to claim the whole province as part of Nicaragua.[19] Estete had ninety cavalry and 110 infantry; the lieutenant-governor in San Salvador went with a mere handful of Spaniards to meet him, and they were promptly taken prisoner. Estete then proceeded to San Salvador and tried to persuade the Spaniards there to join him, but they refused, so he set up a rival 'capital' about 10 or 15 miles away, called

Ciudad de los Caballeros. After no more than a few weeks, however, Estete's position became untenable because his own men, knowing the claim of territory beyond the Bay of Fonseca for Nicaragua to be illegal in terms of the agreements reached, and fearful of a clash with forces sent from Guatemala, became less willing to obey his orders. Eventually Estete himself fled back to Nicaragua, while most of his men went over to a small force which was sent from Guatemala.

When Pedro de Alvarado arrived in Guatemala in April 1530, he decided to found a second Spanish town on Salvadorean territory, in the province of Chaparrastique: a centre of operations against the Lenca still necessary in this province, and a border town against further incursions from Nicaragua. The town was, for this latter reason, called San Miguel *de la Frontera*. No further trouble appears to have come from that quarter, although claims upon San Miguel and its province continued to be made by governors of Honduras.

## 'Individual Military Mercantile Capitalism'

The reason why the *conquistadores* were so anxious to incorporate territories into their spheres of authority, although that authority was only temporarily delegated by the crown, had to do with the financing of the Conquest, an operation which might be called individual military mercantile capitalism. The era of mercantile companies directly operating in overseas empires had not yet arrived; the Spanish crown followed a course which maximized its direct control over its new dominions within the limitations imposed by the need to maintain the loyalty and motivation of the soldiers and those imposed by poor communications; while minimizing the cost to itself in financial outlays. Financial receipts came to the crown, in the form of a fifth part of any bullion obtained; the tribute of a percentage of the villages brought under Spanish rule; and gifts by Spanish captains currying favour. The general method for the initial conquest and pacification of a new region was to draw up an agreement with an individual who was made *adelantado*, a title which might be translated as 'pioneer', 'person placed in a forward position'. This was the title held by Pedro de Alvarado in Guatemala during its conquest and that of El Salvador. The crown would contribute perhaps some of the cost of an expedition, when this was necessary to motivate those who would undertake it; but often it was not, because rich rewards were expected in the form of gold obtained in one way or another from the Indians. The *conquistadores* would obtain the finance themselves, using the wealth they had already amassed and obtaining funds from other individuals, particularly those more wealthy and powerful to whom they stood in a relationship of loose interdependence as patron and client. There were no formal companies, just aggregations of personal capital. The ordinary soldiers, too, had to be attracted by the prospect of a share in the spoils, and could not be expected to undertake expeditions holding out no such prospects, unless it was by the longer-term prospect of advantage in loyalty to the commander. If they contributed their own military equipment, particularly a horse, they could expect a larger share of the gain. Individual contributions to victory were also important: they merited larger shares of the Indian tribute exacted later. There was, of course, endless bickering over the merits of individuals, and accusations of favouritism by *adelantados* and later authorities in the handing-out of the tribute Indians.

For it was not the Indians' tribute which was distributed among the victors, at any rate not at first; but the Indians themselves. In the initial period of a conquest (and this was true of both Pedro de Alvarado and Martín de Estete in El Salvador) Indians were captured and taken as slaves. They could be used as carriers on the expedition and then taken back and sold. But the Spanish crown, worried by the annihilation of the population of Hispaniola and Cuba, was insisting that only rebels could be enslaved. This encouraged some commanders to provoke rebellion by cruelty in order to have legal grounds for taking slaves: whether this was done in El Salvador is uncertain: in any case a very broad definition of 'rebellion' could be made.

Formal slavery, however, was far less important in El Salvador than the initial application of the institution called *encomienda*, which meant vastly different things at different times and places. Etymologically, the word denotes that the Indians were 'recommended into the charge' of a Spaniard, and the most consistent but also the most consistently disregarded provision in grants of *encomienda* was that the recipient should instruct his Indians in the Christian faith. Later, *encomienda* would mean only the right to receive from an Indian village a certain amount in tribute, but immediately upon the Conquest, the *conquistadores* were free of real restraint by the distant authority of the crown, and the *encomienda* grants made in San Salvador in 1528 allowed wide powers to the recipients:

By this instrument you, Miguel Díaz, are put in possession of the town of Nahuizalco . . . with its lords and chief men and with all the lands and villages and inhabitants thereof and subject to it, for you to use them in your house and farms, in conformity with the ordinances of New Spain . . .[20]

Few of the *conquistadores*, however, were really interested in

farming and they did not find very much gold or silver on Salvadorean territory. There were no rich mines, luckily for the Salvadorean
Indians, who would have provided the mineworkers. So El Salvador
attracted relatively few Spaniards in this early period, particularly
when, in 1533, Peru was conquered and there were more hopeful
places for the adventurous to move on to. In 1534 Pedro de Alvarado
himself set sail for Peru from the Bay of Fonseca, taking with him,
among others, at least a majority and probably all of the Spanish
inhabitants of San Miguel de la Frontera, which was repopulated a
year or so later.[21]

The Gulf of Fonseca continued to be used for a few years as a port
of embarkation for Peru, but never gained first-class importance,
having neither the advantage of Panamá with its fairly low and
narrow land-crossing, nor that of Acapulco, of directly serving the
capital of the empire at Mexico. There was, then, every opportunity
of leaving El Salvador for more attractive places, and little reason to
remain there. Those who did remain could each enjoy *encomienda*
jurisdiction over several villages of Indians, though it does not appear
that all Spanish soldiers received *encomiendas*. Some were also
supposed to carry on the artisan trades they had had in Spain, and
were threatened with the loss of their *encomiendas* if they did not do
so: it is unclear how much effect this threat had.

The first decade or two after the Conquest were characterized by
a conflict between the *conquistadores* and new authorities sent from
Spain, centring mainly on the degree of exploitation of Indians as a
labour force serving the colonizers. At first, the latter enjoyed the
advantage that the crown still needed them in case of revolt; and
there was the distance of the *encomienda* villages from any agents of
authority, and the possibility that these agents, because of their
distance from Madrid, would be able and willing to allow the
colonizers to go beyond the law in their use of Indian labour. The
crown wanted the *encomenderos* to reside in the Spanish towns,[22] for
the greater safety of these towns and greater control over their
citizens; but many *encomenderos* preferred to live within their *encomienda*,
where they could directly organize Indian labour for their benefit;
royal decreees prohibiting this were largely inoperative. But the
authority of the crown and its more bureaucratic servants became
stabilized within a very few years: the *adelantados* were replaced by
governors, officials, and judges who had taken no part in the
Conquest, while some of the priests who arrived on the scene took it
upon themselves to curb the colonists. The days of conquest were
over while the *conquistadores* were still young men, and they had to
be content to spend the prime of their lives in obscure provinciality:
they took to writing letters complaining that they were living in

poverty, asking for relief on the basis of their services to the crown in the Conquest. Their letters, detailing their services, are one of the main sources of information about the course of the Conquest.

## The Early Export Products

This poverty, however, perhaps only existed in relation to their expectations. Tribute of local food products could maintain an *encomendero* comfortably, though only gold or exportable crops could bring him wealth. Gold was eventually found by the citizens of San Miguel after 1537, and after persistent efforts involving the employment of Spanish miners and the use of gangs of slaves, Indian and African – for the slave trade had already begun – in the search for deposits.[23] This led to relative wealth for the two or three dozen *encomenderos* of San Miguel in the 1540s: one had extracted over 200,000 *pesos* by 1548, and this compares with the mere 400 (or possibly 800) *pesos* which was the annual value of the tribute from the *encomienda* granted to probably the most high-born citizen of San Miguel in the early 1530s.[24]

Cocoa was the most obvious exportable crop. It was already produced for sale by the Indians, and soon became a popular drink among Europeans too – in Europe itself by the end of the sixteenth century. Cocoa beans were therefore made an item of the tribute which villages had to bring to their *encomenderos*. However, the royal authorities prohibited this practice when it became clear that the quantities demanded were excessive,[25] and although the prohibition was presumably of only limited effectiveness, cocoa was mainly produced thereafter by independent Indian villagers who sold it to Spanish traders in the towns. This allowed the Indian villages in the main cocoa-producing areas of Los Izalcos to remain more autonomous until the late eighteenth century, when the cocoa trade died, and may be the reason why the last pockets of Pipil-speakers are still to be found in this region today.[26] Los Izalcos, at first dependent directly on the Guatemalan capital, its villages granted in *encomienda* to residents of Guatemala, not those of San Salvador, was directly settled by Spaniards soon after San Salvador and San Miguel. In 1532, its port of Acajutla was used as the centre of operations against the Pipil who held out against Spanish authority in the nearby Cumbre mountains until the following year.[27] In 1540 Pedro de Alvarado used the port as one of his bases in his plan to set out for the conquest of the Spice Islands.[28] (It was still one of the main objects of the Spanish crown to get there by the westerly route.) He died, however, in 1541, before he could put the plan into operation. Acajutla remained populated by Spaniards, but in 1552 a Spanish town was also founded inland at Sonsonate,[29] as a centre for Spanish traders in cocoa and in balsam, which was produced from the sap of a tree by Indians on the southern slopes of the Cumbre mountains and sold to the Spaniards in the same way as cocoa. 'Balsam of Peru' was and is only produced in this area of El Salvador, and not in Peru: it is used for healing, and in 1562 was adopted also for church ritual in the making of the chrism. Los Izalcos was granted local autonomy from both Guatemala and San Salvador in 1558, as a reflection of the cocoa traders' political victory over the Guatemalan *encomenderos*; it did not join the rest of El Salvador until independence from Spain, in 1824. Cocoa had been grown all over El Salvador before the Conquest, so it appears conceivable that production became concentrated in Los Izalcos only because this was the sole area in which the interests of traders prevailed over those of the *encomenderos*.

The third and eventually the most important export crop was indigo, a blue dye. The properties of the leaves of the indigo bush were discovered by the Spaniards before 1563, when the authorities, worried that the Indians were being forced to process the plant in unhealthy conditions and were dying in large numbers, ordered that they should not be employed in the work unless they chose voluntarily to do it.[30] Humanitarian but unenforceable laws were the rule in this period. In the case of indigo, all stages of production were directly controlled by Spaniards, employing Indian labour for the cultivation of the plant and the collection and processing of its leaves; perhaps it was impossible to induce Indian villagers retaining any freedom of action to undertake this task because of the hard work required or because the great heaps of rotting leaves lying around after the dye was extracted by steeping in water were a source of flies and disease; or perhaps it was because dye extraction needs large-scale organization of labour and this was inconsistent with the existing social relationships in Indian villages.

The indigo estates were, with cattle ranching, the first form of *hacienda*, a type of agricultural-pastoral estate where a crop for sale (and usually export) occupies only a relatively small proportion of the total area, the rest being given over to a large reserve of fallow and to other crops which make the unit largely self-supporting. The first Spanish settlers had brought cattle – and chickens to supplement the native turkeys – and these became an important part of the *hacienda* economy, especially since they did not eat the indigo plant which therefore did not need to be fenced off from them. The cattle provided meat, milk, and served as draught animals. The Indian labourers were recompensed largely by being permitted to cultivate plots on the estate with their own subsistence crops.

There was, however, throughout the period of indigo cultivation, which lasted until the nineteenth century, a chronic shortage of labour, of which large amounts were required especially for the processing in September and October. Forced labour was extracted under the *encomienda* system at first, but, in the mid-sixteenth century, the crown was making gradually more successful efforts to limit the *encomienda* to a right to receive a stipulated amount of tribute, while the forced labour of the Indians was taken into direct control of royal officials who distributed it (each week, in principle) to the colonists who had farms or other enterprises needing labour. This system of *repartimiento* gave the royal authorities more control over their colonial subjects.[31] However, it was equally open to abuse, in El Salvador by the officials in collusion with the possessors of *haciendas*. The latter might well be *encomenderos* also, but the *encomienda*, which consisted of rights to the labour or tribute of Indians of specified villages, did not evolve into the *hacienda*, which was a stretch of land between Indian villages, and was not supposed to encroach upon the ground cultivated by the villagers. From the provincial authorities colonists received specific areas of land for cultivation, and vaguely designated stretches of land between villages for herding cattle, and it was these larger stretches that evolved into *haciendas*. Once again, as in so many other matters, the local authorities were empowered to favour some individuals over others: the opportunities for nepotism and corruption were wide open.[32]

Some Spanish settlers practised cattle-ranching as a main activity in the early period, at least by 1576.[33] The Indians' pre-Conquest slash-and-burn agriculture had produced grasslands in which cattle now throve. They were marketed locally and in Guatemala, the hides going to Spain. Grazing rights were distinct, as in Spain, from cultivation rights, but whereas in Spain this had meant that relatively poor herders could forage their animals on relatively wealthy farmers' lands after the harvest was completed, in New Spain including El Salvador the same law allowed the Spanish possessors of *haciendas* (*hacenderos* or *hacendados*) further to encroach upon the land of the Indian villages. This land was unfenced, and the cattle did enormous damage to growing crops – a state of affairs which continued throughout the colonial period and into the nineteenth century. In addition there were large numbers of wild cattle, whose proliferation was favoured by the abundant grassland. The cattle also competed with the Indian cultivator for water during the dry season, from October to April. During the course of the colonial period the *hacendado* came increasingly to regard himself, and to impose himself, as the full owner of all the land over which his cattle ranged.[34]

*The Loss of Indian Culture: Direct Rule and the Extinction of the High Tradition*

One important initial effect of the Conquest was that the Indians were immediately required to abandon their religion and cosmology, which were apparently those of the Aztecs with little local variation, and adopt, in form at least, the Catholic faith. All the symbols of the indigenous belief system were destroyed, including the images of the two principal gods and minor deities, and the picture-books recording their 'history'. It is an interesting question why the Spaniards were so zealous in their extirpation of the alternative belief system. In other parts of the world colonizers, and even colonizers of this early date, were quite happy to rule through indirect means, using the existing ruling classes, and to leave the belief system alone as part of this policy. Cortés's original treatment of Aztec Emperor Moctezuma and his later use of other sections of the Aztec hierarchy of officials[35] suggest that he would have wished, if possible, to implant a system of indirect rule. It was, incidentally, Pedro de Alvarado who had sabotaged the policy of working through Moctezuma by leading, while Cortés was temporarily absent from the Aztec capital and in gross defiance of his orders, a treacherous massacre of the 600 participants in an Aztec religious festival;[36] this directly led to the fighting and the mood of last-ditch resistance by the Indians against which their capital was 'won', or rather wiped out.

The fact that this was an unplanned action taken by a subordinate suggests that the system of indirect rule was unworkable because it was contrary to the interests of the *conquistadores*, although it was in the interests of the crown. They intended to profit from the Conquest, and were not going to have their position as the local allies of the crown in the exploitation of the Indians pre-empted by the indigenous élite. They did not see the situation quite like this themselves; but their hatred of the Aztec rulers and the symbols of their dominance can be so explained.

It was, in fact, at the time when the crown was successfully bringing the *conquistadores* under closer control that the system of indirect rule of Indian communities which lasted through the rest of the colonial period was introduced, in or about 1549 in El Salvador.[37] This was through the *cabildo de indios*, or village council, whose members were not elected but emerged in a system of seniority and expenditure on ceremonial occasions. Its establishment was a defence for the Indians against the *encomenderos* and a means by which the crown officials could exercise control over the village.

Another important effect of the Conquest on the Indians was that everywhere, including El Salvador, large numbers of them died:

more than half, according to some authorities.[38] Those who did not
die in resisting the Spaniard militarily, died because they lacked
resistance to his diseases, or because of the physical effects of the
treatment given to them by Spaniards for whom they were obliged
to work, or because of the depression caused among them by their
subjugation and treatment. A report from Nicaragua stated specifically that the Indians were refraining from having children because
these would only grow up to be slaves of the Spaniards;[39] and it can
probably be assumed that, in El Salvador also, there was a drop in
the birth-rate due to this reasoning, in addition to the drop that must
have been caused by dislocation and hardship.

## The Loss of Indian Culture: Ladinoization and the Attenuation of the Folk Tradition

The Spaniards, on the other hand, began immediately to beget
children by Indian concubines. The first Spanish ladies do not
appear to have arrived in El Salvador until Pedro de Alvarado
brought twenty in 1539 to Guatemala, virtually selling them to the
colonists.[40] Some Spaniards were formally married to Indian wives,
but this was exceptional. The social group which immediately began
to grow from the unions with concubines soon came to occupy most
of the intermediate, particularly supervisory, positions in society,
though some of them rose to wealth and position, while many others
became tillers of the soil indistinguishable in standard of living
from the Indians; an effort was made to keep them in separate
villages from the Indians.

Individual Indians were able to incorporate themselves into this
group by shedding their allegiance to an Indian village community
and the outward signs of Indian identity. For this reason, efforts to
distinguish between *mestizos*, which connotes mixed blood, and
*ladinos*, which had a derogatory connotation but etymologically
meant 'Latinized' or Hispanicized Indians, were bound to end in
confusion, and the word *ladinos* gradually acquired an extended
meaning, including eventually anyone, even a full-blooded Spaniard,
who was not Indian in community or custom. Ladinoization, then,
could occur by miscegenation; or by individual adherence to Spanish
ways; or it could also occur collectively as villages gave up their
Indian language and their system of bestowing status and authority
on those who sponsored annual ceremonies. This system was identified as 'Indian' although the ceremonies were Catholic and the status
system may have borne little relation to that of the Pipil or Lenca
before the Conquest. This last manner of ladinoization, gradual but
in the end equally complete, has finally brought confusion even to the
linguistic distinction between *ladino* and *indio*, and led to the present

disuse of the word *ladino*, which is still very much current in Guatemala.

It is not hard to see why, in the early colonial period, the *ladinos* or *mestizos* were treated with scorn and attempts made to keep them out of contact with the Indians. They began as part of no community, and therefore without the strong informal control which communities exercise over their members. Many of them must have had to live by their wits. Something of the flavour of this is conveyed by a passage in one of the first two surviving accounts of travels in El Salvador after the Conquest, written by a Franciscan friar or his secretary in 1586. He mentions the activities of one person of mixed ancestry on one of the islands of the Bay of Fonseca and in the neighbouring mainland. This man went around

> deceiving the poor natives. He sold them health and years of life, so that he became master of their health and master of their lives, and he took a lot of money from them, for there are always plenty of silly people who give credit to this kind of mountebank; news of these matters, and of other dirty and carnal ones which he added in, reached the ears of the judicial authorities, who captured him; but from the prison this evildoer escaped two or three times and was never punished because (according to the friar's informant) the money he had extracted from the Indians served him well.[41]

Meanwhile, the Indians were regarded by such men as this friar, the more educated Spaniards who had been sent out to take over control from the *conquistadores*, as wards to be protected so long as they behaved themselves. He praises the Pipil for showing great devotion to the friars of his order and the Church in general, and for being docile and ready to serve.[42] The Lenca and other tribes east of the Lempa were generally recognized to be more primitive, and there are indications that they proved less malleable and died in greater numbers after the Conquest.[43]

## Sixteenth-century Political Conflict and the Role of Priests

The first priests were probably introduced precisely to help ensure the docility of the Indians. The first one arrived as a salaried participant in the first real settlement of San Salvador in 1528.[44] However, they soon acquired a very important role in the main political conflict of the period: that between the colonists and the crown, principally over the degree of exploitation of the Indians. This conflict came to a head, as in the rest of the Spanish American

Empire, after the passing of the 'New Laws' in 1542.[45] Also, it was in 1541 that Pedro de Alvarado died. He had managed to retain the governorship of Guatemala, including El Salvador, when most *conquistadores* in the area were losing their control, probably because he made a judicious marriage into a very influential family at Court.[46]

It took about six years for the effects of these two events to make a real difference in El Salvador;[47] during this time the area was included in the ephemeral jurisdiction of the *Audiencia* of Los Confines, whose four officials had to rule from the small town of Comayagua[48] in the interior of Honduras an area stretching from Yucatán to Panamá.

Although the promulgation of the New Laws led to a full-scale rebellion of colonists in Peru, and a minor revolt in Nicaragua,[49] by and large nobody disputed the right of the crown to make laws. Therefore, the conflict over the treatment of Indians and the closely related issue of the extent of continuing rewards that the *conquistadores* should get for their past services, was fought out on two levels: one in Spain, determining the climate of opinion at Court in which the laws were formulated; the other in the colonies, over the degree to which they would be implemented in practice. The argument at the first level was of course very much more unfavourable to the colonists – even though the views aired at Court were disparate – than the argument or the practice at the second, colonial, level.

But at this level a lot depended on the particular views of the individual officials put in charge of each jurisdiction. The second president of the jurisdiction of Los Confines[50] arrived in El Salvador in 1548 and immediately freed all the Indian slaves, without compensation to the colonists. In San Salvador the forty or so Spanish heads of household had an average of twelve to thirteen slaves each.[51] In this minor respect the president was actually exceeding the letter of the New Laws, since they did not require the freeing of slaves to whom the masters could show good title. There was never, incidentally, any suggestion that the African slaves should be freed, and the same president asked for many more of these to be sent, for the mines of Los Confines.

At the same time, the president and his officials fixed the precise amount of tribute each *encomendero* was entitled to, in terms of a long list of the agricultural and handicraft products of his villages and a count of its inhabitants. The actual collection of the tribute was left to the indigenous village authorities. In the case of the crops, the amount of tribute was expressed in terms of the amount of seed to be sown by the village for the *encomendero*'s tribute crop, which had then to be delivered to him and which he might sell. In the case of craft articles, a specification of quality had to be included where quality was variable; finally, some tribute had still to be given in the form of domestic service or labour on, for instance, the cultivation of the *encomendero*'s cocoa grove, but the amount of such work was specified.[52]

With the situation more regulated in this way, and with production on *haciendas* and production by Indians for sale to Spanish or *ladino* traders fast becoming as important as production for tribute, the attention of the *encomenderos* became concentrated on having the amount of the tribute set for their villages increased, or maintained in spite of a drop in the number of Indians. The Indians themselves, however, were now in a position to petition the royal officials with less fear of reprisal by the *encomendero*, and could do so in particular when the officials made their head-counting visits, although the *encomenderos* were also present on these occasions. On the other hand, they were not in a position to go to importune the president and members of the *Audiencia* of Guatemala, under whose jurisdiction El Salvador was placed from 1549. Such importuning by the *encomenderos* is reported 'by day and night, with their wives, dependants, and friends', supplicating with tears that they are in great need and that their Indians 'are very well off and can give twice the tribute'.[53] Such supplications did not always fall on deaf ears, if only because the officials wanted to rid themselves of the nuisance.

The arrival of more priests is reported in the same document, a letter sent to the crown in 1594, to have brought allies to the Indians who were in villages paying their tribute to the crown rather than to *encomenderos*. The priests importuned the royal officials as the *encomenderos* did, but on behalf of the Indians in these royal villages; and since there was nobody whose interests were squarely on the side of the crown, they usually got their way.[54] But this document does not mention what effect the presence of priests had on the *encomenderos*' villages.

Monastic orders and therefore larger numbers of priests began to come into El Salvador in 1551, at the same time that the royal officials were imposing a stricter control on the colonists, and this was presumably no accident: the crown was inviting in potential allies. The Dominican order set up the first monastery in San Salvador, to be followed soon after by the Franciscans;[55] both orders built their houses in Los Izalcos[56] in the early 1570s, while the Franciscans were alone in building one in San Miguel, by then the least important of the three cities,[57] in the same period. It is not known whether the rivalry between the two orders was reflected in El Salvador in different attitudes to the political questions of the time, as it was earlier in the Caribbean and Mexico,[58] but it seems no more

likely that the Church should be seen as a monolithic force at this
period than later, when it has often proved divided.

The orders quickly became wealthy, with gifts from the Spanish
citizens[59] and tithes imposed on Indians. The system was, it seems,
for the houses of the orders to be granted a number of Indian
villages in which they would have responsibility for teaching the
Indians Christian doctrine, and would receive the tithes of these
Indians. Thus the Dominican house in San Salvador, with 12 friars,
had 13 villages with a total of a thousand Indian households; the
Franciscan house, with 5 friars, had 9 small villages and 300 households; their house in San Miguel, with 4 friars,[60] had 20 villages out
of the 80 in that province.[61] Some of the friars learnt Pipil, while
others concentrated on preaching to the Spaniards.[62]

It does not appear that in El Salvador either these orders or
those who appeared on the scene later, achieved the *landed* wealth
that the Church and its orders had in Mexico and some other parts
of the Spanish Empire. They received money as tithes from Indians,
as well as a right to the first share in a crop or the first progeny of an
animal[63] (how this was taken in practice is unclear); from tithes of
Spaniards, especially those with mines; from agreements with
*encomenderos* under which they would undertake the responsibility for
catechizing the Indians and would receive payment from tribute;[64]
and from charges for services such as baptism, still made today, as
well as from gifts and bequests.

## More or less Forced Labour: the Repartimiento, Slavery, Debt Peonage

By the end of the sixteenth century, the immediate consequences
of the Conquest had mainly worked themselves out: each of the
social groups that emerged from the Conquest, occupying each
niche in the socio-economic structure of the colony, had achieved
about as much for itself as the natural and technical resources of
which it could dispose, and the power it could exercise, allowed. For
the next two centuries change was to come more gradually, until the
tensions built up which were to overthrow the colonial system.

One last struggle in the shaking-down of the social system after
the Conquest was, however, reserved for the first half of the seventeenth century. The *repartimiento*, under which Indians were forced
to work for Spaniards on their farms and other enterprises, had been
introduced at a time[65] when the colonists still had to be attracted to
settle in a place like El Salvador rather than moving on, when they
were necessary in case of rebellion by the Indians, and when there
was still a recognition of a debt owed to them for the Conquest. They
could not have been expected to remain and to accept a situation

whereby they had to pay an Indian the full market price for his labour. But the *repartimiento* was a step taken by the crown in the direction of just this situation: away from the unlimited power of *encomenderos* over their Indians, and introducing an obligation by the Spaniard to pay, albeit only a small amount, to the Indian for work done.

The fact that in practice this did not usually put the ordinary Indian in any better a position was because his fate was transferred from an *encomendero* whose future income depended on his Indians staying alive and capable of work, to a petty royal official, the *corregidor*,[66] who was himself a colonist with all that that implies in social attitudes, and who had no such interest in the welfare of the Indians he was handing out. Obviously, the system was as open as anything in the empire to corruption, the more so because there was also another person usually involved, namely the *cacique*, who was headman or chief of the Indian village, under this system of partially indirect rule. He was responsible for delivering the complement of labourers to the *corregidor*. All indications suggest that what actually happened in each locality depended far more on the circumstances of that area and on the personalities of the *corregidor*, the Spanish user of labour, and others such as the priest, than on regulations laid down by the authorities on the amount of labour to be requisitioned.

Nevertheless, it was a step in the direction of leaving the labour market to market forces alone. Some free employment of Indians had occurred ever since the Conquest, filling in when cheaper forms of labour were not available. By 1600 the crown was in a position to take the next step. As usual, the method followed was, very sensibly, to issue laws limiting or abolishing the *repartimiento*, which served as an indication to the local authorities of the direction in which they were expected to move, but little more at first. In 1603 travelling inspectors were appointed to impose a ban on the forced labour of Indians in the processing of indigo; the practice continued nonetheless, for in 1630 there were a number of convictions in San Salvador,[67] and the growers of Santa Ana offered the crown 20,000 lb. of indigo in return for the suspension of inspections.

The formal institution of the *repartimiento* remained in existence until near the end of the eighteenth century:[68] its direct descendants, laws against vagrancy, survive even today and were used to some extent as recently as the 1930s. But it does appear that by about the mid-seventeenth century the main battle had been won, the *corregidores* disbanded or absorbed into other functions, and the *repartimiento* reduced to a position of reserve, obtainable by a Spanish employer on application to the authorities if he found himself short of labour, but not so open to the former abuses in terms of wages paid,[69] and not any longer the principal means of obtaining labour. Incidentally, local authorities continued to require unpaid labour on municipal public works.[70]

The *encomienda*, too, survived through the seventeenth and eighteenth centuries; indeed new grants continued to be made, but it became more impersonal, a mere source of income to the holder of the title, who might even reside in Spain and have his tribute collected and sold by an agent.[71]

One alternative to the *repartimiento* as a source of labour was African slaves. The first quarter of the seventeenth century probably saw the largest number of such slaves in El Salvador: now that it was becoming more difficult to force Indians to process indigo, slaves were the cheapest alternative source of labour for this, as they had been for the mines. And whereas there were few mines, indigo plantations were now multiplying. At sales held in San Salvador in the years 1606–10, prices paid for slaves varied from 150 to 500 *pesos* for males and 250 to 500 for females; the median price of a male was 330 while most females were priced at the top end of the range.[72]

But in 1625 an event occurred which must have dampened colonists' enthusiasm for African slaves. About 2,000 blacks gathered in San Salvador in Holy Week with rebellious intentions.[73] But these Africans never came to the point of rebellion and they seem to have been so intimidated by the execution of some of their number as ringleaders that no further riots or risings are recorded. Nevertheless, it does seem that the Africans were in general regarded as more dangerous and likely to rebel than the Indians, which was probably because the crown could never be seen by them as an ally from which they could hope for alleviation of their condition. The Indians could get further, at least in some cases, by appeals to royal officials direct or through priests, so they never threatened rebellion from the 1540s to the end of the colonial system.

If African slaves were dangerous and in any case insufficient,[74] how else could the *hacendados* use their strong local power position to get the labour for their expanding indigo plantations and cattle-ranches[75] more cheaply than by paying the market price? The twin answer was debt peonage and the company store, the *tienda de raya*. It is unclear whether these institutions were ubiquitous or merely widespread in colonial El Salvador, but they must have made their appearance with the decline of the *repartimiento* in the seventeenth century. Under debt peonage, sums of money were advanced to the *peón*, the labourer on the *hacienda*, and gratefully received, for any kind of pressing need for cash. But a debt was thereby established which the *peón* never managed to repay, since it would be very difficult for him to save anything out of his wages. The debt could be inherited, and fleeing debtors apprehended. Clearly, once the practice became general in an area, the customary wage-rate could be depressed below the free market rate, and the *hacendado* would be in such a position of power over his workers that their best course of action would be to show themselves willing to serve him in any way he might wish, to establish a personal link with him in which he would treat them a little better, 'consider' them as the Salvadorean[76] Spanish has it. This, then, is the origin of the so-called 'feudal' aspects of the Salvadorean social structure. Paradoxically, they appeared as a result of the crown's success in abolishing the feudal form of forced labour to replace it by capitalist free labour.

It was not always meekness and humility that was induced in the *peón*: it could also be subservience of a much more active and intelligent kind, a self-interested loyalty that would lend itself to any kind of action, even illegal or immoral, on behalf of the *patrón*. This is the background to *caudillismo*[77] and the so-called patron-client relationship, to the willingness of agricultural workers to follow the bidding of their employers in political matters to the length of taking up arms in the nineteenth century, and still at the ballot-box today. Not that debt peonage itself was responsible for all this: debt peonage was in part just a symptom. The important thing was that there was no other way for the *peón* to obtain alleviation of his condition than by pleasing his employer and gaining his 'consideration'. What he thought about him in private is not recorded.

From the point of view of production on the *hacienda*, there was (and is) a virtue in the fact that the *peones* had a reason to try to please the *patrón*. An *hacienda* with cattle is a mainly self-supporting unit that also produces a surplus for cash. The number of tasks involved, particularly when the upkeep of the mansion is included, is very large and varied, and many of them can be done well or badly in ways that are not strictly quantifiable. The mere payment of day wages or piece rates, where the worker had no interest in the quality of his work, would require considerable supervision and even then would not be entirely satisfactory. A system was needed in which the worker wants a good result, for whatever reason.

Not so necessary from the point of view of production but equally desirable from the point of view of the *patrón* was the *tienda de raya*, the shop on the estate which he owned and whose monopoly of the custom of the *peones* was ensured either by distance – no other selling being tolerated within practicable travelling distance of the *peones*' homes – or by paying his wage entirely or mainly in the form of vouchers which could only be used at the *hacienda* shop. Then the prices at the shop could be set at much higher levels than those current outside. When coupled with debt peonage, with the shop keeping the accounts possibly without ever showing them to the *peón*, the system gave the *hacienda* virtually complete control over the income and expenditure of its workers.

Under this system, the workers were usually living on the *hacienda* rather than coming in to work from their villages. The *ladino* population, that is to say all those not tied to an Indian community, was constantly expanding in absolute terms and as a proportion of the total population, since the various processes of ladinoization, including now miscegenation between African slaves and Indians,[78] were in continuous though gradual operation and were irreversible. Between 1550 and 1650 there was a drastic decline in the population of most Indian villages, and this should not be attributed entirely, or even mainly, to further mortality following the Conquest. Indians living in villages were obliged to pay onerous tribute, so they had every reason to seek to escape from this and evade authority by settling in more remote places, in single family groups without village organization. Since it was their object to escape being recorded by Spanish officials, it is impossible to say what proportion of the population consisted of such 'free' Indians. But the comment of Archbishop Cortés y Larraz, who toured his diocese[79] in 1770, is instructive. Referring to the region of Usulután, he says:

> It is the most level, easily worked, and fertile land in the archbishopric; and to this I attribute the scarcity of Indians and multitude of *ladinos*, for while the latter do not want to live on any lands but good ones, the former only desire to live on bad ones, in broken mountain terrain, on hills and in hidden places.[80]

The villages, then, lost their population primarily to the countryside between villages, and it was on the countryside between villages that the *haciendas* were also established. At first, there must have been room for both, but the *haciendas* tended to expand to occupy all the space between the cultivated village lands. 'Free' Indians must have been absorbed onto these expanding *haciendas* as their labour force, and must have become more ladinoized in the process. Incidentally, occasional attempts seem also to have been made by the authorities to gather the dispersed Indians into new villages, *reducciones*.[81]

In the eighteenth century the process of dispersion was replaced by an unforced process of reconcentration, as the *ladinos* who were growing in numbers moved into the Indian villages, attracted by the fact that village lands were now often more extensive than the remaining Indian population needed for cultivation. Sometimes they were able to take over municipal authority in the villages

entirely, sometimes two parallel organizations coexisted, the Indian
one managing lands vested in the Indian community while the
*ladino* municipal authorities disposed of other common lands.[82] Such
arrangements were possible because the crown still treated the
Indians as its special wards. Yet other Indian villages managed to
avoid the settlement of *ladinos* in them right until the end of the
colonial system.

In the latter part of the eighteenth century the concentration also
took the form of the growth of sizeable *ladino* villages on the
*haciendas* themselves: a number of today's small towns had this
origin.[83]

## The Effect of English Piracy

Another reason for the concentration of population found in
many parts of the world during a long period of history has been
the need for military defence. Surprisingly enough, this was also true
in El Salvador, though no Indian tribes remained unsubdued anywhere in the vicinity. The enemy was the English corsair. Sir
Francis Drake was the first to appear off El Salvador, in 1579. He
and his colleagues had already made Spanish commerce off the
north coast of Central America very dangerous after capturing
Jamaica as a base of operations in 1568. So trade had as far as
possible been redirected to the southern route by the Pacific. But
Drake sailed through the Straits of Magellan and came up the
Pacific coast. In 1579 and again in 1586, when corsairs lay off the
coast in the general region of the port of Acajutla for no less than
eight months, military preparations were made, the colonists
resuming their original role.[84]

It was not until 1682, however, that an actual incursion was
made (if one discounts a possible landing in 1586–87 on the island of
Meanguera in the Bay of Fonseca).[85] In 1682, the whole coastal plain
from the Bay of Fonseca to the mouth of the Lempa was sacked by
the English,[86] and many of the inhabitants fled inland; afterwards,
they were disinclined to return for fear of a repetition. The fear of
such an event being repeated remained in the first half of the
eighteenth century, and this time it was the *ladinos* who were called
upon to provide the military defence. For this purpose, bodies of
soldiers were kept in readiness in a number of villages, some as far
inland as Villa Dolores (then called Titihuapa) in Cabañas or
Tejutla in Chalatenango.[87] Such soldiers engaged in cultivation at
such times as they were not on duty – training or as lookouts on
coastal hills. With their families, they constituted the first large-
scale concentration of *ladinos* in a number of Indian villages: there
were from two to six hundred soldiers in certain villages in 1740. The

*ladinos* living in the Spanish towns, who were otherwise often employed on the *haciendas* outside these towns belonging to their Spanish residents, were also part-time soldiers. Incidentally, a fourth Spanish town had joined San Salvador, Sonsonate, and San Miguel in 1635, with the foundation of San Vicente, intended to draw the Spaniards and *ladinos* from nearby Indian villages where they were living in contravention of the crown policy on such mixing.[88] (The mixing continued, of course, and in 1740 there were small concentrations of Spaniards as well as *ladinos* in the originally Indian villages of Santa Ana and Zacatecoluca in particular.)[89]

The corsairs were not primarily interested in sacking coastal villages. What drew them was the possibility of seizing the Spanish exports from these provinces as they were shipped: not only bullion, but such goods as indigo dye. A capture of indigo is reported as early as the sixteenth century,[90] along with cocoa and other products, but it was not until indigo production greatly expanded in the eighteenth century that a new kind of defensive measure was thought necessary. Until the 1750s, El Salvador's indigo and other exports had taken the tortuous route from Acajutla to Acapulco, across Mexico by land, and then re-embarking from Vera Cruz, whence they went in the great convoys to Cadiz.[91] But in 1751 work began on the port and fortress of Omoa, and in 1760, after a delay due to individuals trying to preserve their monopolies, the crown granted permission for indigo to go via a road from Guatemala to Omoa on the north coast of Honduras, and from there on the route which this fortress protected, to Havana and thence to Cadiz.[92] But Omoa had to be defended, and for this purpose soldiers were called upon from all the regions for which it was now the principal port, including El Salvador. It was in fact temporarily captured by the British in 1780, and in that year and 1782, when there was a campaign to dislodge the British from the Bay Islands of Honduras, militia were sent from San Salvador and Santa Ana.[93] The merchants had to pay for the fortress at Omoa, with an export tariff of 4 *pesos* per *zurrón* (block) of indigo.[94]

## Changes in Export Products

The geographical conditions of El Salvador were particularly suited to the cultivation of indigo. The obstacle which had impeded its expansion for nearly two centuries – from the 1570s until 1737 – was the protection afforded in Europe to its less efficient competitors in the field of blue dyes, particularly woad. In Nuremberg in the 1570s, the dyers met once a year and swore not to use indigo, and anyone who broke the oath was liable to the sentence of death. Strong measures were also taken in other European countries, including England and France. Spain was a small market. Gradually, though, the pressure of the more desirable product became stronger, laws were passed (as in France in 1699) admitting its use if mixed with woad, then finally indigo won the battle in 1737. In 1738 a decision was made by the Spanish crown to allow the use of Indians in the processing of indigo, and finally, by 1763, workers of both ethnic groups were being employed voluntarily in this seasonal work, attracted by the wage.[95] In 1782 the authorities tried to encourage production by small cultivators by establishing a credit fund, but the attempt came to nothing because the large indigo *hacendados* and merchants got hold of all the credits, only allowing them to reach the small farmers through their own hands if at all. The political influence of this class of merchants and *hacendados*, which became preponderant after independence, was already important and held in check only by the crown and its major officials who were sent out from Spain.

Meanwhile, cocoa had suffered a dramatic decline from its sixteenth-century position of pre-eminence as the export product of the province and particularly of Los Izalcos. This secular decline was due mainly to competition from Guayaquil and Venezuela by 1601[96] and later from other places as well. Venezuela was better placed for trade with Cadiz, and the ecological conditions may well also have been more favourable to the plant in South America. There is a certain insect favourable to fruiting but which is absent in El Salvador. However, the decline was sharper in the early eighteenth century than might have been expected to occur just because of competition, since the Indians who cultivated cocoa were also sub-sistence farmers and could have borne a cut in the price they received, while similarly the traders might be expected to become thinner on the ground but not to disappear altogether. The new volcano of Izalco, which arose in the middle of the cocoa-producing area, caused a good deal of destruction in 1722: its ash ruined many plantations,[97] but the Indians were then ordered to replant. How-ever, the authorities would seem to have dealt the death blow to cocoa, probably in order to favour the other regions of the empire where it was now produced. In 1730 an edict was issued by the Captaincy-General of Guatemala prohibiting commerce in cocoa (with effect in El Salvador).[98] It is unclear how long the prohibition lasted or how effective it was, but another act of the authorities seems to have settled the question once and for all, if one accepts a state-ment made in a report to the Legislative Assembly of independent El Salvador by the Minister of Internal Affairs in 1879:

How full of goods of all kinds would the Republic be now if those

Indians had not destroyed their cocoa groves because of the imposition of that most anti-economic tax of one *real* a year per tree![99]

## The Situation in the Late Eighteenth Century

By the second half of the eighteenth century, then, the export economy of El Salvador was dominated by indigo, with some cattle-ranching in association with it, while maize continued to be the basis of local food consumption, cultivated on lines not much changed since before the Conquest. Large numbers of *ladinos*, as well as most Indians, lived by growing maize as a subsistence crop, and there had been some spread of indigo from the large *hacienda* to the small plot for which it was equally suited. The mines had long since been worked out, except for two iron-mines near Metapán.[100]

The social élite consisted of a few officials and priests from the peninsular metropolis, Spain – *los peninsulares* – and a few hundred *hacendados* and merchants[101] in indigo and cattle, also regarding themselves as Spanish still but born and brought up in the colony and therefore called *criollos* (from *criar*, to bring up). The crown allowed the latter to run local affairs through their town councils in the four Spanish towns – with jurisdiction over the provinces in which they were located – but maintained effective control by sending out top officials from Spain, changing them frequently, and having them report on one another. Under a new system San Salvador was sent such a top official, an *intendente*, in 1785, having previously been more dependent on Guatemala.[102]

With such a social structure, no one had much use for education, and there was not a single school in the capital in 1770. There were perhaps 250 school pupils in the whole country, a hundred of them at Izalco.[103] By contrast, Guatemala and León in Nicaragua were meccas of learning, with institutions called universities.[104] Nor was there any newspaper in El Salvador during the colonial period, though in 1741 an instructive booklet on how to process indigo was printed at San Salvador, by a friar who manufactured his own press in order to do so.[105]

All the reports dating from the late eighteenth century emphasize the prevalence of gambling – on card games – in the Spanish towns, particularly San Salvador. It was apparently an activity that consumed large amounts of practically everyone's spare time; but there were few idle or unemployed people in 1765, if a report to the crown by the *alcalde* of San Vicente, referring to all the Spanish towns, is to be believed.[106] He says that those 'plebeians' who were not employed on the *haciendas* of indigo and cattle around the towns were engaged in slaughtering the cattle and making candles and soap from the tallow: returning this and the hide to the *hacienda*, they were paid by being allowed to keep the meat.[107] There were also artisans, of course, and these were kept busy. In 1770 the visiting archbishop does speak of 'many idle and lazy people' in San Salvador;[108] even so, there was clearly not in San Salvador the widespread unemployment or underemployment which is reported for Guatemala City in 1798.[109] Cloth and clothes imported from Spain and from China were reaching even the lower strata of the population in the second half of the eighteenth century, even in the rural areas,[110] and there must have been a number of itinerant and petty traders. At the upper end of the chain of local merchants, however, were none other than the royal officials headed by the *alcalde mayor* of San Salvador. With his connections outside the colony, his ability to bring in a good stock of merchandise on arrival, his power over lower administrators whom he could use as agents, and even his ability to change the rules of the game, he was at a very decided advantage. Since it was the practice for him to sell cloth on credit, and even lend money, to be repaid at the following indigo harvest fair, in indigo at the price obtaining at that fair, he was interested in making that indigo price as low as possible, in direct conflict with the *hacendados* who would want a high price. Now the price at the annual fair was supposed to be set by a committee of *hacendados* and merchants in accordance with the latest information on the prices prevailing in Spain and Mexico. But 'in the last few years', according to the *alcalde* of San Vicente in 1765, 'the *Alcalde Mayor* has been intervening personally in the setting of the price, and if the *Alcalde Mayor* is of corrupt behaviour, obviously the sufferers are the poor processors'.[111] (Some of the processing, as well as the cultivation, was now carried out by small operators.)

It was only the altering of the rules of the game that was regarded as corrupt: the opportunity to make a profit was part of the system under which the crown manned its colonial administration. Things may have changed a little after the arrival of the first *intendente* in 1785, but the kind of activity just described was probably what moulded the attitudes of the local *criollos* to the *peninsulares* and provided the background to the call for complete independence voiced in San Salvador in 1811. The *intendente* system must have added to the grievances of the local élite by removing from them some of the powers they had exercised through their town councils, perhaps also by being less open to bribery by them.

While the *hacendados* and merchants of El Salvador resented the crown's officials on the spot, it is clear that they resented the monopolistic merchants of Guatemala[112] even more, and this provided the background to the eventual separate independence of El Salvador.

All the trade from the north coast of Honduras to El Salvador had to pass through Guatemala, and was controlled by the powerful merchants of that city. Their collective monopoly raised the price of imports; but it seems they exercised a significant control over exports too. In the case of indigo there apparently was a battle for political influence between the *hacendados*, with their monopoly of production, and the Guatemalan merchants, with their monopsony of purchase; while in the case of cattle there is no doubt about the way they organized the monopsony. They would buy cattle only at periodical fairs, and would select a site for the fair, near Guatemala City, which was arid, and would even burn off the existing pasture. Then the drovers, who had brought their beasts from El Salvador or from as far as Honduras and Nicaragua, would be in no position to hold out for a higher price but would have to sell.[113] (This system was abolished by the authorities by the end of the eighteenth century.)

The situation toward the end of the colonial period can be described as one where perhaps half or two-thirds of the land was in the hands of subsistence cultivators;[114] the remainder was occupied by *haciendas* of indigo and cattle, owned by *criollos* and employing Indian and *ladino* labourers. The wealth produced by this agricultural economy was enjoyed partly by the *criollos*, who were *hacendados* and merchants, and by other merchants who were new settlers from northern Spain;[115] there were by now, however, some *criollos* who had fallen into poverty,[116] and probably some *ladinos* who had risen above this level through commerce or the processing of indigo. Another part of the wealth produced was drawn off to Guatemala by the powerful merchants there. A third part went to Spain, both through taxes (and incidentally still the tribute of Indians to the crown) and through the profits made by the merchants in Spain who were the only ones allowed to distribute the indigo to its final destinations in the rest of Europe.

## NOTES

[1] Territory:      El Salvador      8,260 square miles (21,393 km²)
                    Wales & Mon.     8,006 square miles
     Population:    El Salvador      2,510,984 (1961 census); 3,685,000
                                                           (1972 estimate)
                    Wales & Mon.     2,641,000 (1961 census); 2,750,000
                                                           (1972 estimate).

[2] The date of Izalco's appearance is uncertain and disputed, probably because it grew only gradually through the 18th century, from about 1722 to 1790. This is what one concludes from Jorge Lardé: 'El Volcán de Izalco' (1923), in *Obras Completas* (1960: San Salvador, Min. de Cultura), 219ff.

[3] Cocoa beans were still used as an alternative to coins in rural areas in the 1880s. At that time coins were scarce in part because the common method of saving

money was to bury it under the house. Alejandro D. Marroquín: *Panchimalco, Investigación Sociológica* (1959: San Salvador, Ed. Universitaria), 140–1.

⁴ The human sacrifices, performed as in Mexico by tearing out the heart, are said to have been made at several annual festivals related to the planting seasons, at each of which one boy was killed, and in thanksgiving for a military victory, when 15 captured enemies were killed, one each day, if the ceremonies were to the male god Quetzalcoatl, or 5 only if they were to the female Itzqueye. Oidor (judge) Diego García del Palacio, *Carta dirigida al Rey de España* (1576), in *Colección de Documentos Importantes Relativos a la República de El Salvador* (1921: San Salvador). There is an account in Fuentes y Guzmán: *Recordación Florida*, a 17th-century history of Guatemala, to the effect that the Pipil had rebelled against Indian conquerors from Mexico rather than accept the imposition of human sacrifice. However, it is likely that the story is false, arising perhaps because the Salvadorean Indians wanted to justify an earlier rebellion to their Spanish conquerors, known to dislike rebellions but to condemn human sacrifice even more.

⁵ These estimates represent no more than my own reading of the situation. Many authorities accord greater hegemony to Cuscatlán, but this seems unlikely in view of the lack of evidence, the absence of strong neighbouring states, and the state of technical and social advancement. Correspondingly, the largest political units would have had a population of somewhat less than 100,000.

⁶ There were Lenca groups west of the Lempa as well as Pipil groups east of it. Pipil groups had also gone further east, into parts of what is now Honduras and Nicaragua.

⁷ Given by chronicler Juan de Torquemada (1615).

⁸ So thickly were they bound in cotton that when they fell to the ground they had difficulty getting up. Pedro de Alvarado, *2a Carta de Relación a Cortés* (1524) (Edition published in Guatemala, Min. de Educación, Biblioteca de Cultura Popular, Vol. 4, 1967, 115).

⁹ No doubt the exact periods of use and regeneration varied, in accordance with local soil fertility potential, and whether care was taken to uproot rather than merely slash weeds. Today the poorer land, that on fairly steep slopes or rocky terrain, is still rested except where, through extreme land shortage, the farmer is forced to work it every year. In 1955 Adams reported a 'general pattern' of using the land for one to 3 years, then leaving it to rest for 2 to 7 years, as long as it took for a tall growth of weeds to reappear and indicate restored fertility. Richard N. Adams: *Cultural Surveys of Panama – Nicaragua – Guatemala – El Salvador – Honduras* (Dec. 1957: Washington, Pan American Sanitary Bureau), 436.

¹⁰ The distribution of Indian villages in 1550 is shown in David Browning: *El Salvador, Landscape and Society* (1971: Oxford, Clarendon Press), 23, map.

¹¹ The expedition was led by Gil González. The ship which reached the Bay of Fonseca was captained by Andrés Niño. José Milla: *Historia de la América Central*, Tomo I, ch. II (1879: Guatemala; new ed. 1937: Tipografía Nacional).

¹² Pedrarias was already 80 years old at the time of his notorious rule of the isthmus. His name, incidentally, is a corruption of Pedro Arias de Ávila, and it is curious that today once again the most influential family in Panamanian politics bears the surname Arias.

¹³ The effect of Lempira's resistance on Chaparrastique is discussed in Robert S. Chamberlain: 'The Early Years of San Miguel de la Frontera', *Hispanic American Historical Review*, Vol. 27 (1947), 623–46, esp. 628–33. According to Chamberlain, parts of 'San Salvador', the area west of the Lempa, were also involved in the revolt. The failure of the Indians to wipe out San Miguel seems to have been due in large part to the arrival by chance of a party of Spaniards who were on their way from Guatemala to embark for Peru at the Bay of Fonseca.

¹⁴ Pedro de Alvarado, op. cit. For an extended discussion and account of what is known about the events of the conquest from Guatemala, see Rodolfo Barón Castro: *Reseña Histórica de la Villa de San Salvador* (1950: Madrid, Ediciones Cultura Hispánica), a book dealing only with the years 1524–48.

¹⁵ *Proceso de Residencia contra don Pedro de Alvarado*, Anales de la Sociedad de Geografía e Historia de Guatemala, Año 5, Tomo 7, No 1 (Sept. 1930), 115ff.

¹⁶ Barón Castro, op. cit., Part IV.

17 David Luna: *Manual de Historia Económica de El Salvador* (1971: San Salvador, Ed. Univ.), 67.

18 The account is from Milla (op. cit., Tomo I, chs. III–VIII) and Prescott: *History of the Conquest of Mexico* (1843 with later emendations), Book VII, chs. 3–4.

19 There is a document of 1539 which suggests that an attempt had earlier been made by Pedrarias to conquer Chaparrastique, about 1524. This incursion may, in fact, have led to the first establishment of San Miguel by 60 Spaniards under Gil González, the leader of the 1522 expedition. The claim is made by the governor of Honduras in 1539, and it is possible that it was a false claim to justify the incorporation of Chaparrastique into Honduras. The document is quoted in Santiago Barberena: *Historia de El Salvador* (1914: San Salvador, new ed. 1969: Min. de Educación), Vol. II, 316. The account of Estete's expedition is from Milla (op. cit., chs. IX–XI) and Barón Castro, op. cit.

20 Quoted Barón Castro, op. cit. Miguel Díaz was the 'Spanish leader' mentioned above (26) who arranged the deceitful entry to the *peñol* of Cinacantlán.

21 Chamberlain, op. cit., 625–6.

22 Chamberlain, op. cit., 629–30; Browning, op. cit., 34–6; Barón Castro: *La Población de El Salvador* (1942: Madrid, Instituto Gonzalo Fernández de Oviedo), 393, quoting laws prohibiting *encomenderos* from staying more than one night or having a house on their *encomienda*.

23 Chamberlain, op. cit., 636–8.

24 400 *pesos* was the annual value of the *encomienda* of Luis Dubois, who was a Flemish subject of the Spanish crown, born in Lille. Barón Castro, *Reseña Histórica*, Part IV, ch. 3.

25 Browning, op. cit., 53.

26 The possible reasons for the decline of cocoa are discussed below, pp. 46–7. The area where the Pipil language has survived includes also the balsam-producing region where the system of production was similar. Squier, writing in 1855, finds the Indians of the balsam-producing area by far the most retentive of their original culture. In this area, it is clear that the system of autonomous production and trading lasted into the 19th century, while cocoa-production had virtually ceased by the end of the 18th. Ephraim G. Squier (American engineer and envoy in Central America): *Notes on Central America, particularly the states of Honduras and San Salvador* (1855: New York).

27 Jorge Lardé y Larín: *El Salvador, Historia de sus Pueblos, Villas y Ciudades* (1957: San Salvador, Min. de Cultura), 22. Lardé y Larín is the son of the Jorge Lardé mentioned above, p. 49, note 2.

28 Bernal Díaz del Castillo: *Historia Verdadera de la Conquista de la Nueva España* (written in Guatelama 1560s; first published Madrid 1632; new ed. Mexico: Ed. Porrúa 1960), Ch.CCIII, 510–12. Bernal Díaz states that Alvarado invested his whole fortune constructing a fleet of 13 ships at Acajutla: iron had to be brought overland from Vera Cruz.

29 Lardé y Larín, op. cit., 468.

30 Browning, op. cit., 74.

31 James Lockhart: '*Encomienda* and *Hacienda*: the evolution of the great estate in the Spanish Indies', *Hispanic American Historical Review*, Vol. 49 (August 1969), No 3, 411–29, suggests that in many cases the *hacienda* did, in fact, stem from an original *encomienda*. Little of the course of the transition in El Salvador is known. See Browning, op. cit., chs. 2–3.

32 One has to distinguish the kind of systematic corruption and nepotism found in the Spanish American Empire, in which posts of authority were purchased with the intention of making a profit through venal practices, and which was relatively open and acknowledged, from the contemporary examples of 'kleptocracy', as Stanislaw Andreski calls it, in which those who hold state power steal from the state and squeeze the people with demands for bribes. The two types of 'system of corruption' are distinguished mainly by the fact that in the former the topmost authority, the crown, may reasonably have regarded the system as the most rational and efficient means of manning and operating the administration, as imposing the least onerous burden on the people ruled. It might be regarded, in fact, as less harmful to the interests of the population than contemporary 'kleptocracy',

particularly as compounded with gangsterism; one's view must also depend on what one thinks were then, and are now, realistic alternatives. The extent of high-level corruption in contemporary El Salvador is, of course, impossible to gauge with any hope of accuracy. It is clearly widespread at higher levels of financial trans-actions and does impose a substantial burden on state funds, but equally clearly it is not as pervading and overwhelmingly damaging as in some other countries, Latin American as well as African, Asian, and Caribbean; nor is it combined with gangsterism. S. Andreski: 'Kleptocracy or corruption as a system of government', Ch. 7 of *The African Predicament* (1968: London, Michael Joseph), esp. 107–9. See also his *Parasitism and Subversion: the Case of Latin America* (1966: London, Weidenfeld & Nicolson).

[33] Cattle-ranching was already established by the time of Oidor García del Palacio's letter to the king (op. cit.; see above, p. 21, note 4), the first real report about the colony.

[34] Browning, op. cit., ch. 3.

[35] Hernán Cortés: *4a carta de relación* (1524). *Cartas de relación de la conquista de Méjico* (1961: Mexico, Espasa-Calpe, 4a ed., 233).

[36] Prescott, op. cit., Book IV, ch. 8.

[37] Manuel Vidal: *Nociones de Historia de Centro América* (8a ed., 1969: San Salvador, Min. de Educación), 96.

[38] Barón Castro, *La Población de El Salvador*. Barón Castro's estimate of El Salvador's population at the moment of conquest is 116,000–130,000 (p. 124); in 1551, it is 50,000–60,000 (pp. 198–9).

[39] Milla, op. cit., 392–3.

[40] *Carta de Alvarado al Ayuntamiento de Guatemala Notificándole de su Llegada de Regreso de España y de que viene casado; desde Puerto Caballos*, 4/4/1539 (Pedro de Alvarado, *2a Carta de Relación*, 136).

[41] Alonso Ponce: *Relación breve y verdadera de algunas cosas de las muchas que sucedieron al padre Fray Alonso Ponce en las provincias de Nueva España* (1586: San Salvador, Anales del Museo Nacional, Tomo III, No 9, April 1952, 8–102), 51.

[42] ibid., 24.

[43] I make this suggestion for three reasons. First, a general observation that in most processes of colonization from Europe, the indigenous peoples who could not be absorbed so readily into the Europeans' economic system at the bottom levels – those who were at lower levels of socio-economic advance before the Europeans' arrival – tended to disappear unless they could maintain their way of life in places remote from the Europeans. This is what happened, for instance, to the Caribbean island Indians. Secondly, in El Salvador, there was an expansion of the Pipil to the east of the Lempa after the Conquest, suggesting that there was a relative vacuum of population there (Lardé y Larín, op. cit., 42). Thirdly, Ponce reports a con-tinuing decline in at least one place east of the Lempa, as late as 1586: 'This village consists of 7 households, 4 of which speak Lenca and 3 Ulúa; there were originally 2 large villages, but as the people died off more and more, they came together, but even so they go on diminishing daily'. The village referred to is Tzirama, described on p. 54 of Ponce's account. The Lenca are called, in comparison with the Pipil, 'gente más bruta', by Oidor García del Palacio.

[44] His salary was reduced by the *Ayuntamiento*, or council of colonists, from 170 to 140 *pesos* a year, in 1529. He objected, asking for more than 170, and they sent to Guatemala for a replacement. Barón Castro, *Reseña Histórica*, Part IV, ch.3, section 1.

[45] The main points of the New Laws were that: (1) Automatic inheritance of *encomiendas* was abolished; (2) Large *encomiendas* were to be reduced; (3) Enslave-ment, with exceptions, was to cease immediately, and the slavery of Indians was to be ended in future; the release of slaves to whom good title was not held; (4) All church and many government officials were to give up *encomiendas* and slaves who were Indians; (5) Various measures to bring officials under closer control.

[46] To Doña Beatriz, niece of Fernando de Cobos. The twenty ladies whom he brought to Guatemala were attendants of Doña Beatriz.

[47] A representative of San Salvador was commissioned to put the colonists' views against the New Laws at Court. Barón Castro, *Reseña Histórica*, Part IV, ch. 4, section 4.

[48] Or, during part of its existence, from the port of Gracias a Dios on the Mosquito Coast.

[49] An event which is treated in some Central American historiography as a precursor of the call for independence in the 19th century!

[50] Licenciado Alonso López de Cerrato. The first president, Ldo. Maldonado, was clearly much less inclined to press for changes.

[51] Cerrato's own estimates, in his report to the crown; quoted Luna, op. cit., 85, and Barón Castro, *Reseña Histórica*, Part IV, ch. 5. In San Miguel, one colonist had 45 slaves, who had cost him 2,000 gold *pesos* altogether to buy, but who were making that much for him yearly by their work at his mines. Chamberlain, op. cit., 644.

[52] Examples of specifications of tribute are given in Chamberlain, op. cit., 641–2.

[53] Juan de Pineda: *Descripción de la Provincia de Guatemala* (1594), Anales de la Sociedad de Geografía e Historia de Guatemala, Año 1, Tomo 1 (1925), 327–63. The relevant passage is also printed in Julio Alberto Domínguez Sosa: *Ensayo Histórico sobre las Tribus Nonualcas y su Caudillo Anastasio Aquino* (1962: San Salvador, Min. de Educación), 122–3.

[54] ibid., 123–4.

[55] The Dominicans built their house in 1551 (Barón Castro, *La Población de El Salvador*, 320); the Franciscans followed in 1564.

[56] At Sonsonate (Franciscans), Izalco (Dominicans).

[57] Because cocoa was now flourishing in Los Izalcos. Sonsonate was to become larger than San Salvador before the end of the 16th century, with 150 Spanish residents (or households).

[58] The Franciscans siding more with the colonists, the Dominicans taking the part of the Indians.

[59] Vidal, op. cit., 118, quoting chronicler Remesal.

[60] Documents (*memoriales*) of the end of the 16th century, printed in Anales del Instituto Nacional de Antropología e Historia, Mexico, Tomo XVII (1964), 465–6, 475–82.

[61] Lardé y Larín, op. cit., 374.

[62] Documents of the end of the 16th century (above, note 60).

[63] Vidal, op. cit., 117.

[64] ibid., 98. It is unclear to what extent at that time and indeed more recently members of the clergy have conducted profitable, even illicit, businesses on the side. There is considerable anti-clericalism in El Salvador, based on the belief that such activities are widespread and continuing.

[65] The 'other enterprises', apart from indigo processing, included sugar-mills. There is some confusion over when the *repartimiento* was introduced. There had been an institution called *repartimiento* (sharing-out, of men) since the days of Christopher Columbus's rule in Hispaniola. But at that time what actually happened, the virtually uncontrolled use of Indians by the colonists to whom they were assigned until they all died, had even fewer built-in checks than the *encomienda* system of the first years in El Salvador. It seems certain that the milder *repartimiento*, in the controlled form described here, must have been introduced to El Salvador either shortly before or at the time that *encomiendas* were more closely regulated, i.e. 1548, and not as late as the 1560s as suggested by Napoleón Rodríguez Ruiz: *Historia de las Instituciones Jurídicas Salvadoreñas* (1951; new ed. 1959: San Salvador, Ed. Univ.), Vol. I, 52.

[66] Called also by other titles. They were often the hangers-on or menial servants of the *Audiencia* members, the higher officials. Thomas Gage: *The English–American, a new survey of the West Indies* (1648; new ed. 1958: Chapel Hill, University of North Carolina Press), 216.

[67] 92 convictions in what was apparently a new drive by the crown, now in earnest. Browning, op. cit., 74–5.

[68] Rodríguez Ruiz, op. cit., 54.

[69] i.e., the wage he had to pay was a wage customary for free labour, though presumably recourse to the *repartimiento* would mean he could not get any at that price just then.

[70] Those who could afford it could pay for a substitute.

[71] The last 5-year period in which extensive grants of *encomienda* were made was 1641–45, with 38 grants. Thereafter until 1680 about 11 were made every 5 years, and after that only 2 per 5-year period until 1726, after which only 3 were made altogether, the last in 1800. Browning, op. cit., Fig. 1, 95.

[72] A list of prices of slaves is quoted by Barón Castro, *La Población de El Salvador*, 155, from García Peláez: *Memorias para la Historia del Antiguo Reino de Guatemala* (1851: Guatemala).

[73] Barón Castro, *La Población de El Salvador*, 154.

[74] And their importation was eventually prohibited by the crown (Browning, op. cit., 45).

[75] In 1612, Antonio Vásquez de Espinosa noted extensive indigo plantations and, in lowland El Salvador, extensive cattle ranches, on his journey through the country. This compares with Oidor García del Palacio who in 1576 noted that there were fewer cattle than there might be. Vásquez de Espinosa, *Compendio y Descripción de las Indias Occidentales* (1629; 1948: Smithsonian Institution, Washington), Vol. 102, chs. 15–16.

[76] Perhaps in other countries also the verb *considerar* denotes that a more powerful person is disposed to favour a less powerful one. I am certainly not suggesting that these social processes were unique to El Salvador.

[77] It is not easy to convey the connotation of *caudillo* and *caudillismo* to one unfamiliar with these terms. The *caudillo* is a leader, acceptance of whose absolute authority is based on a rational calculation of interest on the part of those led, rather than psychological subordination as to a *Führer*; voluntary and provisional acceptance as to a 'leader'; or mere subordination within a hierarchy of authority as to a *jefe*. The leader of bandits is a *caudillo*, but also, as the Spaniards are reminded if they read the inscription on their coins, General Franco is '*Caudillo* of Spain by the Grace of God'. *Caudillismo* was often blamed by 19th-century Latin American liberals for the failure of their constitutions, modelled on that of the United States, to work as well in practice; and sometimes this has been seen as the cause of all other troubles.

[78] The African genes have become so interspersed in the Salvadorean population that it is now very rare to see a Salvadorean much more African in appearance than everybody else.

[79] That of Guatemala, including El Salvador.

[80] Pedro Cortés y Larraz: *Descripción Geográfico-Moral; Provincia de San Salvador* (1768–70; 1921): in *Colección de Documentos Importantes Relativos a la República de El Salvador*. Quoted Lardé y Larín, op. cit., 523. Neither Cortés y Larraz nor Lardé y Larín mentions the explanation given here for the Indians' strange predilection, but it seems the obvious one.

[81] Sometimes these were concentrations of *ladinos*, too; in some cases, apparently, to prevent them from living in the Indians' villages. Barón Castro, *La Población de El Salvador*, 394.

[82] Browning, op. cit., 90.

[83] About 10 out of the 33 *municipios* of Chalatenango; one or 2 out of the 9 of Cabañas, for instance. Fuller information could be extracted from Lardé y Larín, op. cit., who has attempted to give the origin of each town. See also Browning, op. cit., 125–7, who mentions an immigration of *ladinos* to Chalatenango in this period, probably from Guatemala.

[84] Lardé y Larín, op. cit., 23; Barón Castro, *La Población de El Salvador*, 590, quoting a petition to the king of 1594.

[85] The official publication *El Salvador 1969* (San Salvador, Casa Presidencial) says on p. 9 that Sir Francis Drake disembarked at Tonalá in the Department of Sonsonate and begot a child there by an 'honourable matrona'. The raider of 1586–87 is mistakenly thought in El Salvador to have been Drake himself returning. Thus Vidal (op. cit., 107) asserts that Drake used the island of Meanguera as a base, while Lardé y Larín (op. cit., 23) says he disembarked at Tonalá. Thus the story of the honourable matron, while certainly not true of Drake, could conceivably be true of the raider of 1586–87.

[86] Lardé y Larín, op. cit., in his descriptions of a number of the coastal towns, including Conchagua and Usulután.

[87] Manuel de Gálvez: *Relación Geográfica de la Provincia de San Salvador* (1740: Boletín del Archivo Central del Gobierno, Guatemala, Vol. 2, No 1, 1936, 20–34).

[88] Lardé y Larín, op. cit., 450.

[89] Manuel de Gálvez, op. cit.

[90] From Puerto Caballos, Atlantic coast of Honduras. Jorge Alberto Escobar, 'El añil en la economía de El Salvador', *Economía Salvadoreña*, Año XI, No 25–6, 1962, 25.

[91] Certain other routes were also tried, e.g. via Panamá, with the land crossing there, or by land from Guatemala to Vera Cruz.

[92] Escobar, op. cit., 26–7.

[93] Lardé y Larín, op. cit., 418.

[94] Escobar, op. cit., 27–8. One *zurrón* weighed 214 lb. The following information on indigo is mainly from Escobar; see also Browning, op. cit., 66–77.

[95] *Carta de don Manuel Fadrique Goyena a don Basilio de Villarraza Vanegas*, 19 Aug. 1765, reprinted in Domínguez Sosa, op. cit., 127–8.

[96] Browning, op. cit., 59.

[97] Jorge Lardé, op. cit., 232, quoting a contemporary document.

[98] Gustavo Denys: *El Cultivo del Cacao y Algunos Trabajos y Observaciones Llevados a Cabo en El Salvador*. Tesis doctoral, Escuela de Ingeniería Económica, Univ. de El Salvador, 1962, 10; Alejandro D. Marroquín: *Apreciación Sociológica de la Independencia Salvadoreña* (1964: San Salvador, Ed. Univ.), 52. Marroquín gives the following explanation of the edict: '. . . the flourishing cocoa industry of Sonsonate, whose entire output was bought by New Spain [i.e., Mexico], paying for it with cloth and materials which had a high demand among the *mestizos* and *ladinos* of Sonsonate and San Salvador. The authorities of Guatemala, with the object of favouring the local textile industry, prohibited the entry of cloths and materials from New Spain; for this reason she ceased to buy the cocoa of Sonsonate, and this product was ruined for the remainder of the colonial period'.

[99] *Memoria que el Ministro del Despacho de Gobernación presentó a la Asamblea Legislativa*, 1879, 5. Unfortunately the Minister does not mention the date when the tax was introduced. On the decline of cocoa, see also Browning, op. cit., 59–64. I do not, however, accept his thesis that the final eclipse can be 'explained in terms of the final incompatibility between the grower's perception of the function of the land he used and the demands made upon him by an alien system'. There is, in fact, no need to posit that the Indian had any less instrumental an attitude to his land than anyone else.

[100] Manuel de Gálvez, op. cit.

[101] ibid. Gálvez in 1740 counts 299 Spaniards (families), and 267 *haciendas*, in the area for which he was responsible: for which, see below, note 102.

[102] Until then, the main permanent official in El Salvador seems to have been the *Alcalde Mayor de San Salvador y Teniente de Capitán General de las Provincias de San Salvador, San Miguel y Villa de San Vicente de Austria*, which was Manuel de Gálvez's title. Sonsonate was still administratively directly dependent on Guatemala, although its economic ties were probably mainly with San Salvador. There is a large body of literature on the administrative policy of the Spanish crown in the Indies.

[103] Cortés y Larraz, op. cit.

[104] In Guatemala, the Colegio de Santo Tomás was founded in 1620 by the bishop there. It was elevated to university in 1676. In 1795, chairs of Natural Sciences and Exact Sciences were established there, said to be 'an indication of the penetration of liberal ideas and rejection of scholasticism'. Some Salvadorean colonists attended this college. Domínguez Sosa, op. cit., 60.

[105] The *Puntero Apuntado con Apuntes Breves*, a very complete and well-written account of the process, reprinted in Ítalo López Vallecillos: *El Periodismo en El Salvador* (1964: San Salvador, Ed. Univ.), 25–35. López Vallecillos argues convincingly against an alternative thesis that it was printed as early as the 1640s; unfortunately the press was rather rudimentary and the date got blurred.

[106] Francisco Quintanilla, report to the crown, 21 Aug. 1765. Reproduced in part in Domínguez Sosa, op. cit., 128–33.

[107] ibid., 130.

[108] Cortés y Larraz, op. cit.

[109] 'There being few Spaniards who need them [i.e., artisans], in a short time they are unemployed . . .' Fray Matías de Córdoba: *Utilidades de que Todo. los Indios y Ladinos se Vistan y Calcen a la Española, y Medios de Conseguirlo sin Violencia, Coacción ni Mandato*; Memoria premiada por la Real Sociedad Económica de Guatemala, 13 Dec. 1797. Anales de la Sociedad de Geografía e Historia de Guatemala, Año 14, Tomo 14, No 2, 214.

[110] Quintanilla, op. cit., 130.

[111] Quintanilla, op. cit., 131–2. Another document estimates the amount that an *Alcalde Mayor* can make out of his commercial and financial operations in a 5-year term of office as 45,000 or 50,000 *pesos*, unless it is wartime, when business slumps because the routes to Spain are cut off. (*Carta de don Manuel Fadrique Goyena* . . ., in Domínguez Sosa, op. cit., 128). A third document, of 1776, puts it at 20,000 per year (Barberena, op. cit., 313). By way of comparison, Quintanilla (140–1) puts the number of *hacendados* in the province whose capital reaches 50,000 *pesos* at 10.

[112] Sofonías Salvatierra: *Compendio de Historia de Centro América* (1946: Managua), quoted Domínguez Sosa, op. cit., 57–8; Pedro Molina (1827), quoted Ramón Salazar: *El Marqués de Aycinena* (1899; 1952: Guatemala), 23; and see also Ralph Lee Woodward: *Class Privilege and Economic Development, the Consulado de Comercio of Guatemala, 1793–1871* (1966: Chapel Hill, U. of N. Carolina P.). It appears from these sources that it was only the Guatemalan merchants, led by the marqués de Aycinena, who benefited from the system of making advances to indigo-producers and collecting a very handsome profit.

[113] Rodrigo Facio: 'Trayectoria y Crisis de la Federación Centroamericana', *La Universidad*, Año LXXXV, 35–6 (1960: San Salvador). According to Facio, however, the export of hides had ceased and the commerce was merely for the purpose of supplying Guatemala with meat.

[114] Browning, op. cit., 84–7.

[115] From Santander, the Basque region, Galicia, and Catalonia mostly. Antonio Gutiérrez y Ulloa: *La Provincia de San Salvador* (1807; 1962: San Salvador, Min. de Educación), 12. Some new arrivals also became *hacendados*. Rodolfo Barón Castro: *José Matías Delgado y el Movimiento Insurgente de 1811* (1962: San Salvador, Min. de Educación), 62.

[116] Gutiérrez y Ulloa, op. cit., 10–12.

# Chapter 2

# Historical Background: 1800 to 1871

AFTER TWO AND A HALF CENTURIES during which there had been no questioning of the crown's authority from any quarter, at the end of the eighteenth century it became possible once again to think in terms of achieving political ends by removing the rulers rather than merely by pleading with them, winning them over with gifts, or otherwise influencing them in petty ways. The desire began to grow among sections of the *criollos* to get the officials from Spain off their backs altogether. This did not necessarily mean complete independence, but rather more local autonomy, the participation of *criollos* in government, and concessions by the crown to the economic interests of the colonials. From these *criollo* circles the demand for change spread to the *ladinos*, where it was taken up with considerable enthusiasm.[1]

The dates of the most conspicuous events in the struggle which led to independence are: 1799, when a dispute arose between the governor of Guatemala and the *criollos* of San Salvador over the question of who was entitled to exercise the functions of *intendente* after the death of the incumbent until a new man was appointed from Spain – the *criollos* won this dispute on legal grounds and, for the first time, a local-born man was in charge of local affairs as acting *intendente* until 1802;[2] 1807–08, when Napoleon overran Spain and the authorities in Guatemala recognized the sovereignty of the parliament which was organized in Cadiz in opposition to Napoleon; 1810, when the first rebellion occurred in Mexico, and two Salvadoreans were arrested in Guatemala for sedition;[3] November 1811, when the *intendente*'s rule in San Salvador was overthrown in an uprising and, for a month, the *criollos* were in control there; January 1814, when a second uprising was quashed, while in Spain Ferdinand VII reasserted his absolute control after the defeat of Napoleon; 1820, when a liberal uprising in Spain forced the king to establish parliamentary rule; and 1821, when a declaration of independence in Mexico was followed a few months later by one in Guatemala which covered El Salvador also.

But a timetable like this gives a false impression of importance to certain moments of greater confrontation within a period when the strength of the different political forces was changing more gradually and subtly. To understand the events it is necessary to put them in the context of these changes.

## Background to Independence

First, the international background was one in which Spain had for long been growing weaker in relation to the other great European powers, having used the wealth of the Indies to finance wars and to buy the luxury products first of the Orient and then of northern Europe, instead of developing her own production. With the industrial revolution, it was only a question of time before the interests of the industrially more developed countries like Britain and of the local élites in Latin America would come together to circumvent the restrictions of the Spanish monopoly on trade with the Indies, so that the area would come to depend economically on these more advanced countries even if formally it continued to depend politically on Spain and Portugal.

Meanwhile, the *criollos* in Latin America no longer had to depend on a great imperial power to provide them with security against the possibility of an uprising by Indians, except perhaps in Peru where the division and antagonism between the races were still very sharp. In this situation, many *criollos* responded to the American War of Independence with thoughts of emulation, and were receptive to the ideas of freedom of the writers associated with the American Revolution, and even more the French Enlightenment, particularly Rousseau; and copies of this literature circulated throughout the continent, including El Salvador, in spite of the prohibitions – the 'Inquisition' – which were more severe in the colonies than in Spain.

In the last thirty years before 1810, discontent in the colonies had also increased because the crown had imposed new taxes, and in particular introduced a major new means of collecting funds, through a state monopoly on alcoholic spirits. (This was later to prove an important source of funds for governments of independent El Salvador.)

It was against this economic and ideological background that the major event occurred which precipitated the whole process of independence: the crisis in Spanish authority at the centre, with the imprisonment by Napoleon of the Spanish king, Charles IV, and his son, Ferdinand VII, and the installation in Madrid of Napoleon's brother as King Joseph I; resistance against this imposition, particularly among the populace and the liberals; and the setting-up of a rival government in control of only a small enclave of southern Spain, but recognized by most of the colonies.

The beleaguered parliament of Cadiz of 1808–13[4] was more

liberal in mood than any Madrid government could have been expected to be at the time: it was in an extraordinary position, with the king whose legitimate authority it upheld a prisoner of the French, and a Frenchman sitting on the throne in Madrid. Its main aim *vis-à-vis* Spanish America was to get as much help as possible from the colonies in the fighting against the French. For these two reasons, it acceded to the colonials' wish for representation, and *criollo* delegates attended from all over Latin America including San Salvador. Moreover, being a liberal body, it decreed in its Constitution of 1812 that all were equal before the law, and established the popular election of town councils: this meant that *ladinos* were admitted onto the council in San Salvador. Indians benefited too: their tributes were abolished[5] and they were freed from their previous obligation to give free services to priests.

When Ferdinand VII took power in 1814, he had the enormous popularity of one who had been a symbol of legitimacy and resistance to the French but whose own qualities as a ruler had never been tested. His initial popularity allowed him to rule autocratically for six years before the liberal tide returned with a revolt in the army, and he was forced to restore the abrogated 1812 Constitution.

In Guatemala, the balance of forces in the period of Spanish weakness, 1808–14, was extremely delicate. The number of *criollos* who were favoured by the Spanish system of restriction on trade was greater than in El Salvador, and the opposition to Spanish rule was correspondingly rather weaker. The only attempt to throw off this rule, in 1813, was nipped in the bud while still at the stage of a conspiracy.[6] Nevertheless, the Spanish governor had to tread warily in this period.

## Rebellion in San Salvador

In San Salvador, opposition to the officials from Spain was getting much stronger in the year 1810, after outbreaks of revolution had occurred elsewhere in Latin America. It was only the extreme wing of the movement, which even contemplated total independence at that time: what was more general was a dislike of *peninsulares* and a demand for the freeing of trade; among the *ladinos*, for whom change could mean the end of the racial discrimination against them, and who stood to lose less in an uncertain future situation, there was full support for the leaders of the *criollo* movement but, as yet, no separate *ladino* leadership.

Thus, upon the announcement of the arrest of two *criollo* leaders who were priests as well as *hacendados* the *ladino* crowd gathered on 4 November 1811 in San Salvador which precipitated the overthrow of *intendente* Gutiérrez y Ulloa. Popular indignation had boiled over and spoilt the balance which had been maintained between the *criollo* leaders, in control of the town council, and the *intendente*. This balance was the one that corresponded to the overall situation, since Spanish authority held in the rest of the colony and military forces could be sent to crush a rebellion. The *criollo* leaders knew this, and their actions reflect the fact. First, they established their orderly rule by representing themselves as the leaders of the movement and promising to carry out the popular demands. They formally deprived the *intendente* of his office and conferred it upon one of themselves. At the same time, they took every precaution to ensure that the popular indignation against the *peninsulares* did not result in any harm to the few such persons who were in the town. Most interestingly, they continued to address notes to the *intendente*, who was now both in their custody and under their protection, as if he were still in office. They did try, or some of them at least tried, to rouse the neighbouring cities to a rebellion like their own, in the hope of being able to turn the tide in the whole of Central America against the authorities in Guatemala, but this was a forlorn hope. On hearing the news from San Salvador, the great majority of towns, including all the four other important centres in El Salvador, responded by sending letters to Guatemala reaffirming their loyalty. There were internal struggles in a few small towns and uprisings in a few villages in El Salvador, and there was a response in two important towns of Nicaragua; but in El Salvador, the response came, overwhelmingly, from *ladinos* and Indians, probably less aware of the hopelessness of their action in view of the general balance of forces, and probably acting mainly from dislike of some increased taxes that had been imposed in the previous few years.[7]

With the delicate balance of forces in Guatemala, the governor there found it more prudent in this situation not to send an army against San Salvador, but rather to despatch two Guatemalan *criollos*, acceptable to the rebels, to take over the government peacefully. One of these was appointed *intendente*, thus confirming the rebels' deprivation of the *peninsular* occupant of this office and his replacement by a colonial.[8]

So a balance was restored in San Salvador, but in 1812 and 1813 the opposition between the *intendente* Peinado and the majority of *criollos* backed by overwhelming popular support from *ladinos* became steadily more bitter and open. The *intendente* escalated the confrontation by organizing a corps of volunteers to add to his regular army – he had enough supporters among the *criollos* to provide officers for the corps – and then by three times annulling the municipal elections which were held under the new Cadiz constitution, for no better reason than that the results were favourable to the 'subversives'.

(There were still no real names for the two parties although they were now very clearly delineated.) Eventually he had to let the elections stand, and the most prominent *ladino* in the events of 1811, Pedro Pablo Castillo, became one of the two *alcaldes* of the town. The constitution also provided for *alcaldes* of wards, and *ladinos* were elected to these positions too. It was Pedro Pablo Castillo who precipitated and led the confrontation of January 1814. Once again, he and his *ladino* supporters went too far in terms of the balance of forces. The *intendente* had gone too far on his part by arresting some opponents, including two ward *alcaldes*, for organizing a meeting. Then Castillo and his *criollo* friends were able, amid popular tumult, successfully to put pressure on the *intendente* to release the prisoners. At this point most of the *criollos* realized that nothing more was possible, but Castillo, still with one or two of the most extreme of them and with his *ladino* supporters, organized the populace to form a great cordon across the city[9] with the object of forcing the disbandment or physical disarming of the volunteer corps. This failed, however, because after two people had been shot dead by a patrol of the corps while the crowd was trying to disarm it, the whole cordon sat out the rest of the night but refrained from advancing any further.[10] Castillo realized his failure in time, and was able to escape to Jamaica, but the repression which fell on other organizers, following as it did the restoration of Ferdinand in Spain and the consequent fundamental change in the balance of forces, was much more severe than after the 'rebellion' of 1811.

## Independence Comes from Outside

Between 1814 and 1820, with Ferdinand tolerating no compromises like *criollo* representation in government, the conflict became a clear-cut question on a continental scale of submission to Spain or independence, fought out under Bolívar in the northern part of South America and San Martín in the southern. A few attempts at armed rebellion were made in Mexico too, but they were comparatively insignificant. In Central America nothing was even tried: the advocates of independence waited for a more hopeful situation to arise.

In 1820, with the conflict in South America still unresolved, liberal dominance was restored in Spain and with it the parliament and the representation of the colonies. The result of this in Mexico and Guatemala was consternation among many of those who had been the staunchest supporters of Spanish hegemony. They stood to lose their privileged position in trade and with it all that they stood for ideologically, in terms of a monarchical system of government and the entrenchment of the Church.

For the leading *criollos* of Mexico and Guatemala formed minor aristocracies, enjoying monopolistic advantages in the trade of the large areas under their control. They therefore tended to be conservatives, in the nineteenth-century meaning of that term. The Salvadorean élite, with their indigo estates, was on the whole much more receptive to liberal ideas: they wanted representation in government, even if in turn they had to grant some of it to *ladinos* too. Their commercial interest was in trading direct with the foreign buyers of indigo, not through Guatemala and Spain; and in paying the lowest possible prices for imports, not protecting any home industries with tariff barriers. They therefore tended to oppose monopoly and protection in principle, as well as the Spanish and Guatemalan practices: to be liberals in the nineteenth-century sense. So too were many of the less privileged *criollos* in Mexico and Guatemala.

The liberal government in Spain led to a *rapprochement* between the forces of independence and conservatism in Mexico, a *volte-face* by the commander of the royal armies, General Iturbide, and the declaration of the Independence of Mexico, in February 1821, without serious opposition.

In Guatemala preparations had been going on for the elections under the restored 1812 Constitution. These elections were contested by two parties, one of which represented the forces of the government then in control and the moderates or Centre; while the other was an alliance of the forces now more in favour of independence: both the more extreme liberals and the aristocrats. This unnatural association broke up after the government party won the elections, and when the news of Mexican independence arrived, reducing the strength of the forces loyal to Spain, Guatemala became once again divided in two main ways rather than three: there were those who wanted to declare the independence of Guatemala (with Central America) separately from Mexico – the liberals – and those who wanted to join a conservative Mexico. It took a few months for Iturbide to establish his control over Mexico; meanwhile, all support disappeared in Guatemala for the maintenance of the Spanish yoke, and independence, separate from Mexico, was declared with the assent of all parties in September 1821.[11] However, by November Iturbide was strong enough to menace Guatemala with an invasion if she did not join Mexico.

## After Independence, Which Country to Belong to?

Thus the first question to be settled after independence, by the new ruling groups not only of Guatemala and El Salvador but of the other towns of Central America, and indeed in one form or another by all Latin America, was the size and composition of each independent unit. One ideal, actually realized in the former Portuguese Empire – a single state covering the whole area – was out of the question in the case of the Spanish Empire because of its vastness and its shape. Even Bolívar, the leading advocate of a greater union, argued for no more than a united Spanish-speaking South America, not for the inclusion of Mexico and Guatemala too. And even his actual achievement, the *República Grancolombiana*, soon broke up into its constituent areas of Venezuela, Colombia, and Ecuador – and Panamá broke away later too. Throughout the first hundred years or so of their independent existence, the rulers of the capital cities of the larger countries, particularly those with poor communications systems due to mountain ranges, always had difficulty in controlling the provinces. Local *caudillos*, with their petty armies, preserved a good measure of local autonomy and could even descend on the capitals to take over the national treasury.

In the case of Central America, the alternatives were incorporation into Mexico, continuation as a unit, or break-up into smaller units. In the last case, the composition of the smaller units still had to be decided and there was the possibility of any combination among these. More remotely, there was even the possibility of adhesion to Britain or the United States as a protectorate.

The conservative *criollo* interests which existed in all the towns but were strongest in Guatemala were inclined at first to favour inclusion in a conservative Mexico, as a strong state in which their local interests would be respected and preserved. The liberals of the rest of the isthmus, whose main fear at first was a Guatemalan hegemony, assented to this inclusion in Mexico, and Central America became a part of Mexico from 5 January 1822 until 1 July 1823. The single exception to this consent was San Salvador with San Vicente: the dominant liberals here were just as opposed to a conservative Mexican régime as a Guatemalan one, and perhaps saw sooner than other liberals that a Central America which was united, even with its capital at Guatemala, did not necessarily mean Guatemalan conservative hegemony, since the liberal forces in the rest of the isthmus would also have considerable strength. They were confirmed in this point of view when Iturbide proclaimed himself emperor of Mexico in May and dissolved the representative Congress, with its delegates from Central America. But this episode was brought to a close as soon as the army sent from Mexico and Guatemala had defeated Salvadorean resistance in February 1823. Iturbide was overthrown in the same month by the opponents of his Napoleonic aspirations in Mexico, and after that little support remained in Central America for the incorporation into Mexico. Full independence was once again proclaimed in Guatemala, without opposition from the Mexican army.

It was during the period of liberal ascendancy, when San Salvador was for a time successfully resisting the onslaught of the Mexican and Guatemalan forces, that the curious idea arose of requesting the admission of El Salvador into the United States of America as a member state. The motion was carried on 5 December 1822, by the Legislative Congress that had been convened, and five of the leading liberals went to Washington.[12] But they did not set off until after the fall of San Salvador to the Mexican army and the overthrow of Iturbide; these events changed the situation and they waited for four months in the United States while it became clearer: they never made the request.

After the abdication of Emperor Agustín I (Iturbide), the Mexican General Filísola who was in command of the army in Guatemala, and in El Salvador where it was particularly resented,[13] recognized that the opposition to union with Mexico was now almost unanimous throughout Central America; and preferring a peaceful process of succession, he himself summoned representatives from Guatemala, El Salvador, Honduras, Nicaragua, and Costa Rica to a National Constituent Assembly in Guatemala, where they sat from June 1823 until January 1825 and where they declared, on 1 July 1823, a new absolute independence as the United Provinces of Central America, covering these five states. The state of Chiapas, however, which had been part of the kingdom of Guatemala during the colonial régime, adhered at this time to Mexico with which it has since remained.

In November 1824 the Assembly renamed the state the Federal Republic of Central America and promulgated a federal constitution. The five states were each to have their own legislatures and executives ('heads of state') while the Federation was to have a Congress and a President. Both states and Federation could raise taxes. Each state was declared 'free and independent in its internal government and administration',[14] and each would have its own armed forces in addition to the armed forces of the Federation. The stage was set for wrangling over the spheres of competence of Federal and state governments, particularly over whether state or Federation could claim certain traditional sources of government income such as the tobacco monopoly.[15] The stage was also set for these disputes to be fought out with arms when the party (liberals or conservatives) in control of a state government was the ideological opponent of the party in control of the Federal government. In reality, the sway of the Federal authorities, whose seat was first established at Guatemala City, was not peacefully accepted in the whole of Central America for more than a few months after the end of the Constituent Assembly and the election of the first President, the Salvadorean Arce, in April 1825.[16] Arce attempted to bring liberals and conservatives together and to impose strong central control on the states. Having begun as a liberal, however, he only succeeded in becoming closely aligned with the Guatemalan conservatives and leading them in a civil war against the liberals, who were concentrated in El Salvador: he commanded the first, unsuccessful, attack on San Salvador in May 1827. But this was only the second[17] of a long series of civil wars which reflected the impossibility of reconciling the divergent political forces in Central America into a stable union. The Federation became weaker until in 1838 the last Federal Congress adjourned, declaring the states free to govern themselves independently, and, in April 1839, with a conservative victory in Guatemala, El Salvador was left as the only state supporting the Federal President, the liberal Morazán. With the defeat of Morazán in 1840 El Salvador became *de facto* an independent republic.[18] There were many attempts to re-establish the union, the last ephemeral federation being formed as late as 1921, but none achieved any real ascendancy over the constituent states.

## The Bones of Contention after 1823: Liberals and Conservatives

The whole period of El Salvador's political history from 1823 to 1871 was characterized mainly by the struggle between liberals and conservatives heavily overlaid by the personal rivalries of the leaders. It was a struggle general to Central America, and it was carried on largely at a Central American level; but there was a gradual tendency during the period for the participants to realize more and more clearly that dominance could not be achieved over the whole of the isthmus, and the concept of Central America as the political unit gradually changed to one of the individual state. However, this change was so slow that it was not completed until well after 1871; the last wars of intervention in neighbouring states did not take place until 1906–07. The ideal of Central American unity is still proclaimed to this day, and has wide acceptance among the educated classes of all political persuasions; but in the course of the nineteenth century its futility was already becoming increasingly obvious. The collapse in 1839–40 of the original Federation of Central America set up in 1823 did not mark a sharp break in this process, but only a milestone along the road.

Among the populace of the five states there has never been the same enthusiasm for Central American union as among the élites, and it was probably a growing sense of national consciousness among the uneducated which gradually made intervention in other states more difficult. In the early 1840s, Salvadoreans had been willing to follow

Honduran leaders,[19] but by the 1870s it was always necessary for those who imposed their rule by force on neighbouring states to install a suitable local man as President.[20]

Differences in economic policy between the conservatives and the liberals were always present. The latter advocated free trade more unreservedly, while the conservatives wanted to raise a tariff wall to protect local textile production.[21] Nevertheless, this dispute was entirely overshadowed by attitudes towards the Church. This was because Central America had very little manufacturing above the level of handicrafts, and there was no thought even among the conservatives of transforming these handicrafts into machine-powered industry. They, as much as the liberals, accepted the incorporation of the Central American states into the world economy as producers of raw materials and tropical foods, and for the most part they accepted the extinction of local handicrafts under competition from Britain and other industrial countries. At times they sought the support of the handicraftsmen by opposing the trade with Britain,[22] but they were by no means the spokesmen of the artisans, still less identified with them. They were a wealthy landowning and merchant group, and they obtained their political support among the populace largely by exploiting religious fanaticism. The liberals were opposed to church privileges, and could be represented as enemies of religion itself. The polarization on this religious issue was exceptionally great (by comparison with the rest of Latin America) in Central America at this time; and some of the most advanced contemporary anti-clerical legislation was passed by the liberals in 1826, with the reduction of tithes by one-half and other measures.[23]

Apart from the antagonism between liberals and conservatives, there were also certain other oppositions in this political system: although elections continued to be held at frequent intervals, power usually changed hands by *coup*, military uprising, or invasion from a neighbouring state. There was the opposition between Guatemala and the rest of the isthmus over Guatemalan political and economic hegemony; there was the similar opposition between the capital of each state and its other towns, over the political and economic hegemony of the capital. This was still a period when poor communications kept the wealthy classes resident in, and identified with, the local area from which they derived their wealth. And then there were the purely personal rivalries between *caudillos* over the territories in which they held sway.

For El Salvador, the opposition to Guatemala was focused for a long time on the question of the establishment of a separate episcopal see. This had been a bone of contention ever since San Salvador was given an *intendente*[24] but not the bishop that usually went with this degree of independence within the Spanish Empire. The most important mandate assigned to the San Salvador representative at the Cadiz parliament in 1810–11 had been to ask for this ecclesiastical separation.[25] By this time the question of personalities and their followings was involved also, since the obvious candidate for bishop was the 'parish priest' of San Salvador, José Matías Delgado, and he was the most popular man in the country: a key figure – as a moderate – in the events leading to independence, and the main opponent of the Mexican army. During this resistance, the Salvadorean Legislative Congress did in fact create the bishopric and confer it upon him, so the subsequent argument was about the legality and validity of this act. Pope Leo XII declared it null in 1826. In this dispute, the liberals supported Delgado, while the conservative opposition was led by the archbishop of Guatemala:[26] thus the prevailing sentiment in San Salvador shifted further towards the liberals. After Delgado died in 1832, the position was changed, and in 1842 it was the conservatives who successfully requested Pope Gregory XVI to establish the bishopric, and a conservative who was made bishop.[27]

Although, at Federation and individual state level, there were one or two occasions when temporary coalitions were effected and conservatives served in moderate liberal governments,[28] or vice versa, on the whole the polarization between the two parties was so great that the issue was fought out by force of arms. At first the turmoil was constant, and the wars decreased in frequency only gradually between 1823 and 1871. For they became more unpopular with the extra taxation and economic dislocation they caused, and it became slowly clearer that military control could only be maintained effectively over individual states where there was at least some popular support, and not over larger areas of Central America.

## The Means of Political Struggle

The means used to gain ends in this political system was principally military force. Much destruction and loss of life among the 'cannon fodder' resulted. But the outcome was not necessarily less 'democratic' than it would have been if decided by elections alone. Indeed, given the fraudulence of elections, which could almost always be controlled by the party in power – as they still can – the system may be said to have reflected popular will comparatively well. Later, when armies were larger and discipline was maintained more thoroughly, the army came to be the agent of permanent imposition.

In the period before 1871 armies were generally small. Some important battles were won by as few as 600 men;[29] the largest force on record in the period is a Guatemalan one of about 18,000 in 1863.[30] The ease with which such small forces could be raised was one of the reasons why they were raised so frequently to challenge an incumbent government. They were assembled by calling for volunteers and by shanghai. Indians, in particular, were pressed into service by all parties. Obviously, the rate of desertion was high and this was one way in which the pressure of a sort of public opinion could make itself felt: only a popular general could retain his troops. It became particularly difficult in the invasion of another state.

Similarly, like Napoleon on his Hundred Days, a popular general could attract a volunteer army merely by his presence, as Morazán, the liberal and unionist hero, did when he reappeared from exile in 1842.[31] Also, groups might organize themselves and take up arms even in the absence of a popular leader, to attack the town's barracks.[32] The spirit of resistance of an urban population was particularly important in the event of an attack from outside: a siege might last several months,[33] or be called off, if the citizens of the besieged city were determined to resist, while otherwise the attack would be quickly successful.

Seeing that the differences in policy between conservatives and liberals were not particularly deep – especially in El Salvador where the Church did not at any time have the great wealth or privileges which could elsewhere be taken away from it – it is interesting to look at the arguments used to attract support to one side or the other. The themes, apart from religion and anti-clericalism, were patriotism, legalism, personal qualities, and the perennial themes of war: honour, accusations of savagery on the part of the foe, and so on.

Local patriotism could be aroused for the defence of a town, and both liberals and conservatives used the theme of Central American unity and the need to restore it, by military means if necessary. But the most effective patriotism was that aroused for the state, among, at first, the population of the capital cities of each state, and later among the people of the state as a whole. Legalism, and particularly respect for constitutions, was a very strong sentiment particularly among educated classes, and throughout the period Congresses and Assemblies were meeting to give the stamp of legitimacy to the governments whose real power emerged from the battlefield. The extreme verbal respect for constitution and law – they are referred to as 'holy' in documents of the period[34] – probably stemmed in part from the knowledge that, if every side were to obey them, the disastrous warfare could come to an end. But they were not obeyed when they could not be enforced, so it was always possible to argue that one's enemies were acting unconstitutionally and that one had to take up arms to restore constitution, law, and peace.

This attitude to constitutions, a respect disproportionate to what they could achieve in practice, survived to later periods and has influenced historians to accord considerable importance to the Federation of Central America which existed formally from 1823 to 1838 or 1840. But it was only in the first two years or so of its existence that the Federal government was able to exercise any authority at all over the states by virtue of voluntary acceptance. After that, it became little more than a legalistic justification for intervention, and the justification did not end with the demise of the Federation. It continued to be used in the only slightly different form of the re-establishment of the union of Central America. New federations and confederations continued to be formally established from time to time during the rest of the nineteenth century, none of them with any greater power over the constituent members.

Another mode of argument most frequently used in the nineteenth century was personal invective against one's opponents and, to a rather lesser extent, glorification of one's friends and particularly the leaders – a cult of personality which encouraged the tendency to *caudillismo* already present. The denigration of opponents was exemplified even in the names by which the liberals and conservatives were known: *servil*, which carries a connotation of boot-licking servility to the rich and powerful; and *exaltado*, which connotes being carried away by passion and therefore irresponsible.[35] A vivid example of the way opponents might be vilified is provided by a speech made by the Salvadorean General Gerardo Barrios about the Guatemalan Rafael Carrera in 1863: 'General Carrera', he tells his troops,

> giving himself up to his vices and disorders, has made no use at all of the long period in which he has dominated Guatemala. He is still the same savage aborted by the mountains of Mataque-scuintla at the time of the cholera plague, and it's no use talking to him of peoples' rights or conventions. A public figure who does not know how to read or write is an armed Hottentot who, dominated by his passions, is a threat to order and civilization. . . .[36]

Rafael Carrera was, in fact, a *ladino* who came to power in Guatemala in 1838–39 by leading an Indian revolt instigated by the conservatives: they used the fanatical religiosity of these Indians, spreading the rumour that the cholera epidemic had been deliberately started by the liberals – at least, so it is stated by the liberal historians.[37] His long domination of Guatemala – until his death in 1865[38] – was made possible by the greater strength of conservatism in that country, and it was an important factor in the politics of El Salvador, since Carrera was ready and able to intervene there.

In El Salvador, with the forces of liberalism internally rather stronger than those of conservatism, but with the presence of the powerful Guatemalan neighbour, power changed hands more often than in Guatemala. It is interesting to compare the manner in which these changes took place.

The liberals gained control on the following occasions:

*1821*, when in November José Matías Delgado, coming as *intendente* for the Federation, received a general welcome;[39]

*1832*, when Francisco Morazán, a Honduran who was now President of the Federation with headquarters in Guatemala, entered San Salvador by force;[40] this was the only occasion on which a *liberal* invasion of El Salvador from Guatemala took place;

*1845*, when the Vice President, General Joaquín Guzmán, whom the conservative President Malespín had left in charge to go to fight against the liberals in Nicaragua, carried off a *coup* against him;[41] Guzmán had previously fought on the liberal side, and now once more co-operated with that party;

*1846*, when after an internal struggle in the capital during which, for a few days, the liberal President Aguilar was forced out of office, he was brought back through popular demonstrations;[42]

*1858*, when a moderate conservative President, Rafael Campo, relinquished power peacefully to an elected liberal, in circumstances where it would probably have been impossible to control the election to prevent a liberal victory;[43]

*1871*, when a revolt of Salvadorean liberals succeeded with Honduran military help.[44]

The conservatives gained control on the following dates:

*1821*, when in September the last Spanish *intendente*, Pedro Barrière, on hearing of the Declaration of Independence in Guatemala, arrested the liberal leaders in San Salvador;

*1831*, when José María Cornejo, who had been elected in 1829, turned toward the conservatives; this change may well have been due to fear of Guatemalan hegemony, which at this time, exceptionally, had a liberal guise;[45]

*1840*, when the Guatemalan conservative Carrera defeated

Francisco Morazán and virtually imposed the rule of
Salvadorean conservative General Francisco Malespín;[46]

*1846,* when for a few days only the conservative bishop Viteri y
Ungo raised enough support to oblige President Aguilar to
step down from office;[47]

*1851,* when Carrera defeated an invasion force into Guatemala
from El Salvador and Honduras with ignominy for the
incumbent President; although Carrera did not intervene
openly after this, the liberal government of El Salvador fell
and was replaced by a moderate conservative régime under
Francisco Dueñas;[48]

*1863,* when Carrera defeated the liberals of El Salvador and
Honduras in yet another war, and this time clearly
re-imposed Dueñas.[49]

Such, then, was the political system which prevailed in El
Salvador for about fifty years. Liberals were in power for about
twenty-nine years, conservatives for about twenty-one. Like most
two-party systems, it tended to produce intense antagonisms but
not striking changes in policy when the régime changed, because
too sharp an alteration would cause a movement of support to the
opposing party.[50] The exception to this was some of the measures
taken against the power of the Church by liberal régimes, such as the
abolition of monastic orders, the establishment of civil marriage, and
moves toward state education, taking it out of the hands of the
clergy. The system was Central American in scope, but a union was
impossible largely because the forces of conservatism which were
strong in Guatemala were weaker elsewhere, and preferred to
dominate Guatemala rather than risk total eclipse in an attempt to
dominate the whole area.[51] This was why the liberals were able
to claim that the conservatives were 'separatist'.

## Threats to the System: Indian Rebellion

The whole system was occasionally challenged: by the gunboat
diplomacy of the British, by the American adventurer William
Walker, and by Indian uprisings; but since these threats were
usually met by a closing of ranks and were defeated, they can be
thought of in isolation to the 'normal' political system.

The most significant of these threats for El Salvador was the
Indian rebellion of Anastasio Aquino in 1833, in the region of
Los Nonualcos. In this region the antagonism between Indians and
*ladinos* was apparently particularly strong. The first fighting between
the two ethnic groups took place in 1814, at the time of the revolt led
by Pedro Pablo Castillo in San Salvador. At that time the Indians

were demanding the return of the tribute they had paid to the local
authorities. Tribute had been abolished by the Cadiz parliament in
1811, but it appears that in Los Nonualcos, and possibly in the rest
of El Salvador, the authorities had continued collecting it: its
abolition was not a measure that would recommend itself to the
*intendentes* then in power in San Salvador. The Indians, without any
leader, then descended on the town of Zacatecoluca and threatened
to kill the *alcalde* if he did not return the tribute. But they were
beaten back by a crowd of *ladinos* led by market women and armed
with knives and stones. It seems that the parish priest of Santiago
Nonualco had told the Indians of the illegality of the continued
collection of tribute.[52]

During the period 1814–20, when Ferdinand VII asserted his
control in Spain, all the acts of the Cadiz parliament were declared
void and tribute was reintroduced, or perhaps one should say its
continued collection was re-legalized. There were during that period
some rebellions in Guatemala by Indians who had apparently not
paid tribute in 1811–14 and who thought that the re-imposition was
an arbitrary act of local authorities;[53] it does not appear that any
such revolt occurred in El Salvador at that time. It is interesting to
note, however, that both in a rebellion in the Totonicapán district of
Guatemala in 1820 and, at least according to the hostile accounts, in
that of Anastasio Aquino in El Salvador in 1833, the rebel leaders
had themselves crowned *kings* of their followers.

Similarities between the two uprisings, one just before and one
soon after independence, are not very surprising; for despite the
final abolition of tribute at independence, the situation of the
Indians probably got worse rather than better in the ensuing period.
The basic reason for this was that they no longer enjoyed the special
protection that the crown had previously reserved for them. The
government was in the hands of the Salvadorean landowners and
other wealthy citizens, whether liberal or conservative, and they
now had no external restraint to prevent them from seizing those
Indian lands that had remained in the hands of the Indian village
communities. It is not known how many were seized at this time, but
a number came under a decree which ordered that all unappropri-
ated or unused land should be reduced to private property.[54] Given
the fact that slash-and-burn cultivation, still widely practised,
requires that land stands unused for several years while it regains
fertility, there was every scope for the seizure of this land, essential
for the cultivation system of the subsistence farmer. Moreover, it is
likely that the indigo *hacendados* were able to impose more onerous
working conditions on their Indian workers, and that they were
inclined to do so in order to pass on the ill effects of the chaotic

economic conditions caused by the long series of wars,[55] which had begun in earnest in 1826. Aquino and his brother were, in fact, workers on an indigo *hacienda*, and one of the more detailed versions of the rebellion has it that it began when the brother, Blas Aquino, was put into stocks by the *hacendado*'s agent or factor. This provoked a violent reaction from Anastasio and the other workers because they thought it unjustifiable.[56] At the time, it was normal for landowners to keep stocks on their *haciendas* to punish workers who misbehaved. It would appear also that although there was no legal provision for it, the colonial practice of recruiting Indians for forced labour on private estates was still maintained.[57]

Another cause of discontent at the time was that in 1832 the state government had introduced new taxes in order to supplement the income it received, most of which had come, until then, from the liquor monopoly.[58] The treasury had been exhausted in part by a new war against the Federal government.[59] Insurrections occurred in October and November in several towns, including the capital.[60] These probably involved mainly *ladinos*, but Indian troops were used to put them down. This forced recruitment of Indians for the army, to fight battles in which they had no interest, was another of the main grievances which led to the uprising of the Nonualcos. At the end of December 1832 a force of just over a hundred Indians from Santiago Nonualco and San Juan Nonualco formed the garrison maintained by the government in the city of San Miguel, which was hostile, having been the scene of one of the November insurrections. Tension gradually rose between the Indians of the garrison and the *ladino* population of the city, and culminated in an organized attack on the Indians on 3 and 4 January 1833, and the death of most of the Indians.[61]

The rebellion of Anastasio Aquino began in Santiago Nonualco soon after news of this event must have reached there. The Indians were determined that no more of their fellows should be conscripted; their first acts, therefore, were to attack the escorts for parties of new recruits, freeing the latter and seizing arms.[62] Then, when about a hundred strong, they successfully attacked small army posts; after this, the movement grew rapidly and attracted the allegiance of all the Indians of the Nonualco region, the poorer *ladinos* of that region or at least a majority of them, and a number, apparently of both ethnic groups, who joined the rebellion from further afield, including from the capital itself.[63] In the first encounters with larger government forces, Aquino's forces were again successful, and it is thought that, with the government already weak as a result of the previous disturbances, it would have been quite possible for Aquino to have marched on the capital after these early victories, and to have taken it virtually without resistance.[64] Instead of San Salvador, however, the Nonualco Indians marched on the more familiar towns of Zacatecoluca and San Vicente, and the government had time to reorganize.

The actions of the rebels in the areas they controlled show that they were motivated more by aspirations for social justice than by mere ethnic antagonism. The estates of the wealthy *ladinos* and *criollos* were attacked and sacked, but other *ladinos* served as cavalry in the movement, which called itself an 'Army of Liberation'. According to some accounts at least, a careful record was kept of the goods confiscated from the rich, and they were distributed among the poor. At the same time, a puritan discipline was maintained within the movement: decrees provided for amputation of a finger or an arm for minor or major theft, and of an ear for unjustifiably beating one's wife.[65] One of the actions which most incensed the opinion of established society, and of nineteenth-century writers, was the sacking of the church of San Vicente with the rich treasures it had accumulated.

Aquino's troops entered San Vicente on 15 February, and won another battle on the 27th, but on the 28th they were decisively beaten.[66] Although Aquino was not captured until mid-April, the rebellion proper lasted only just over a month. If Aquino was a 'primitive rebel', the treatment he and his followers were given after capture was also primitive;[67] after his execution in July, his head was placed in a cage and publicly exhibited. According to one author, after his death a party of Indians arrived from the highlands of western Guatemala, having heard about the rebellion, in the hope of concerting with Aquino a plan for a general rising of Indians.[68] It is interesting to speculate how formidable such a combination might have been, particularly in view of the fact that a few years later, in 1837–38, a movement that started as a rebellion by the Indians of western Guatemala, deftly manipulated by the conservatives, ousted the liberal Guatemalan government and inaugurated the quarter of a century of rule by Rafael Carrera.[69]

## Anglo-American Rivalry and William Walker

Small Indian insurrections, about which there is little information, continued to occur sporadically during the rest of the century; but none of these constituted a threat to the established political system. The other threat which did have to be met came from the Great Powers and their agents, and from an American adventurer backed by powerful financial interests.

In order to understand the rivalries of the Great Powers it is necessary to consider the position of Central America in international trade and as a possible site for an inter-oceanic canal. The British (and the Dutch),[70] who after independence took over from Spain most of the trade with the area, were happy to see it independent either as a single state or as five small states, so long as there was freedom of trade. As the most advanced industrial country, Britain had every reason to support free trade everywhere, in the knowledge that her better techniques would give her a competitive advantage. Independent Central America offered freedom of trade with all countries, except Spain for a period when Spain refused to recognize that independence; and the tariffs against imports were so low as to allow British and other European manufactured goods, particularly cloth, to displace the local product from the local market. Thus, whereas at the end of the eighteenth century only the few who could afford a luxury product were wearing European or oriental cloth, and others were dressed mainly in locally made cloth, by 1830 the majority of *ladinos* were wearing mainly British cloth.[71] The import tariff on this cloth was only 14 per cent. (Damage was similarly caused by this freedom of trade to the more developed cloth manufacture in Peru and Chile, and since a fair proportion of the indigo produced in El Salvador had gone there for use in that manufacture, some transitory difficulties were caused to the Salvadorean export of indigo.)

The British were also interested in retaining the centre for entrepôt trade at Belize, later known as British Honduras, and, though the matter was accorded little importance, in supporting the interests of the settlers at Belize who had established a profitable business cutting mahogany both in the area around Belize itself and in other parts of the Atlantic coast of Central America, where the Spaniards had only maintained posts at certain ports and the Indians had by and large escaped Spanish domination. British influence in these regions was so strong that at the time of Central American independence the British were crowning at Belize each successor to the unfortunate title of king of the Mosquitos, which was conferred on the Indian chief whose authority throughout the whole coast the British recognized in return for his subordination to the British governor of Jamaica; at Jamaica also the royal Mosquito princes were being given an education.[72] These extensions of *de facto* British sovereignty irritated the Central Americans, and although the dispute did not involve El Salvador directly, it did affect the attitude of educated Salvadoreans to Britain, creating a resentment which has still not been dispelled because of the continued British 'occupation' of Belize.

The other British interests were finance and the possible canal. At first these were closely linked, since the finance house which made the first loan to the Federation of Central America in 1824[73] also tried at the same time to obtain a contract for the exclusive right to build a canal. Such a contract could be sold at a profit to those who would actually undertake the construction.[74] The loan proved extremely profitable to the British company and correspondingly onerous to the Central Americans,[75] and inaugurated a period of chronic foreign indebtedness which continued in El Salvador for over a hundred years, mainly to the benefit of Britain; but the contract for the canal went to the company's American rival.

Anglo-American rivalry became more acute after the American acquisition of California in a treaty imposed on the Mexican government by force of arms in 1848, and the gold rush which began almost immediately afterwards. The means of transport and communication across the North American continent were very poorly developed and one of the most convenient ways to get to California from the east coast of the United States was by crossing Central America. The route across Panamá, then still part of Colombia, was the narrowest land crossing, and was the one adopted first for a railway, completed in 1855, and later for the canal which was finally built in 1903–14. But there were several other feasible routes, including one for a canal across Nicaragua near and perhaps partially running along the Costa Rican border, and one for a railway across Honduras joining the Pacific at the Bay of Fonseca.[76] This last possibility directly interested El Salvador.

However, El Salvador also became directly involved with events in Nicaragua and American activities there. The Californian gold rush had created a pressing need for a means of transport across Central America which could start operating at once. Nicaragua offered the most convenient route, because all that needed to be constructed was a road 13 miles long from the Pacific coast to the Lake of Nicaragua. Passengers could be taken by water across the lake and then down its river outlet to the Atlantic – or, more important, in the reverse direction, since most passengers were going west. Cornelius Vanderbilt was the entrepreneur who carried out this project, obtaining at the same time the concession for a canal across Nicaragua. His Accessory Transit Company was in operation by 1851.

Then in 1855 William Walker was invited by the liberals of Nicaragua to recruit a small army[77] of mercenaries to help them defeat the conservatives. Walker was a well-educated adventurer from Tennessee, son of a Scottish immigrant. He began his military activities in Nicaragua by helping the liberals, and continued by uniting majority factions of both liberal and conservative parties in a government under a moderate conservative, with himself as commander of the army. He ended by alienating support through a series of political mistakes,[78] getting himself elected President of Nicaragua by force of his American army and a few Nicaraguans loyal to him. He finally incurred the wrath both of Vanderbilt and of conservatives and liberals in the rest of Central America, thus uniting all the mutually antagonistic political forces of Central America against him. The Salvadorean liberal Gerardo Barrios was the commander of the Salvadorean army, sent by a conservative régime, which entered Nicaragua to attack Walker, and fought alongside the armies sent by Costa Rica, Guatemala, and Honduras. After this Walker's cause was lost and he soon had to flee to the United States in 1857. (Persistent to the point of self-delusion, he made two attempts at a comeback. The second time, in 1860, he was under the curious impression that he could combine and use to his advantage the disparate and irrelevant political aspirations of, first, the English-speaking inhabitants of the Bay Islands of Honduras, who had just been finally abandoned to Honduran rule by the British government after an ephemeral 'Bay Islands Colony' had been given up, along with the Mosquito kingdom, and second, a desire among Southerners in the United States, just before the civil war, to extend slaveowning territory.[79] His landing, on the north coast of Honduras with a small band of troops, turned into a flight; then he was handed over to the Honduran authorities by the captain of a British warship which picked up the group, and summarily executed on the orders of the Honduran conservative government.)[80]

## Changes below the Surface of Political Contention

All the political activity described above (except the Indian rebellion) can, from a different perspective, be viewed as merely the internecine squabbles of a group of wealthy families so small that it might be called a ruling coterie rather than a ruling class. The conservatives who ruled Guatemala and intervened freely in the rest of the isthmus from 1838 to about 1863 were called by one author no more than four families aided by Carrera and the Jesuits.[81] Some have even suggested that the Guatemalan conservatives were no more than the Aycinena family and its relatives and friends[82] – and the rumour was started that Carrera was really an Aycinena himself.[83] Similarly, the liberals have been said to be merely those men of substance who were excluded from positions of privilege in the Guatemalan commercial, military, and priestly guilds before independence.[84] And certainly also, there is evidence that almost all the politicians of the period used both position and policy as a means of increasing their individual wealth.[85] One of the most revealing

passages illustrating the way the ruling group saw its relationship to
the rest of society is to be found in the second of the Dutch consul's
three reports on Central America, published in Holland in 1828.[86]
He recounts a conversation he had at a ball in San Salvador with a
lady to whom he had asked to be introduced because he found her
the most beautiful he had seen in Central America.

> She had a command of literature far greater than I had ever
> encountered before in any Spanish lady. She entertained me on
> the subject of a number of Spanish authors and gave me an idea
> of their literary works. She had a knowledge of French works
> translated into Spanish and even spoke to me of Kotzebue's
> *Misanthropy and Repentance*. Finally she asked me if I could let her
> have Baron d'Holbach's *Universal Morality*. I answered her by
> asking if she knew the nature of the work. 'Very well', she replied,
> 'I have already read it and because I liked it so much I wanted to
> read it again'. 'But don't you think it contains extremely danger-
> ous principles?' 'Dangerous perhaps for the vulgar crowd, but
> no less true for that'. 'Should each class of society have its own
> particular ethic, then?' 'You Europeans must take us for very
> ignorant people, if you imagine that we haven't been convinced
> of that for a long time. The common people must be reined in,
> with the fear and the hope of a life beyond the tomb; but we
> who know that the after-life is just a myth of that common people,
> like that man sitting opposite for example' (alluding to a Guate-
> malan monk who had just come in and was behaving with the
> utmost indecorum; not only did he attract the glances of the
> whole company by pouring out liquor in navigable quantities
> but, on top of everything, he joined in a bacchanalian chant
> sung in the manner of sacred music of Praise) 'just in order to
> indulge their laziness and libertinage at the expense of others – we
> who know this must at least take advantage of the knowledge and
> use our understanding to attain all the pleasures that this world
> has to offer'. On hearing these words, I felt a shudder run through
> my whole body, and had difficulty in hiding my disgust, for I did
> not have the courage, before this woman and in this place at
> least, to come to the defence of the right. I changed the subject,
> but for me her beauty had vanished, for when are systematic
> indecency and immorality more abominable than when they
> come from the lips of a woman?

The social and economic policy which accompanied such attitudes on the part of the ruling group, both liberal and conservative,
was aimed at the expansion of the agricultural exports that brought

them their wealth. The Spanish crown, if for no other reason than that its own income in the region came largely from tribute, had been concerned about the health of all branches of agriculture including subsistence crops, and had maintained and controlled fairly well-adjusted systems of communal landownership with individual land use. There was one system for Indian communities, and a parallel one for *ladino* villages under which any village of more than 500 inhabitants, with a church and a council, had a right to be granted land, and the villagers paid into a communal fund an annual sum for the use of their individual part of this land for cultivation. This was similar to the Indian system, but the two were kept separate to the extent that where Indians and *ladinos* both lived in the same village, they were supposed to have, and sometimes did have, separate lands, separate authorities, separate corporate existence. This situation lasted until the late nineteenth century, even into the twentieth, but after independence there was less interest in the healthy or honest operation of the communal system. The goal was at first diversification of export crops, and the measures taken to encourage economic development were the free distribution of seedlings of a number of possible new crops; tax exemptions for those who planted them; the provision that a user of communal land could obtain title to the land by planting such permanent export crops; and grants of land to men of substance who would undertake such cultivation; and as a necessary corollary the improvement of the transport routes for these exports, the ports, and the roads to the ports.[87]

Another measure generally thought desirable was to attract colonists from the more advanced European countries: it was thought that they would introduce improved methods in the cultivation of export crops. At this time inducements for such colonists were being offered by most Latin American countries, and consequently remote and obscure El Salvador attracted hardly any agricultural colonists.[88] The Europeans who did come were primarily merchants, apart from a few military officers who found high positions open to them in the unsophisticated armies of Central America. However, the merchants tended to expand their activities into export agriculture, and about a dozen of the immigrants of this period became rooted in El Salvador and founded families which became part of the Salvadorean élite. They came from several different countries,[89] and they merged into the existing élite rather than forming their own separate group, as did for instance the German settlers in Guatemala.[90]

A small number of immigrants also came from South America, some of them contracted by the government to give expert instruction in various fields – military, educational, musical – and it was one of these, a Brazilian named Coelho, who is said to have made the first planting of coffee in 1840. He thus provided the future basis for the Salvadorean economy and, more immediately, for a change in government policy from diversification of export crops to concentration on the encouragement of the most successful of these – coffee. In fact, plantings of coffee had been made at least as early as 1804,[91] before colonial rule began to crumble, and in 1826 very good coffee was being produced;[92] but its local price was higher than the price in Europe.[93] This must mean either that a good commercial opportunity was being missed because of a lack of price competition, or else that cultivation or processing methods – perhaps the varieties planted or the altitude at which they were planted – were so poor that production costs were very high. Assuming this to be the case, Coelho's contribution must have been to show Salvadoreans how to cultivate coffee rather than to make the first planting.

There was a reluctance among many landholders, both large *hacendados* and holders of communal plots, to plant coffee at first. For the former, indigo and cattle were showing satisfactory returns, while the latter did not have permanent title, so were chary of planting a crop which requires five years of growth before it begins to give a return. However, governments took energetic measures to encourage the new source of wealth, by granting land, distributing coffee saplings free through local authorities, and then even fining those landowners who failed to plant. In 1860 one wealthy landowner, Antonio Zaldívar, who refused to plant coffee even after being fined, was thrown into jail and claimed to have been beaten there: after that, he submitted to the pressure, and had the satisfaction a few years later to find that his coffee was giving him a handsome profit.[94] Those who were not so lucky, perhaps because their land was at an altitude too low for successful coffee-growing, were to suffer before very long from a sudden decline in indigo because of the invention of synthetic blue dyes in Germany in 1879–82.[95] Thus the rise of coffee to replace indigo also meant some changes in the ruling class: a number of families whose wealth had been based on indigo faded into the background, while others who had been early to see the opportunity presented by coffee took their place. These came primarily from the ranks of foreign immigrants and urban middle classes, not from rural origins.[96]

Such, then, was the birth of the 'coffee-planters' oligarchy',[97] which came to exercise almost complete control over the country in the early years of the twentieth century, and still has enormously strong influence today.[98]

## NOTES

1 Bustamante y Guerra, governor of Guatemala 1811–18, reported to the crown in 1814 that the dissension had started among *criollos*.

2 Barón Castro: *José Matías Delgado*, 62–4. Presumably the 'civil disorder' which is already mentioned by *intendente* Gutiérrez y Ulloa in his report of 1806, op. cit., 10, is connected with these events or their aftermath.

3 The first such arrests in Central America, according to Manuel Vidal, op. cit., 127.

4 Simplification: it did not sit throughout the period, and sometimes it sat elsewhere than at Cadiz.

5 J. Daniel Contreras R.: *Una Rebelión Indígena en el Partido de Totonicapán en 1820* (1968: Guatemala, Univ.), 9.

6 The 'Conspiración de Belén' of December 1813. Alejandro Marure: *Bosquejo Histórico de las Revoluciones de Centroamérica* (1837; 1960: Guatemala, Min. de Educación), Tomo I, ch. 1, 55–7.

7 A number of new taxes and state monopolies had been introduced throughout the Indies since about 1780.

8 The account of the events of 1811 is based on: Alejandro D. Marroquín: *Apreciación Sociológica de la Independencia Salvadoreña*, 59–71; Barón Castro, *José Matías Delgado*, 145–52; and Miguel Ángel Durán: *Ausencia y Presencia de José Matías Delgado en el Proceso Emancipador* (1961: San Salvador, Tip. Guadalupe). However, there is a basic disagreement between these sources on the question of whether on the crucial night of 4 November 1811, after the crowd had dispersed, Manuel Arce and other *criollo* leaders went around organizing the reconcentration that took place in the morning, i.e., encouraging the indignation of the populace, as Barón Castro has it without quoting evidence; or whether, as Marroquín says, their aim throughout was to put themselves at the head of the movement in order to contain it. It is perfectly possible that the truth lies in between the two accounts, in particular that only Arce and perhaps one or two others of the *criollos* wanted to stir things up while the rest were trying to cool them down.

9 Across the central part of the town where it was divided into square blocks – across about 11 blocks. The town had a population of somewhat over 10,000 by this time.

10 The account of events in January 1814 is based on Durán, op. cit., 73–105.

11 This account is based on Marure, op. cit., 58–66.

12 The account of the period 1821–23 is based on: Durán, op. cit., 123–262, for a narrative of events in Guatemala and San Salvador, and some analysis; Lardé y Larín, 'Período de la Independencia', *Anales del Museo Nacional* (San Salvador), Tomo VI, Nos. 23–4, 5–6, for some dates; Alfonso Teja Zabre: *Historia de México* (1935: Mexico) for events there; also David Luna: *Manual de Historia Económica de El Salvador* (1971: San Salvador, Ed. Univ.), esp. 141–4; and Marure, op. cit., ch. 2, 71–104.

13 Marure notes that there were continuous complaints from the Salvadorean provinces about the garrisons of Mexican troops who had entered as victors in February, and that these complaints were particularly strong in San Vicente. He says that on the one hand the noble families of Guatemala were working secretly to retain the army as long as possible in Central America as a protection. Marure, op. cit., 126.

14 Ricardo Gallardo, *Las Constituciones de la República Federal de Centro-América* (1958: Madrid, Instituto de Estudios Políticos), Vol. II, 705.

15 Louis E. Bumgartner, *José del Valle of Central America* (1963: Durham, North Carolina, Duke University Press), 220.

16 The election itself was acrimonious, with the supporters of the defeated candidate, José del Valle, a respected Guatemalan intellectual, claiming that he had been cheated. The division between Valle and Arce was not on clear liberal-conservative lines. Bumgartner, op. cit., 236–42.

17 The first was in 1824–25 in Nicaragua, where Arce intervened to end warring among various factions, or perhaps to ensure the victory of the faction which he and

the Salvadoreans favoured. Bumgartner, op. cit., 223–9; Marure, op. cit., 194–5.

[18] It was only in 1849 that the official designation was changed from 'Independent State' to 'Independent Republic' of El Salvador.

[19] Francisco Morazán 1839–40; Juan Lindo 1841–42.

[20] As Guatemalan strongman Justo Rufino Barrios found to his cost. He was killed in an attempt to impose himself directly on the neighbouring states, in 1885.

[21] Woodward, op. cit., 42–3, 54, 115–16.

[22] Marure, op. cit., 59.

[23] J. Lloyd Mecham: *Church and State in Latin America: a history of politico-ecclesiastical relations* (1934; 1966: Chapel Hill, Univ. of N. Carolina P.), 308–26.

[24] i.e., in 1785. But even in 1770 Archbishop Cortés y Larraz had recommended the establishment of a bishopric. So far as I know, the question of why the crown was unwilling to grant it has not been investigated, though it must have been due in part to opposition from Guatemala.

[25] He duly asked, but it was not granted then either; apparently this was because of a delaying tactic by the Guatemalans. Barón Castro, *José Matías Delgado*, 87.

[26] Fray Ramón Casaus y Torres, of the Dominican order, a peninsular Spaniard appointed before independence, in 1811, and a power in the land.

[27] Dr Jorge Viteri y Ungo. He was hounded out of El Salvador in 1846–47, and made bishop of León in Nicaragua.

[28] And there were important personalities who changed sides, perhaps because they judged it in the interests of unity in the particular situation; notably Manuel Arce as President of the Federation of Central America in 1826, and José María Cornejo as Chief of State of El Salvador in 1831: both moved from liberal to conservative.

[29] e.g., the army sent from Mexico to El Salvador in 1823.

[30] For a list of El Salvador's wars since Independence in 1821, see below, pp. 264–67. There was almost certainly a gradual increase in usual size.

[31] In El Salvador and then in Costa Rica. In El Salvador he attracted a number of officers and men after landing on the coast, but left again for Costa Rica with 500 of these men because he was too near the centre of conservative strength in Guatemala. In Costa Rica he was at first successful and took over the government (April 1842), but was soon after defeated and executed (September 1842). He had made the mistake of trying to send the Costa Ricans into war again against Nicaragua, as a first step in a reconquest of the rest of Central America. Ricardo Dueñas Van Severén: *Biografía del General Francisco Morazán* (1961: San Salvador, Min. de Educación), 333–45 (El Salvador), 349–68 (Costa Rica).

[32] They did so, to the number of about a hundred, in San Salvador in January 1842, according to Vidal, op. cit., 231. This does not seem to have been an isolated event, but a typical form of uprising.

[33] In 1828 a Guatemalan force of about 3,000 laid siege to San Salvador for 7 months without success. Vidal, op. cit., 169–81.

[34] José Antonio Cevallos: *Recuerdos Salvadoreños*, Tomo III (1920; 1965: San Salvador, Min. de Educación).

[35] These terms were not used only in Central America.

[36] Emiliano Cortés: *Biografía del Capitán General Gerardo Barrios* (1965: San Salvador, Ed. Lea), 146–7.

[37] The Salvadorean historians who deal with the period, almost without exception, take the liberal side. Moreover, it is only now that the university is starting to train academic historians, and much of the writing is partial in an unsophisticated way.

[38] With only one short break.

[39] Durán, op. cit., 158ff.

[40] Dueñas Van Severén, op. cit., 183–9.

[41] Emiliano Cortés, op. cit. It is probably significant here that a daughter of Guzmán had recently married the rising liberal leader Gerardo Barrios.

[42] Ítalo López Vallecillos: *Gerardo Barrios y su Tiempo* (1967: San Salvador, Min. de Educación), Tomo I, 158–9.

[43] ibid., 260–84, esp. 282–3.

[44] Isidro Martínez Vargas: *Cien Años de Actuaciones Presidenciales 1862–1962* (1962: San Salvador), 7.

[45] I have not been able to find an adequate account of the Presidency of Cornejo.

[46] A large number of the most prominent liberals fled with Morazán after his defeat; the list is given, for instance, in López Vallecillos, *Gerardo Barrios*, 108–9.

[47] ibid., 158–9.

[48] ibid., 164–5; Sandas L. Harrison: *The Role of El Salvador in the Drive for Unity in Central America* (1963: Ann Arbor Microfilms), ch. 2.

[49] López Vallecillos, *Gerardo Barrios*, 420.

[50] This was only learnt by experience; when Morazán gained control of the Federal government and Guatemala in 1829, the changes made were far-reaching and did provoke a strong reaction. Durán, op. cit., 374–8; Mecham, op. cit., discusses the moves against the Church.

[51] This point is made by David Luna, op. cit., 167.

[52] Francisco Gavidia: *Historia Moderna de El Salvador* (1918: San Salvador), quoted Julio Alberto Domínguez Sosa, op. cit., 45.

[53] Contreras, op. cit., 9, 37–8, and passim.

[54] Domínguez Sosa, op. cit., 83–4.

[55] ibid., 84.

[56] Coronel Julio César Calderón: *Episodios Nacionales: el indio Anastasio Aquino y el por qué de su rebelión en 1833 en Santiago Nonualco* (1957: San Salvador, Imp. Moreno).

[57] Domínguez Sosa, op. cit., 84, quoting the statement of a priest who attempted to mediate between the authorities and Aquino.

[58] The tax most objected to was a head-tax on all males of productive age, the *Ley de Vialidad*. It was, it seems, abolished in January 1833 because of the strength of the protests (Cevallos, op. cit.), but reintroduced later and still in existence.

[59] This war was to prevent the transfer of the Federal capital from Guatemala to El Salvador! The Federal government, then liberal, could not control the conservative-inclined régime of Cornejo in El Salvador, but hoped to be able to do so by transferring its own seat to San Salvador. The Federal capital was in fact moved to San Salvador after a further campaign in 1834, and remained there until the Federation finally broke up at the end of the decade.

[60] Including Izalco and also Zacatecoluca, which is in Nonualco country.

[61] Cevallos, op. cit., Tomo I (1891), 48–54. Strangely enough, a number of authors who write about the Aquino rebellion, possibly all those writing in this century, ignore the clear connection between the events in San Miguel and the rebellion. Cevallos, who is usually far less concerned with causes and limits himself to the detailing of events, makes the connection quite clearly (229–30).

[62] Fernando Cañas y Cañas: *El Caudillo de los Nonualcos, una epopeya naciona* (1939: San Salvador, Imp. Arévalo), 7ff.

[63] Cevallos, op. cit., Tomo I, 231.

[64] ibid., 235–6.

[65] Tomás Guerra: 'Actualidades de Aquino', *Ciencias Jurídicas y Sociales*, Tomo VII, No 34 (San Salvador, April–June 1962), 58.

[66] Cevallos, op. cit., Tomo I, 239–54.

[67] ibid., 254. It would appear that the killings of Indians, after the revolt had been thoroughly defeated, presaged the massacre under similar circumstances a hundred years later (see below, pp. 100–1).

[68] ibid., 262.

[69] Chester Lloyd Jones: *Guatemala Past and Present* (1940; 1966: New York, Russell and Russell), 42–3.

[70] The British, Dutch, and Americans were the first to send diplomatic representatives to Central America, in 1825–26. The French appear, if Central American fears had any foundation, to have been toying with the idea of helping Spain to reconquer the area, presumably in order to establish a monopolistic trade position *vis-à-vis* her main commercial rivals. There might also have been ideological reasons: 1815–30 was the period of the restoration of the Bourbon monarchy in France.

[71] Jacob Haefkens: *Viaje a Guatemala y Centroamérica*, 290, 295. This is a translation (1969: Guatemala, Ed. Univ.) of three publications printed in Holland in

1827, 1828, and 1832. These data are from the third of the three, entitled *Centraal-amerika uit den Geschiedkundig, Aardrijkskundig en Statistiek Oogpunt Beschouwd* (1832: Dordrecht). Haefkens was the Dutch consul-general.

[72] R. A. Humphreys: 'Anglo-American Rivalries in Central America', in *Tradition and Revolt in Latin America and Other Essays* (1969: London, Weidenfeld and Nicolson), 158.

[73] Barclay, Herring, Richardson, & Co.

[74] Haefkens, op. cit., 161.

[75] R. S. Smith: 'Financing the Central American Federation 1821-1838', *Hispanic American Historical Review*, Vol. 43 (1963), 483.

[76] This route was advocated by Squier, who said he discovered it while walking in the Salvadorean port of La Unión and feeling a stiff north breeze, which he surmised must mean there was a gap in the Honduran mountains to the north, low enough for a railway. He then surveyed the route, and published his findings in France. E. G. Squier: *Notes sur les Etats de Honduras et de San Salvador, dans l'Amérique Centrale* (1855: Paris). See also Charles L. Stansifer: 'E. George Squier and the Honduras Interoceanic Railroad Project', *Hispanic American Historical Review*, Vol. 46 (1966), 1-27.

[77] At different times there were from 50 to over 600 American soldiers under Walker: more were attracted by widely-publicized stories of his early successes. The Salvadorean army under Barrios, sent against him, had 800 men.

[78] The worst of these mistakes were: (1) executing two prominent conservatives, one, it seems, merely in retribution for an attack on Americans with which he had nothing to do; (2) snubbing the liberal President of Honduras, Trinidad Cabañas, who was the most revered liberal in Central America at the time, as a veteran of earlier struggles; (3) making an enemy of Vanderbilt; (4) having one of his American followers, Parker H. French, an adventurer of less education than himself, appointed as Nicaraguan ambassador to Washington, where he was not recognized and alienated a considerable part of American opinion. The British and the Costa Rican conservative government were opposed to Walker from the start.

[79] He had conceived and publicized a plan to reintroduce slavery into Nicaragua, and had thereby gathered some Southern support for this expedition. Slavery had been abolished in Central America as one of the acts of the Federal parliament when it was a reality in 1823-24. There had been fewer than a thousand slaves by then anyway, the majority belonging to the Dominican order. In 1824 slavery was still an important institution in the economy of Belize (British Honduras), and the slaves began to flee to Guatemala; the British authorities pressed for their return, and there was an internal dispute in Guatemala over whether to accede to the request. Haefkens, op. cit., 148, 316, 161.

[80] The story of William Walker only concerns El Salvador peripherally, but it is referred to there as the 'National War' against the American Filibusters, and is remembered. The above account is, in fact, based largely on a Salvadorean history of the events: Ricardo Dueñas Van Severén: *La Invasión Filibustera de Nicaragua y la Guerra Nacional* (1959; 1962: San Salvador, Min. de Educación).

[81] Lorenzo Montúfar: *Reseña Histórica de Centro América*, Tomo I (1878: Guatemala), 10. Quoted Rodrigo Facio, op. cit., 87.

[82] Possibly the Salvadorean conservatives also, at least in large part. The Aycinena family possessed half a dozen *haciendas* in El Salvador as well as their Guatemalan properties. For an *exposé* of the Aycinena family, see Salazar, op. cit. They had bought the title of marqués, the only title in Central America.

[83] 'Un verdadero descubrimiento de la descendencia del Sor. Gral. de la armas de Guatemala, Rafael de Ayzinena, conocido anteriormente con el apellido de Carrera', printed in Dueñas Van Severén, *Biografía del General Francisco Morazán*, 248-57.

[84] Woodward, op. cit., 127.

[85] This aspect of the period is emphasized by Robert Gregg: *A History of the Republic of El Salvador* (unpublished mss. written San Salvador *c.* 1965).

[86] Haefkens, op. cit., 73-4. The original title of this second report is *Reize naar Guatemala, tweede stuk* (1828: The Hague).

[87] See Browning, op. cit., esp. ch. 4, for a more detailed discussion of the matters mentioned in this paragraph.

[88] There were no organized colonies promoted by colonization companies as there were elsewhere, including Guatemala, where a Belgian colony was founded in 1850 and granted a monopoly for its proposed port on the Atlantic; the port idea failed, however, and the colony was unsuccessful.

[89] Including Britain. Also France, Germany, Italy, Spain.

[90] In 1939, 50 per cent of Guatemalan coffee plantations were owned by foreigners, mostly Germans, compared with only 12 per cent of Salvadorean plantations. Wilhelm Lauer: *Vegetation, Landnutzung und Agrarpotential in El Salvador* (1956: Kiel, Univ.).

[91] A planting by a Spaniard in the region of Usulután is reported for that year by Lardé y Larín, op. cit., 524.

[92] Haefkens, *Viaje a Guatemala*, 68. Haefkens was writing about the region of Ahuachapán, and his failure to say that coffee was a recent crop there indicates that it was probably grown in that area before 1804.

[93] ibid., 300. He notes that coffee was not drunk in Central America in 1830, except by foreigners; the universal drink was still cocoa, though by now it had in part to be imported (from Ecuador). It would be interesting to know how soon after its planting as an export crop coffee came to replace cocoa as the only important hot beverage locally. Gregg affirms it was 'in the latter part of the century' (op. cit., 319).

[94] Cortés, op. cit.

[95] Escobar, op. cit., 35.

[96] At least this is my impression. A number of cases are mentioned in the historical literature of doctors or other professionals, as well as foreigners, planting coffee in large amounts. It is a great pity that Robert T. Aubey, in his study of the branches of activity in which the wealthiest families engage today, did not find out how each family first acquired its wealth. Aubey: 'Entrepreneurial formation in El Salvador', *Explorations in Entrepreneurial History*, 2nd series, Vol. 6, No. 3 (1969).

[97] Abel Cuenca: *El Salvador, una democracia cafetalera* (1962: Mexico, Costa-Amic), passim. Abel Cuenca was one of the few communist leaders of the 1932 rebellion who managed to escape after its failure. By the late 1950s, when he wrote his book, he had mellowed sufficiently to be arguing that the best course for El Salvador would be a strengthening of an industrial bourgeoisie which recognized the divergence of its interests from those of the coffee-planters, particularly over the level of wages, which they should want to raise in order to provide a market for their goods.

[98] A detailed account of Salvadorean history from 1811 to 1890 is to be found in Gregg, op. cit. The typescript has been placed in the manuscript collection of the library of University College, London.

# Chapter 3

# Historical Background: The Last Hundred Years

FROM THE OVERTHROW of the last conservative President, Francisco Dueñas, in 1871, a new period of Salvadorean political history, which was to last until the late 1920s, can be said to have begun. This was characterized by general acceptance of the liberal position that the state should not interfere with the economic mechanism of market forces. Its role was to ensure in every possible sphere the free operation of market forces. In this period communal landownership was abolished and replaced by full individual ownership. This included the right to sell the land, which often meant to lose it to moneylenders or lawyers. It was a period during which the increasing strength of the national army and the improvement of communications led to a gradual decrease in the frequency of armed uprisings and minor civil wars. In particular, popular opposition was extremely ineffective, while the greater strength of the regular army meant that there was less need to seek popular support, to enlist volunteers in a cause, or retain the voluntary loyalty of soldiers behind a leader.

With conservatism a spent force, and no effective challenge to the ruling classes from the popular masses, it might be thought that there were few political issues to divide the liberal élite in power. Much of the division which did exist centred on personalities. More fundamentally, however, one can distinguish an opposition between two different groups of liberals: pragmatists who laid emphasis on the economic themes of the liberal creed; and idealists who stressed the political themes, particularly free speech.

## Pragmatic and Idealist Liberals

There was little else to disagree about. The scope of interest was no longer primarily Central America, but El Salvador, and there was no serious political opposition from the pro-clerical forces of the Right nor, until the end of the period, from the rising popular forces of the Left. The liberal élite which monopolized power for

these fifty-five or sixty years, with the exception of the government
of Carlos Ezeta (1890–94), agreed on the most basic policies: the
encouragement of coffee; the development of railways to the ports,
carried out at great cost and financed by the contraction of foreign
loans, but considered necessary for foreign trade and therefore
national prosperity; and the elimination of communal landholdings
because they were not used for growing export crops; laws against
vagrancy so that the rural population could be forced to work for
the landowners at the low wage rates they paid; and repression of
any outbreaks of rural discontent.

Carlos Ezeta seems to have been an exception in one important
respect: he is said to have enforced a minimum wage, or rather a
minimum piece-work rate, for agricultural work, much higher than
previous or subsequent rates. The author who reports this also says
that the redistribution of income to the rural working classes meant
also that the prices received by artisans were greatly increased and
they were much more fully employed. Their income is said to have
gone up six or seven times, falling to its previous level after the fall
of Ezeta.[1] Unfortunately, almost all other sources are hostile to
Ezeta, and there is no confirmation of this account of a striking
temporary improvement in the lot of the poor. If he was indeed an
exception, it is not surprising that Carlos Ezeta was obliged to rule in
a despotic manner with his brother Antonio, relying on the armed
forces rather than the élite for support.[2]

The policies of the idealists and the pragmatists do not seem to
have differed very much when they held power, although the two
camps opposed one another vocally. The idealists appear to have
found it difficult to live up to their ideals once in power, finding it
necessary to control elections and limit free speech to some extent in
order to retain this power.[3] They were not particularly successful in
retaining the Presidency, however, as can be seen from the following
classification of Presidents between 1860 and 1927:

| Pragmatic reformist | Idealist liberal | Pragmatic liberal | Conservative |
|---|---|---|---|
| | | Barrios 1860–63 | |
| | | | Dueñas 1863–71 |
| | González 1871–76 | | |
| | Valle 1876 | | |
| | | Zaldívar 1876–85 | |
| | | Figueroa 1885 | |
| | Menéndez 1885–90 | | |
| Ezeta 1890–94 | | | |
| | Gutiérrez 1894–98 | | |

| Pragmatic reformist | Idealist liberal | Pragmatic liberal | Conservative |
|---|---|---|---|
| | | Regalado 1898–1903 | |
| | | Escalón 1903–07 | |
| | | Figueroa 1907–11 | |
| — Manuel Enrique Araujo 1911–13 — | | | |
| | | Meléndez, C. 1913–18 | |
| | | Meléndez, J. 1918–22 | |
| | | Quiñónez 1922–27 | |

Each period of rule by the idealist liberals saw an initial step toward liberalizing the political process, but later curtailment of freedoms. On attaining power, Santiago González reduced the Presidential term of office from six years to two. He then not only prolonged it again to four, but after serving his four years arranged the election of Andrés Valle as President and continued himself as Vice President and commander of the armed forces.[4] In 1885 Francisco Menéndez called for the election of an Assembly to write a new constitution, but when he did not approve of the document produced, he had it disbanded and a more pliant one elected;[5] in spite of this, Menéndez is revered by many who follow in the idealist liberal tradition as having been perhaps the best President El Salvador has had, certainly since Barrios or the earlier more legendary heroes of liberalism. Rafael Antonio Gutiérrez actually went so far as to abolish the police force, but soon found that he had to re-create it.[6]

It is probably not a coincidence that some of the main efforts to achieve Central American union through political agreement were made while these liberal idealists were in power in El Salvador: in 1872, a pact of union was signed by Guatemala, El Salvador, Honduras, and Costa Rica; in 1876, before Valle and González were ousted, a congress was held in Guatemala attended by all five states; in 1889, a provisional pact of union of the five states was signed, creating a 'República de Centroamérica'; in 1895, the Pact of Amapala was signed, between El Salvador, Honduras, and Nicaragua, establishing the 'República Mayor de Centroamérica'; in 1897 both Costa Rica and Guatemala seriously considered joining this union; in 1898, the name was changed to 'Los Estados Unidos de Centro América'; and provision was made for a capital and federal district at Amapala, a port on the Gulf of Fonseca.[7]

None of these attempts at union survived the replacement of idealist liberals in El Salvador by pragmatic liberals. It was recognized, however, that the sentiment in favour of union was greater in El Salvador than in any of the other states, and that much of the initiative for achieving union by peaceful means came from El Salvador.

It seems likely that the idealists really believed in both the desirability and the practicality of such a political union; whereas the pragmatists, while not denouncing the idea, knew that it was not to be achieved by peaceful agreement. In 1860 Gerardo Barrios proposed smaller unions between El Salvador and Guatemala and between Honduras and Nicaragua, explicitly recognizing that the establishment of a comprehensive union would rekindle the former jealousy against Guatemala.[8] In 1883 Zaldívar ordered the first minting of Salvadorean coins – previously those of neighbouring countries, of the United States, and of France had been used – and these were first issued by Ezeta in 1892. This practical step and every monetary transaction now showed that El Salvador was to be thought of as a political unit rather than as part of Central America. Finally, Regalado reaffirmed Salvadorean sovereignty on coming to power in 1898, and sabotaged a new effort at political union in 1902 by insulting the Guatemalan delegate: he told him that El Salvador should annex (the Guatemalan Atlantic port of) Puerto Barrios forthwith, and so get her Atlantic outlet.[9]

To draw a further distinction between the idealist and pragmatist camps, it is instructive to look at the ways in which new régimes were inaugurated in this period. Like the conservative Francisco Dueñas in 1863, the pragmatist Rafael Zaldívar achieved power as a result of El Salvador's military defeat by the Guatemalan liberal strongman Justo Rufino Barrios. Zaldívar, who had served in Dueñas's government, professed to belong to neither conservative nor liberal parties, but proposed to found a 'national' party: he did not, however, alter the liberal legislation passed after the overthrow of Dueñas. He was chosen as President by a more or less informal meeting of the rich and influential men of El Salvador, and he was acceptable to Justo Rufino Barrios who then removed his troops.[10] Zaldívar then retained power for nine years, the longest period for any President until Martínez in 1931–44.

Carlos Ezeta in 1890 and Tomás Regalado in 1898 achieved power by internal and bloodless, or almost bloodless, *coups d'état* in the Salvadorean capital. In contrast, on all three occasions when idealist liberals captured power, they did so by launching a small military movement from across a friendly border and issuing a proclamation calling for support. These tactics were not always successful: unsuccessful revolts against Zaldívar took place in 1877, 1879, and 1883.[11] An unsuccessful revolt was also staged against Menéndez in 1889, clearly incited by disillusioned idealist liberals[12] who thought that Menéndez had betrayed their cause.

In 1907 the failure of one of the last classic Central American invasions, with Nicaraguan help,[13] put an end to the idealists' hopes of mounting a successful uprising. They continued to exist, however, and to identify themselves as 'oppositionists' against the *gobiernistas* (government-ists) who held power. Their policies ceased to have real relevance after the rise of demands for economic and social reforms, but they played a part in the overthrow of President Martínez in April and May 1944, and in the attempted invasion from over the Guatemalan border in December of the same year (the *Jornada de Ahuachapán*). Some of them maintain the tradition to this day: an inherited allegiance. I was told by one man in 1971 that he had refused to accept a ministerial position under the 1960 junta on account of his being an 'oppositionist' and therefore unable to associate himself with such a government. This man was a coffee-planter from Ahuachapán, the department of Francisco Menéndez, and he said that the 'liberal', that is idealist liberal, tradition had always been strong in this region.[14]

This idealist-pragmatist division seems to have been the Salvadorean equivalent of the inherited party allegiances which are such a curious feature of the politics of a number of widely separated Latin American countries: Colombia and Nicaragua with their Liberal and Conservative parties; Uruguay and Paraguay with the *Blancos* and *Colorados*; and Honduras with her Liberal and National parties.[15] This is not to suggest that these other countries still live in a political epoch which in El Salvador ended about 1927 (though something of the sort might be argued for Honduras and even for Nicaragua and Paraguay); but that in these other countries the inherited allegiances had grown so strong that the new ideological divisions, on the question of reforms and the reduction of inequality, appeared within the ranks of each of the traditional parties rather than between them or replacing them.

These political systems – two deeply divided parties, inherited party allegiances, but minimal ideological differences between the parties, and no prospect of free elections leading to a change of party control (the situation in Nicaragua and Paraguay) – remind one of dual dynastic 'systems' in autocratic monarchies.[16]

## Stirrings of Reform, 1911–18

Significant early stirrings of the new direction in Salvadorean politics came in 1911, the centenary of the first call for autonomy in San Salvador, celebrated as a proclamation of independence. In that year Manuel Enrique Araujo arrived in the Presidency by the usual route, imposition by his predecessor through an election in which opponents were allowed to participate but not allowed to win.

But Araujo was in some ways atypical. With his reputation for respecting the freedoms he had more support from idealists. Moreover he was to some extent a reformist, questioning the wisdom of contracting foreign loans to finance the state or the development of railways. In 1911 the first references are found to associations of workers: artisans engaging in some semi-political activity, though well within the range of respectability and the established structure. Workers made official speeches at the centenary celebrations.

In 1913 Manuel Enrique Araujo was assassinated after only two years in office. The evidence is inconclusive, but it can be assumed that the man behind the assassination was probably Prudencio Alfaro,[17] a veteran leader of the idealist liberals, and that the motive was exasperation at the impossibility of achieving the overthrow of the entrenched pragmatists any other way. On this basis, the murder was counter-productive, for it brought about the return of pragmatists like Araujo's predecessors. A minor dynasty, in fact, since Carlos Meléndez, who emerged as strongman from Araujo's legislature, was succeeded by his brother Jorge and then by brother-in-law Alfonso Quiñónez.

It was Quiñónez who formed the *Liga Roja* (Red League) for the purpose of electing Jorge Meléndez in the 1918 election.[18] This was a further development of the kind of official party which already existed. It aimed to work not merely through the channels of administration to ensure the election of official candidates, but also attempted to acquire a mass membership or following by appealing to a popular demand for the improvement of living standards. This election propaganda may have helped to give the masses the idea that it might lie within the scope of political action to improve their lot. In the past government had usually so far abstained from any intervention in the economy – except to collect minimal funds for the maintenance of the state and its agencies, and a few measures to encourage export agriculture – that the populace had not been made very aware of what reforms could be introduced by government on its behalf. Appeals for support on a platform of promised improvements were also made at the 1918 election by the opposition, the idealist liberals, whose standard-bearer was Tomás Palomo; and both he and Jorge Meléndez promised freedom of trade union organization.

## Laissez-faire: *Good for the Rich but Bad for the Future*

Economic liberalism, reforms, and particularly unionization have different connotations in a country like El Salvador than in more advanced countries.

The doctrines of economic liberalism, of free trade, and a minimum of state intervention, were commonly justified on the grounds that it was by following such policies that Britain had become wealthy. Thus economic activity would automatically tend to be engaged in areas where each country had a comparative advantage, so that every other country following Britain's example would become wealthy as quickly as possible. The comparative advantage held by El Salvador and similar countries was, of course, in agriculture and particularly in certain long-living plants requiring a tropical climate, such as coffee.

Almost everybody accepted this point of view towards the end of the nineteenth century. It did not have to be imposed by British or American imperialists. It was in the immediate interest of the Salvadorean ruling class as it was in that of the ruling classes throughout most of Latin America. The planters sold their coffee and bought imported luxuries with minimal loss to the state in tariffs or duties. The merchants were even more obviously favoured.

But the effect, as in most other parts of the 'third world' of Africa, Asia, and Latin America, was to cause a decline in handicrafts and prevent the establishment of industry, or prevent the gradual transformation of handicrafts into industry, as had taken place in Europe. The doctrine of comparative advantage might lead to universal benefit if there were full and easy mobility of all 'factors of production', particularly the workers. But this is a totally unrealistic requirement, as can be seen today with the universal shutting of doors to unskilled immigrants throughout the advanced industrial world, or their admission when urgently needed only on a temporary and conditional basis.

Surplus labour could not emigrate from El Salvador, except to neighbouring countries and in particular the north coast of Honduras where commercial agriculture was being started without an indigenous labour force locally available; it was also being created both by the replacement of handicrafts by imported products and by the introduction of improved medical techniques which reduced infant mortality rates. The supply of labourers thus exceeded the demand. This happened earlier in El Salvador than in most other parts of the third world because of the greater shortage of land. Wage rates had probably been depressed by 1890, and the reforms of Carlos Ezeta most likely consisted of re-establishing by decree the wages that had previously been paid, at the same time as maintaining the traditional free meals.

The only kinds of government activity between 1894 and 1911 which had some effect in alleviating the condition of at least some of the masses, so badly affected by the market forces in operation, were the extension of the public school system particularly at low primary level – it was thought unwise to educate the masses further[19] – some provision of medical care, and the public works on which labour was given employment. The reforms of Manuel Enrique Araujo consisted of furthering public works, abolishing imprisonment for debt, obliging employers to pay indemnity for work accidents to rural workers, and raising the status of the Department of Agriculture to a Ministry.

In the same period the abolition of communal landholding (begun in 1880 and completed in 1912) had its usual effect of exposing the ignorant to the unscrupulous, as large numbers of small parcels of land were bought up for very small amounts and amalgamated to form many of the thriving *fincas* (coffee plantations) of today.[20] 'The easiest way to deprive a peasant of his land is to give him title to it', a remark made in the context of contemporary Africa, was also true of late nineteenth-century Latin America.

Market forces were being reinforced by singular state action to the detriment of the rural masses. Vagrancy laws obliged poor peasants to work for landowners. Such laws and practices continued to exist up to the régime of Maximiliano Hernández Martínez.[21] But because of the greater pressure on land which forced men to seek paid employment anyway (since the price for which land could be rented for a season was higher), such laws have been invoked much less regularly in the twentieth century than in neighbouring Guatemala, where they were an important institution right up to the overthrow of Jorge Ubico in 1944.

The opposite measure, rural unionization, which, if effective, would modify the operation of market forces in favour of the rural workers – and by extension of the masses as a whole since the rural workers would buy more local products, and the whole labour market would be changed to benefit the workers – is still not permitted, although it might be allowed in the not too distant future. Rural unions have never been formally permitted, although in contrast to the usual contemporary suppression there was a short period of only half-repressed formation of such unions from 1929 to early 1931, under Presidents Pío Romero Bosque and Arturo Araujo.

## The Rise of the Left Reorients the Political System

Freedom to organize unions and the improvement of rural living standards were promises made at the 1918 elections. At the same time the first effects of the Russian Revolution reached El Salvador in the shape of underground copies of a newspaper, *El Submarino Bolchevique* which came through Panamá. Unlike the 'Bolshevik sweets', 'Bolshevik shoes', and 'Bolshevik bread' popular at the time, the *Bolshevik Submarine* had a political content, not merely a catching name. Also in 1918 there probably took place the first secret meetings at which thoroughgoing social reforms were advocated, mainly to groups of artisans and workers in San Salvador, by a few persons of middle-class origin who had been educated in Guatemala or else-where outside the country.[22]

From these embryonic beginnings, workers' organization gathered momentum throughout the 1920s. Between 1920 and 1922 there were still one or two unsuccessful attempts at military uprisings.[23] But in 1921 something unprecedented happened: a demonstration by market women in San Salvador was fired upon by troops with machine guns and a number were killed. The women, who were demonstrating in favour of the opposition leader Miguel Tomás Molina, attacked the police post of Barrio El Calvario, and, according to the autobiographical account of ex-shoemaker Miguel Mármol, executed several policemen. According to Mármol, a strike of shoe-makers had just the same day ended with an official commission finding in favour of a raise in wages; but after the bloody con-frontation with the market women, the government of Jorge Meléndez threw aside this conciliatory finding, terrorized the leaders of the strike, and sanctioned a reduction of wages and massive dismissals of shoemakers.[24] The shoemaking trade, like other handicrafts, was in decline, because of competition from imported factory-made shoes – and later a local factory. This decline led to the replacement of the larger workshops by small firms, so that now a third of all shoemakers are their own bosses.[25]

In 1923 the first permanent trade unions were founded, in the form of general unions in the smaller towns, by separate trades in the cities. By 1924 there was already a Regional Federation of Workers of El Salvador, within a Central American Workers' Confederation. Anarcho-syndicalist and communist lines soon emerged and separated within these bodies, however poorly under-stood the different doctrines may have been.

The National Guard (*Guardia Nacional*, modelled on the Spanish *Guardia Civil*), formed by Araujo in 1912 to combat crime in the countryside, came increasingly to be used as an agent of repression against the proletarian agitators, wherever they went outside the largest cities. But the fact that the Quiñónez government or its legislature contemplated concession as well as repression is shown by a decree of May 1926 regretting the rise in rents, and facilitating the formation of private corporations to build cheap housing. No such corporations were in fact set up, perhaps because the interest rate that they would have been allowed to charge was only 9 per cent.[26]

At the end of his term of office in 1927, Alfonso Quiñónez installed in the Presidency his friend and fellow-townsman from Suchitoto (*paisano*, a person who hails from the same part of the country – a significant connection in El Salvador as in many other countries) Pío Romero Bosque. Quiñónez, like Regalado, Escalón, and the Meléndez brothers, was a member of the planter élite;[27] Pío Romero Bosque was his inferior in wealth and social position, and he expected to be able to control him. In this he was mistaken. The wide powers accorded to Latin American Presidents, and the great dislike of re-election, make it difficult for a strongman to continue in office himself; usually the puppet behaves tamely enough;[28] but on this occasion, as in Mexico seven years later when Lázaro Cárdenas turned on his protector Calles and changed the course of the Mexican revolution, it did not work for Quiñónez; and in December 1927 an attempt by Jorge Meléndez and his friends to overthrow Romero Bosque by military means failed.[29]

One can say that the course of Salvadorean history changed at the accession of Pío Romero Bosque to the Presidency; or at least it was the beginning of a period of transition ending with the suppression of the rebellion of 1932, after which the new order of things was apparent. After this change Salvadorean history has been above all else a series of moves or shifts made in relation to a basic conflict between the privileged attempting to maintain their privileges and the representatives of the interests of the underprivileged – between oppressor and oppressed in fact. Before 1927, the masses had few spokesmen; their dissatisfaction with their poverty, when it attained political expression, took the form of sporadic revolts. These were not effective enough to force the ruling groups to give their main attention to their tactics in dealing with the challenge. Since 1927, Presidents have had a measure of freedom of choice in the policies they have adopted, in conformity with the traditions of the Latin American Presidential system, with its background in *caudillismo*.[30] They have nevertheless been obliged to adhere fairly closely to the particular stance toward the masses which is imposed on the ruling classes by the logic of their situation at any particular time, given their determination to hold on to their privileges. A President who deviates too far from the balance of concession and repression called for by prevailing conditions invites a *coup d'état* which will restore the correct balance. The balance may not necessarily be anything like an even one: there have been periods of almost total repression. President Arturo Araujo, who followed Romero Bosque, was ousted by *coup d'état* in December 1931 for erring on the side of concession; General Hernández Martínez fell after more than twelve years in power, in May 1944, for too much repression; Menéndez in October 1944 for concession; Castaneda Castro in December 1948 for repression; Lemus in October 1960 for repression. The most recent

*coup* occurred three months later in January 1961 when the junta
which had toppled Lemus were themselves ousted for making too
many political concessions to popular aspirations.

Throughout this period there have always been groups within the
ruling classes seeking greater use of repressive measures, and other
groups favouring more concession. Political tension results and
minds are made up by external events, which are not within the
control of the Salvadorean ruling classes. Such matters as the
current international price of coffee, which, if it rises, gives greater
opportunity for concessions; the degree of political awakening
among the masses or sections of the masses, questioning the unequal
distribution of wealth; and the United States government's current
policy on social questions in Latin America as a whole and in El
Salvador in particular all play their part.

Changes in these external conditions are usually gradual, so that
the balance of opinion only changes slowly. I would suggest that this
balance, crucial to the thinking of the ruling classes at any given
time, corresponds well to the particular combination or 'mix' of
concession and repression which best answers their interests at the
time: this 'mix' can be seen, then, as in a sense imposing itself upon
them, as the natural policy for them to follow in view of the circumstances to which they are adapting themselves. Indeed, one can
think of ruling-class policy as having been consistent ever since
1927 if one sees it as applying in each of the changing sets of circumstances a 'natural mix' – the minimum of repression judged necessary
to maintain the bases of privilege and in particular to prevent the
representatives of the underprivileged from attaining state power; a
corresponding degree of political concession, aimed at attracting as
many popular representatives as possible to work within the formal
political system (although their effect is small) rather than to adopt
revolutionary means. A degree of economic concession to at least
some sections of the masses – enough to give the impression of a
government favouring the populace, without seriously eating into
privilege – may also be applied.

Consistency in this fundamental position leads me to date the
present political system of El Salvador from 1927 rather than from
the advent of military rule in December 1931. The coming of
military rule does not contradict the 'balance' thesis. The 'natural
mix' in the depression conditions of 1931 required considerable
repression, and the military are the instrument of repression. But
why 1927? The régime of Pío Romero Bosque which began in that
year marked a sharp break with its predecessors – he held the freest
municipal and then Presidential elections in Salvadorean history –
and it was in the late 1920s that popular forces, demanding radical

changes in the economic system – redistribution and the reduction of privilege – began seriously to challenge existing political assumptions, particularly the liberal idea of the state.

## Short-lived Democracy and the Uprising of 1932

Don Pío, as he was called, inherited a relatively comfortable national economic position: coffee prices were high. He also inherited the growing problem of unrest among the urban workers, which was spreading to some rural areas as well. His policy, as far as political organization was concerned, was to allow free elections with the participation of all political views – six *ad hoc* parties were formed – except those which sought the overthrow of the political system. The meeting which founded the Communist Party in 1930 had to be held in secret, in a wood near Lake Ilopango.[31]

Within the limits of a non-interventionist liberal policy Romero Bosque made some economic concessions too. In 1928 he decreed tax exemption for income derived from the cultivation of maize, beans, rice, and other cereals.[32] Two other events occurred during the Presidency of Don Pío which tend to reinforce the impression that times had changed or were at least changing. The first was the dismissal in 1928 of José Gustavo Guerrero from the Foreign Ministry after Guerrero, an influential man who went on to become a leading international jurist, had had an altercation with the United States Secretary of State, Charles Evans Hughes, over the American intervention in Nicaragua.[33] The Salvadorean élite were greatly disturbed about American involvements in that country. A long period of some tension between El Salvador and the United States therefore resulted. But it seems that from this time on, the ruling classes and government could not allow themselves to come into conflict with the American government, their natural ally against the aspirations of the masses for fundamental social change.

The second event was the formation in late 1929 of the Society for the Defence of Coffee by the leading coffee-planters, who must previously have assumed that their interests would be adequately defended by the government direct. They had not set up any formal organization before: informal influences on the government had been enough. The new organization, later called the *Asociación Cafetalera de El Salvador*, constituted a body within which the planter élite could more or less autonomously control the production and marketing of coffee without interference from the government, and after 1932, from the military. This position was somewhat modified under the short-lived 1960 junta, which enabled smaller-scale coffee-planters to take the place of the élite in control of the *Asociación*; but the *status quo ante* was pretty well restored by the succeeding régime, which gave the planter élite control of the semi-governmental agency, *Compañía Salvadoreña del Café*, which has taken over the regulating function while the *Asociación* has withered.

For the 1930 elections Don Pío issued strict, and totally un-precedented, instructions to every provincial governor to be impartial and not to assume that there was any official candidate. The result was a victory for the man who promised most in the direction of reform, Arturo Araujo. He was a landowner who had acquired a reputation for generosity toward his workers, paying them, it is said, double the going wage-rates; an engineer; and an accomplished linguist. According to one source, he had prepared in 1920 an invasion from over the Honduran border in typical idealist-liberal fashion, but it came to nothing.[34] At the election, what was left of idealist sentiment was divided between Araujo and two other candidates, Enrique Córdova and Miguel Tomás Molina, with Córdova the main beneficiary. Araujo had also acquired an admira-tion for the British Labour Party while studying in England, where, extraordinary for a Salvadorean aristocrat, he had stayed in Liver-pool in the house of a shop steward and Labour Party activist. From England also he brought in 1900 his wife Dora (née Morton, of respectable middle-class family) who was to stay with him through the vicissitudes of his career for fifty years. The name that Araujo gave to the party he founded for the purpose of his candidacy was *Partido Laborista Salvadoreño*, a name that in Latin America carries a clear reference to the British party. Moreover, his candidacy had the strong backing of a well-respected writer and educator, Alberto Masferrer, who advocated in a number of works, for which 'tender-minded' seems the best description, a voluntary sharing of privilege and reduction of inequality.[35]

Although Araujo allowed some of those reformist-minded working-class activists who had rallied to his cause to make large election promises on his behalf,[36] there is no evidence that he wanted to carry them out. He was not a traitor to his class, and his class accepted his assumption of office. Agustín Farabundo Martí, the colourful communist leader, had joined the legendary Sandino's guerrillas in Nicaragua after being exiled by Jorge Meléndez, but had quarrelled with Sandino over the merely nationalistic, non-revolutionary nature of his struggle against the Americans. He had been expelled again by Pío Romero Bosque in December 1930 but returned secretly in February 1931. Now, after Araujo's inaugura-tion in March, he went to the President's office to try to persuade him to implement reforms. Araujo's reaction was to call him a fanatic[37] and, soon after, to have him imprisoned.

But Araujo's actions cannot be analysed except as reactions to the worsening economic situation following the onset of the Depression and to the fact that popular revolutionary organization had been proceeding at an accelerated pace since the Wall Street crash had caused a sharp fall in coffee prices and coffee-workers' wages. In 1931 the coffee export price fell as low as ₡18 per quintal (1 quintal=100 lb.=46 kilograms)[38] as compared with ₡32 in 1927 and ₡39 in 1928, and rural wages are reported to have dropped as low as 20 *centavos* a day in 1930, which would be substantially less than half the figure obtaining before the stock market crash. It is not surprising, therefore, that the revolutionaries were able to organize an estimated 80,000 agricultural labourers, mainly coffee-workers in western El Salvador, into militant unions. There were strikes and, in May 1930, a mass march was organized in San Salvador. Pío Romero Bosque addressed the marchers, but without offering concessions.

By 1931 these activities had increased, and in May Arturo Araujo began to repress them with bloodshed, the first such case being a demonstration at Sonsonate. However, Araujo did announce that the Communist Party would be allowed to participate in the municipal elections scheduled for December. There was still an attempt to balance concession with repression.

Araujo was overthrown on 2 December, by a large number[39] of young army officers. Since the army has occupied the government ever since – the only case of such permanent occupancy in Latin America – it would be particularly important to establish the causes of this *coup* and whether others were involved, elements of the civilian or military élites and particularly General Martínez, who emerged the beneficiary. However, the officers still maintain that they acted without any such connivance, and that their imprisonment of Martínez during the violent course of the *coup* – several regiments were loyal to Araujo and it might have failed – was genuine. They installed Martínez as President, they say, because under the constitution he was the legal successor and, they thought, the only person who would receive diplomatic recognition. Martínez, who seems to have been an accomplished serendipitist if nothing else, had attached himself to Araujo's ticket as Vice Presidential candidate in the election of 1930, after having found that he himself did not stand a chance as a Presidential candidate: he was running fifth or sixth in a field of six, according to all prognostications. It is astonishing that Araujo accepted him as running-mate and afterwards had full confidence in his loyalty.[40]

The officers who overthrew Araujo say they did so because he was obviously inept and ineffective, and this verdict has acquired almost the status of accepted fact in El Salvador today. A main reason may have been Araujo's refusal to pay military salaries any sooner than those of civilian officials. (It had been traditional to do so, perhaps an essential part of maintaining military goodwill. The proud boast of a good outgoing President had been that payment of civilian salaries was no further in arrears upon his leaving office than it had been when he entered the Presidency.) It was certainly true to say that Araujo had been ineffective in dealing with the growing unrest. Although he had repressed it, he had not repressed it enough to prevent it from growing again.

When Martínez took over a few days after the *coup*, the extent of the change from Araujo's régime did not make itself immediately apparent. University students were able to publish a newspaper which was openly revolutionary and communist, but in which they avoided mentioning Martínez.[41] The municipal elections were put off, but only for a month and the Communist Party was allowed, for the only time in Salvadorean history, to participate. Martínez might have wanted to find out who his enemies were. At all events, the communists won some of the towns in the west but were denied their victory and not allowed to take office. This denial finally persuaded the party to launch the rebellion for which it had been preparing the rural workers. It was a desperate move, because the party was strong only in certain areas, and Farabundo Martí is recorded as having said in mid-1931 that there was no hope of success.[42] A few days before the agreed date for a simultaneous uprising in a number of towns, Martínez's police captured Farabundo Martí and two student companions, editors of the newspaper, in a hideout. When this news reached the other communist leaders, they made a last-minute attempt to call off the revolt; but they were unable to establish communication with many of the towns where it was to take place, and the only result was that the effectiveness of the rebellion, which started in most places as first planned, was reduced. The failure to establish communication may have been due to some individuals preferring to save their own skins by going into hiding in the capital, rather than return to the west to spread the news that the rebellion had been called off.[43]

The rebellion took the form of concerted attacks by *campesinos* (agricultural workers and peasants), armed almost exclusively with *machetes*, during the night of 22–23 January 1932, on the public buildings of the western towns. The towns of Izalco, Sonzacate, Nahuizalco, Juayúa, and Tacuba were captured, but the soldiers in the largest cities of Sonsonate, Santa Tecla, and Ahuachapán were able easily to repulse the attacks; in San Salvador a mutiny in the principal barracks had been part of the plan, but it came to nothing.[44] Then the carnage of *campesinos* began. Seventy-two hours after the revolt began, almost all the small towns had been re-captured by the army,[45] and the massacre took the form of mass executions of suspects, which could often mean anyone wearing Indian dress[46] or indeed almost anyone at all. Estimates of the number who died vary widely, but 15,000 to 20,000 is likely. The figure of 30,000 is often used by the political Left. The repression can be described as a massacre, because of the undoubtedly large numbers killed in cold blood after resistance had ended. There was an attempt to justify it on the other side with stories of murder and rape, but these have been investigated by the politically impartial American historian Thomas P. Anderson, and found to be unfounded:[47] in all probability, not more than half a dozen civilians were killed by the rebels, and certainly not more than thirty.

The ethnic cleavage between Indians and *ladinos* played a part in the revolt, particularly since the only Indian *caciques*[48] remaining in El Salvador, Feliciano Ama of Izalco and Felipe Neri of Nahuizalco, supported it. But the revolt covered areas where the cleavage was already much less strong than at Izalco, and numerous *ladinos* took part. There was almost no echo of the revolt to the east of Lake Ilopango,[49] either in the Nonualco region or elsewhere. It was concentrated in the western coffee-growing areas, where coffee had already spread to cover most of the ground in the areas of suitable altitude, and the rural population was already almost completely dependent on seasonal wage labour on the coffee plantations; there was no space left for them to plant subsistence crops. This process had not gone so far in the eastern coffee-producing zone where there was no revolt. It appears also that in the places where the coffee-planters were not quite so cut off socially from the bulk of the rural population; where they did not own such large estates and generally resided in the local area rather than in a city; and above all where they had cushioned the workers from the blow caused by the fall of coffee prices, the rebellion did not occur; this would explain why Ataco, an otherwise typical small town in the western coffee-producing area, did not join the revolt.[50]

## The Firm Hand of General Maximiliano Hernández Martínez

It remained Martínez's policy throughout the rest of his Presidency to prevent any political activity by advocates of structural reform. He founded an official party, called *Pro-Patria*, on the lines of the *Liga Roja* which had been disbanded by Pío Romero Bosque after it had helped him into office. Under Martínez, all other political organizations were banned, as well as trade unions, and there were a number of violations of university autonomy, an extreme measure in Latin America. In these acts of repression Martínez was at first supported wholeheartedly by the ruling classes in general, who had been frightened by the rebellion. But as time went on the economic situation gradually improved; there were no further outbreaks of unrest;[51] and the first conspiracies began to appear, aimed at replacing Martínez by a more relaxed régime.

Meanwhile, Martínez did make some economic concessions. First, in March 1932, he demonstrated his willingness to depart from liberal orthodoxy by declaring a moratorium on debts. (He also devalued the *colón* which has stayed at the rate of ₡2.50 to the U.S. dollar ever since 1934.) This was followed by a law providing for partial liquidation of the debts, particularly welcome to the smaller coffee-planters who had gone heavily into debt in the boom years before the crash.[52] In 1933 he founded *Mejoramiento Social* (Social Improvement), a general-purpose government institution to help further the standard of living of the poor. In 1936, continuing with a policy started under Araujo,[53] the government authorized the buying of land to redistribute to small farmers who would pay by instalment. Such schemes were continued by later régimes but always on a very small scale; very often it was a matter of legalizing squatting and making the squatters pay.[54]

In 1939 a new constitution included for the first time the idea of state intervention in the economy, for instance to protect the small trader – though this amounted to discrimination against the Arab and Chinese traders, who had come to El Salvador since the last years of the nineteenth century, not a help for small as opposed to large merchants.[55] Martínez also passed laws prohibiting the use of powered machinery to manufacture shoes and certain other items, including sisal sacks for the export of coffee, which could be produced by handicraftsmen.[56] As a protectionist measure it seems partial, too late, and ill-conceived, since it made no provision for the gradual transformation of handicraft production into a competitive modern industry. It was, however, a concession to the economic aspirations of at least a section of the poor, and he is remembered with gratitude for it, as he is for keeping down the crime rate. He also took steps to provide credit for agricultural operations of different sizes, with the foundation of a mortgage bank (*Banco Hipotecario*) in 1935 for large-scale operations, and the *Cajas de Crédito Rural* in 1943 for the small farmer or *campesino*.

A *modus vivendi* between his military régime and the civilian élite seems to have been established with little difficulty, and has survived in subsequent régimes. The military occupy the Presidency and a number of positions in the government, most of the remainder being given to civilians who are not members of the élite but are rather more dependent for their career prospects on their relations with the military. On the other hand, key positions in the economy are occupied directly by the civilian economic élite. This applies especially to coffee, which does not come under the control of the Ministry of Agriculture at all, and also to the Central Reserve Bank which was founded in 1934. The *Banco Hipotecario*, though controlled by civilians, has distinguished itself by its advocacy of reform measures, at least in 1944 and again at the present time; perhaps this is a consequence of the nature of its operations.

There has not been a significant cleavage between the civilian and military élites: they have coalesced to form a single ruling class in which the military reserves for itself the positions of political power, above all the Presidency, but carries out a policy which does not deviate from the general interests of the civilian élite. In this situation, the differences of opinion over the appropriate balance of concession or repression, in face of the claims advanced on behalf of the masses, find supporters on both sides among civilians and military. Thus the conspiracies which aim to oust a President who is thought to be going too far in one direction or another are generally joined by both civilian and military men. The first large-scale conspiracy against Martínez was led by Colonel Asencio Menéndez in 1938, on the occasion (always a spur to conspiracies) of Martínez's announcement of his intention to get himself re-elected. This was uncovered and the conspirators exiled. After El Salvador had entered the Second World War, on the side of the United States and 'democracy'[57] immediately after Pearl Harbor, and the economic position had begun to improve, Martínez's repressive régime came to be seen as less and less desirable or necessary. Conspiracy spread among both civilians and military in 1943. Some civilians were imprisoned, and one was executed.

## *1944–61: Relaxation, but Two More Régimes are Overthrown when they Propose to Hold Free Elections*

In March 1944, with another re-election, discontent became more general. It erupted in a revolt in the capital on Easter Sunday, 2 April 1944. The revolt took the form of a military *coup* which did not succeed, but the city became a battlefield for two days and there were many wounded and dead. When Martínez reasserted his control, he blundered by continuing to repress and executing captured rebel leaders. This provoked a strong reaction, a strike begun by the students being taken up by the rest of the city population. The final blow came on 7 May, when a student, José Wright, a member of the Salvadorean élite, although an American citizen, was shot dead by a policeman. The following day the American ambassador[58] advised Martínez to resign, and the advice was taken.

The period from 8 May to 21 October 1944 was one of political freedom in anticipation of free elections. Martínez's Vice President, General Andrés Ignacio Menéndez, had assumed the Provisional Presidency, but did not attempt to continue a policy of repression. The hopes of reform were placed in the most outstanding civilian leader of the revolt of April and May, Arturo Romero, a doctor.[59] Romero was the hero of the hour and was expected to win the election. If he had been allowed to do so, his régime would doubtless have resembled that of Juan José Arévalo in Guatemala, which grew out of a similar and parallel revolt against a similar dictator, Jorge Ubico, in the same year.

But he was not allowed to do so. A *coup* took place on 21 October 1944 without any resistance from the Provisional President, who may even have requested it[60] because he could not take the necessary measures himself. The *coup* was executed by the Chief of Police, Colonel Osmín Aguirre y Salinas, who had played an important role in the pacification of the 1932 revolt. Arturo Romero was expelled to Costa Rica, and with only minor right-wing opposition candidates left in the field, victory in the election could not but go to the candidate with the support of Osmín and the military, General Salvador Castaneda Castro.

A last-ditch attempt was made to reverse the situation. An invasion was prepared in traditional style from across the Guatemalan frontier. Called the *Jornada de Ahuachapán* it involved the crossing of the border by between 500 and 800 men, some soldiers and others armed civilians. They went to Ahuachapán, where the commander of the barracks was a conspirator and was expected to open the fortress and its arms supplies to them. However, he did no such thing and in a short battle they were easily defeated.[61] Among the organizers of the *Jornada de Ahuachapán* were such diverse figures as Arturo Romero; Miguel Tomás Molina, the now eighty-year-old survivor of the idealist liberal tradition, who had been a member of the Constituent Assembly in 1886; had been the candidate around whom the whole opposition to Meléndez and Quiñónez had gathered in 1922; and had seen practically all that support vanish by the 1930 election, although he retained considerable respect; Colonel Félix Osegueda, one of the young officers who had overthrown Arturo Araujo; and Julio Adalberto Rivera, who was later to be the leader of the *coup* from the Right against the 1960 junta, and President from 1962 to 1967.

Castaneda Castro's régime was a static one: while he did not go to the repressive extreme of Martínez and allowed some of the organizations formed in 1944 to continue some form of existence, he did not make any real economic or political concessions, and when he made known his intention to prolong his period of office, he was overthrown by another *coup*, on 14 December 1948. This *coup*, carried out by younger officers against the older generation, resulted in the Presidency of one of the majors involved, Oscar Osorio. His régime can be said to have been the one which worked out the more stable political system which still exists today. Although there were to be two more *coups* in 1960 and 1961, the system implanted by Osorio was sufficiently open and flexible to allow an incumbent President to judge the way the balance of opinion was moving on the basic question of the 'mix' of concession and repression in face of the challenge from the advocates of structural reform to reduce inequality. The 'mix' applied by Osorio was appropriate in the circumstances: open revolutionaries were still repressed, but an opportunity was provided for those who were content merely to advocate milder reforms to do so through opposition parties. The formation of trade unions was allowed, and all kinds of opposition organizations were given more freedom to operate than they had had since May–October 1944; but in contrast to the relatively full freedom of that period, each organization had to tread carefully, and the régime applied flexible reins to the activity of each one. In the economic sphere, the moves made both by Osorio and by his successor, Lemus, in the direction of concession had two main tendencies. In attempting or appearing to effect a general expansion and improvement through industrial development, they tended to achieve only an expansion of job opportunities for a new salaried middle class; and in attempting or appearing to introduce modern government provision for social development, they tended to create a relatively privileged sector within the working class, those with access to such innovations as social security, collective wage bargaining through the legal unions, and the government urban housing and rural land settlement schemes. These benefited a very small percentage of the poor, but could be presented demagogically as a social revolution being carried out by the government; the *coup* of 1948 was presented as a revolution comparable with the Mexican Revolution or that of Guatemala in 1944. One consideration which must have influenced Osorio's régime to take this attitude was the growing radicalism in Guatemalan politics between 1948 and 1954. The demand for far-reaching reform was growing again under the impact of the Guatemalan example, and Osorio was concerned to keep control of the situation in El Salvador.

The Osorio régime took the first important steps towards the encouragement of industry: exemptions from import tariffs on equipment, and on raw materials for an initial period, and exemption from taxes for a similar period, for those setting up certain new industries. Such steps began piecemeal in 1949 and have been extended since. Government departments were set up to stimulate growth in areas other than agriculture; and this is another policy which has been steadily widened under successive régimes since 1948, along with minimum wage legislation, extended to rural labour in 1965; the control of prices of basic grains; increased state provision of education; and increased availability of state credit to small farmers. In general, such economic concessions have accumulated, each President wishing to mark his régime with some new measures to attract popularity, and tending usually to carry on the measures of his predecessor in broad outline. However, the most demagogic of the innovations begun by Osorio and expanded by Lemus, the *Procuraduría de Pobres*,[62] which had a number of functions, not merely legal, and which might be described as a government agency to help the poor conspicuously, had its budget drastically cut by Rivera. The demagogic style of Lemus in particular has not been wholly imitated by his successors.

Colonel José María Lemus came to the Presidency in 1956 as official party candidate, all opposition candidates having withdrawn in protest that the election was not really free. His initial attitude on the question of political freedom or repression was rather more permissive than Osorio's had become; but by 1960, confronted by an increasingly militant Left, which included for the first time since 1932 an influential Communist Party, Lemus turned more and more to repression. On 2 September he finally sent his police into the university building, usually a safe sanctuary, where they manhandled a number of lecturers as well as students.[63] In contrast to the mistreatment or even murder of working-class or particularly rural agitators, this type of repression provoked an immediate outcry and widespread condemnation among the ruling classes. After two months of extreme tension – September and October 1960 – Lemus fell to a *coup*.

Lemus had also fallen out with his predecessor, Osorio, and the *coup* was the result of a conspiracy between at least two clearly separable groups: supporters of Osorio and advocates of gradual but far-reaching structural social reforms in the direction of equality. This was the first and only time in the country's history that such 'Bernsteinian socialists', as some of them have been heard to refer to themselves, have had any share in state power. It appears there was also a third group, with a political position akin to Osorio's but owing no allegiance to him.[64] The junta, during its three months of power, did not attempt to carry out any major reforms, but it made clear its intention to hold really free elections, allowing even the Left to organize. While the Communist Party itself was not legalized, the *Partido Revolucionario Abril y Mayo*, of clear left-wing orientation and including communists, was to be permitted to participate in the election. When this became clear, the junta was overthrown, on 25 January 1961, by a movement supported by a majority of army officers and the civilian élite. It is true that opposition to the pro-Osorio elements also played a part in this *coup*, but even without this, it is hardly conceivable that the army would have allowed a left-wing government to take power: a *coup* was inevitable while the junta persisted in its policy of free elections.

## The Régime Stemming from the 1961 Coup

The régime resulting from the 1961 *coup*, led by Colonel Julio Rivera until 1967 and by Colonel (now General) Fidel Sánchez Hernández since the election of that year, has continued the pattern laid down by Osorio, achieving stability by adopting a flexible policy of varying the degree and the form of repression and economic concession according to the political exigencies of the moment. The policy has also been made more sensitive, in that considerably more freedom of political activity is allowed in forms which are judged to be innocuous, while left-wing proselytization in the countryside, for instance, is still rigidly repressed. Over and above the temporary cycles of relaxation and retightening of control, the political policy has tended to ease with time since 1961 (and overall since 1948), as the economy has grown and given rise to a new middle class, and as the 'revolutionaries' have been increasingly occupied either in pursuing partial economic gains for a section of the working class through trade union organization and wage claims, or in internal politicking at the National University. Indeed, one might describe the present situation as the result of a successful strategy on the part of the ruling class to incorporate its opponents into the formal political system without allowing them to have any really significant effect (up to now at any rate) on the outcome. The strategy has been particularly successful since 1963, when Rivera introduced a form of proportional representation for the Legislative Assembly and so gave the reformist opposition a chance to have a number of seats, while the government could be sure, through its control of rural voting, that this need never mean opposition control of the Assembly. Before 1963 the reformist opposition had on several occasions boycotted elections, including the one at which Rivera himself gained the Presidency, but not since then.

Paradoxically at first sight, university autonomy has been strengthened during the 1960s, and the university's funds from the state greatly increased, allowing the building of an attractive new campus. At the same time, the university has tended to move in a more revolutionary direction – staff and ruling bodies as well as students. The paradox can be explained on the assumption that if the revolutionaries are not interfered with on their own territory, and are enabled to live more comfortably, they are not so likely to make revolution.

The treatment of proletarian revolutionaries in the trade unions has been a little less kind, but the same trend can nevertheless be observed. On the one hand, would-be agitators have been discouraged by what can only be described, as all the evidence seems to indicate, as a regular pattern of occasional brutal murder by the police of a worker who has achieved some prominence though not pre-eminence in the revolutionary or strongly reformist organizations. These executions without trial, of which there seem to have been three in the late 1960s,[65] were not specifically or immediately provoked by particular acts by the victim. They have been a general disincentive to revolutionary proselytization among workers, and have performed this disincentive function through the publicity that the Left has given them. On the other hand, the majority of leaders have been allowed to survive and, within the urban areas, to organize, to make public speeches, and to lead illegal strikes to a successful conclusion. It is likely that the apparent policy of occasional police murder has now stopped, because the man chiefly identified with it in the public mind, General José ('Chele') Medrano, Chief of the National Guard, was dismissed from this and all posts in December 1970. It is interesting to note that a few days after the dismissal, the National Guard was sent to break up a strike at the country's largest shoe factory in San Salvador, a kind of action unusual in recent years. It was as if President Sánchez Hernández were reassuring the ruling classes that despite the departure of Medrano the government was prepared and able to use repressive measures.

## The Contrast with Guatemala since 1944

It is worthwhile to compare the present success of the Salvadorean 'mix' with the situation in Guatemala, the country with which El Salvador has always had most in common politically, with parallel economic structures and parallel discontents. In Guatemala General Jorge Ubico, whose rule was similar to that of General Martínez in El Salvador and covered exactly the same years, 1931–44, fell in a similar situation and through a similar process, which culminated in a general refusal to go to work. In Guatemala, however, the fall of the dictator was followed for a few months by another very repressive régime, and then by a popular reaction and a successful *coup* or revolution from the Left, in October 1944 – the reverse of the sequence in El Salvador. The revolutionaries were in power until 1954, moved further to the left during that time, and although they were then defeated by an invasion of right-wing exiles with American as well as Honduran help, they were in power long enough to achieve an impact which is remembered. And it is perhaps this fact, as well as the existence of suitable mountainous terrain for guerrillas, which has led to the recent extreme and unmanageable polarization of Guatemalan politics. No 'mix' of concession and repression has been able to hold the line since the beginning of relaxation after the death of Castillo Armas in 1957; only his unmitigated repression of 1954–57 worked. At the present time there are considerable pressures for this policy to be adopted again. President Carlos Arana Osorio, the right-wing colonel elected on a minority vote in 1970,[66] made no secret in his election campaign of his willingness to use extreme methods to deal with communists, and had demonstrated his tough tactics against guerrillas when he was commander of the Zacapa army base.[67] However, although he leads the movement founded by Castillo Armas, he has not as yet returned to the complete clamp-down against any form of opposition which obtained in 1954–57; the repression is sharp, but it may get even sharper.

If greater polarization and sharper repression have been the result of the stronger discontent with the present distribution of wealth in Guatemala than in El Salvador, one wonders whether the policy of the ruling class in El Salvador can successfully continue much longer. For with even the present degree of freedom of political organization and proselytization, the level of discontent and its reflection in support for the reformist parties are bound to rise, so that it will become necessary either to dismantle privilege to a significant extent – perhaps as it has been done in Peru or perhaps by allowing a reformist party to rule – or else to face a situation of polarization, tension, and sporadic bloodshed as exists in Guatemala.

## NOTES

[1] Roque Dalton: *Miguel Mármol, Testimonio Político-Autobiográfico*, to be published in Cuba and Italy. I am grateful to Roque Dalton, the Salvadorean poet and writer resident in Cuba, for showing me the manuscript. Miguel Mármol, a shoemaker who was one of the founding members of the Salvadorean Communist Party, would have been recounting what he heard from the generation of his parents in the early years of this century. He says that under the Ezetas the wage of rural workers went up from about 35–50¢ to ₡2 per day, while instead of 75¢ the urban artisan could earn ₡4 or even ₡5. I can, however, find no corroboration of this picture, nor any reference to wages in the *Diario Oficial* for January–June 1891. The French visitor Laferrière, who gives full economic data for El Salvador in 1875, says that the day wage in agriculture was then 4 *reales* (50¢), and at the same time that the full cost of employing a hand on an *hacienda* for a month, including meals – which all rural employers provided in addition to wages – was 10 *pesos*. Joseph Laferrière: *De Paris à Guatemala* (1877: Paris).

[2] But Carlos Ezeta was ousted and has gone down in Salvadorean history merely as a drunken tyrant. Salvadorean history has been written almost exclusively by the idealist liberals, and their hero was Francisco Menéndez, who died, they say, of a heart attack when he learnt of the *coup* which his trusted lieutenant, Carlos Ezeta, was carrying out against him. Francisco Castañeda, *El General Menéndez y sus victimarios* (1893; 1966: San Salvador, Min. de Educación), 153–61. A most curious note in this connection is that Carlos Ezeta had lunch on the day of the *coup* with Rubén Darío, the great Nicaraguan poet, on the occasion of Darío's marriage; the *coup* took place later, in the evening, while Menéndez was holding a celebration dance to commemorate the fifth anniversary of the fall of Zaldívar and his own assumption of power.

[3] 'If an insurrectionary movement is liberal, then when it ceases to be merely an aspiration and achieves power, this power must remain in liberal hands, just as it would have to go to conservative hands if the movement were conservative. And it is strictly logical that it should be so'. Castañeda, op. cit., 61–2. Castañeda, a qualified supporter of Menéndez, was criticizing him for allowing too much freedom to other factions, and for being too idealist at the beginning of his period in the Presidency.

[4] *Diario Oficial*, early months of 1876.

[5] Julio Alberto Domínguez Sosa: *Génesis y Significado de la Constitución de 1886* (1958: San Salvador, Min. de Cultura), esp. 38–9, 49.

[6] Isidro Martínez Vargas: *Cien Años de Actuaciones Presidenciales 1862–1962* (1962: San Salvador, own press), 20.

[7] Harrison, op. cit., esp. ch. 1; Thomas L. Karnes: *The Failure of Union: Central America 1824–1960* (1961: Chapel Hill, Univ. of N. Carolina P.), esp. ch. VII.

[8] Emiliano Cortés, op. cit., quoting Barrios.

[9] Martínez Vargas, op. cit., 24.

[10] *Diario Oficial*, 1876.

[11] Led by Francisco Menéndez. Martínez Vargas, op. cit., 13–14.

[12] Led by General Rivas and Dr Prudencio Alfaro. The group known as *chachacasteros*, led by Rivas, had been the most vocal among those in the 1885 constituent assembly which Menéndez had disbanded by force. Alfaro was to remain the extremist leader of the idealist liberals until he was executed for the assassination of President M. E. Araujo in 1913.

[13] The background was as follows. Ex-President General Regalado led an invasion of Guatemala by El Salvador in support of Guatemalan insurrectionaries, in 1906. This war ended in stalemate, with a peace treaty achieved by the mediation of Mexico and the United States. Then in March 1907 a new war broke out with an invasion of Honduras by Nicaragua, which El Salvador entered on the side of the Honduran President Bonilla. This gave the Salvadorean idealist liberals a chance to fight on the side of Nicaragua and the Honduran rebels, against the Salvadorean army sent into Honduras. This war ended with the fall of Bonilla and a compromise Honduran President was installed (Dávila). Then the Salvadorean revolutionaries, led by Rivas and Alfaro, launched an invasion from the sea, with Nicaraguan help and apparently some also from Dávila under Nicaraguan pressure. They captured the port of Acajutla in June 1907, but only reached as far as Sonsonate before being put to flight. Gregorio Bustamante Maceo: *Historia Militar de El Salvador* (1951: San Salvador, Imp. Nacional), 99–103; Percy F. Martin: *Salvador of the Twentieth Century* (1911: London, Edward Arnold), 61–79, an account highly biased in favour of Figueroa; Alfredo Parada: *Etapas Políticas* (1950: San Salvador), ch. 7.

[14] These allegiances, like those to conservatism or liberalism in the 19th century, are often stronger in some areas than in others, but one still finds that there is a minority in each place which adheres to the other party, and this was certainly the case in Ahuachapán.

[15] I have benefited from discussion of this topic with Odin Toness, who has done research in Nicaragua and Paraguay.

[16] The kinds of ways in which the Karadjordjević and Obrenović families replaced one another on the throne of Serbia in the 19th century, by enlisting sufficient military support for an uprising or *coup*, are similar to events in Latin America. And the persistence of support for a dynasty which is out of power for

decades, like that of the Al Wazirs in the kingdom of the Yemen before the 1962 revolution, parallels the resilience of the Liberals in Paraguay today. Perhaps the Wars of the Roses were an English version of this phenomenon in an earlier period; and perhaps they should be thought of as an alternative version of wars for succession within a single dynasty, which according to Max Gluckman, in the context of the tribes of south-eastern Africa which had developed autocratic kingdoms before the arrival of Europeans, served as a check on the oppressive rule of the king, where few other checks existed, since he knew he would have to maintain some support, or rely entirely on spies. See Dana Adams Schmidt: *Yemen, the Unknown War* (1968: London, Bodley Head), 37–8; Max Gluckman: *Order and Rebellion in Tribal Africa* (1963: London, Cohen and West), esp. 87.

[17] Francisco Lucientes: *El Crimen del Parque Bolívar*. Araujo was attacked by two hired assassins while sitting in a 'park' – a square in San Salvador where he liked to listen to the band in the evening. Thomas Hohler, the British *chargé d'affaires* in Mexico, who had an appointment with Araujo at the time of the assassination, reports in his book *Diplomatic Petrel* (1942: London, John Murray), 181, that he was told he had been killed for purely private reasons, and this is repeated by Peter Calvert in *Latin America: internal conflict and international peace* (1969: London, Macmillan; New York, St Martin's), 72, but Hohler did not know El Salvador or her politics. According to David Luna: 'Owing to the President's activities à la Don Juan, there was more than one offended and resentful father. The Alfarist groups pushed one of these into avenging himself. The labourers who carried out the deed did not know the political importance of their victim'. David Luna, 'Análisis de una dictadura fascista latinoamericana, Maximiliano Hernández Martínez 1931–44', *La Universidad*, Año 94, No 5 (San Salvador, Sept.–Oct. 1969), 44.

[18] David Luna: 'Un heroico y trágico suceso de nuestra historia', *El Proceso Político Centroamericano*, Seminario de Historia Contemporánea de Centro América (1964: San Salvador, Ed. Univ.), 49–50.

[19] 'The education of the lower classes has been purposely restricted to a few fundamentals, because the authorities have desired to discourage the tendency, so harmful in all parts of Central America, towards the adoption of the learned professions at the expense of agricultural pursuits'. Dana G. Munro: *The Five Republics of Central America* (1918: New York, Oxford Univ. P.), ch. 5 (El Salvador), 110. One need hardly add that the restriction also served to hinder any challenge to the social position of the people who were the 'authorities'. Munro continues: 'No government aid is now granted to poor children for advanced study either at home or in foreign countries, and every effort is made rather to encourage those who have completed their primary course to fit themselves for the cultivation of the soil or for some trade'.

[20] Browning, op. cit., 212–21. A similar reform had been undertaken in Mexico rather earlier, with similar results.

[21] The laws, brought together as *Ley Agraria* in 1907, were strengthened in 1942, and include the article: 'The agents of the National Guard shall, immediately upon the demand of any *hacendado* or farmer, arrest the person or persons whom he indicates to them as suspicious'. These laws still apply today. David Luna, 'Análisis de una dictadura fascista . . .', 55–7.

[22] Data for this and the subsequent account of the beginnings of workers' organization are mainly from Dalton, op. cit., and Thomas P. Anderson: *Matanza, El Salvador's Communist Revolt of 1932* (1971: Lincoln, Univ. of Nebraska Press), ch. 2. Also from a taped conversation with one of the proselytizers mentioned.

[23] Bustamante Maceo, op. cit., 103–4.

[24] Dalton, op. cit. (n. 1). The various accounts or rather mentions of the demonstration leave the exact course of events unclear, and most people only remember the 'massacre' of the women. One writer says that the troops also fired at Dr Miguel Tomás Molina, but missed; he survived, indeed, to a ripe and active old age. Martínez Vargas, op. cit., 28.

[25] In 1961, of 3,450 shoemakers and repairers in San Salvador and its suburbs, 230 were 'employers', 880 self-employed, while 2,110 worked for others, 180 were apprentices, and 50 worked as part of a family business. Information from a 10 per cent sample of 1961 census cards.

[26] Harold Albert Sumner: *La Vivienda Popular* (1947: doctoral thesis in civil engineering, Univ. de El Salvador), ch. 6.

[27] Figueroa, too. Only M. E. Araujo is reported to have annoyed the oligarchy, and is said by some to have been killed by them.

[28] It may be worth noting that Quiñónez himself appears to have fallen out somewhat with Jorge Meléndez after taking over the Presidency from him. Of the previous hand-overs, it seems that Escalón allowed Regalado to retain considerable power, even virtually to rule, until his death in the war he provoked in 1906; M. E. Araujo did not have any trouble with ex-President Figueroa; Carlos Meléndez was in poor health and died during the Presidency of his brother Jorge, in 1920.

[29] Bustamante Maceo, op. cit., 104–5.

[30] Including the conditional nature of the loyalty it implies, see above, p. 54, note 77.

[31] Dalton, op. cit.

[32] José Eduardo Reyes: *Criterio de Inversiones, sugerencia de un sistema de prioridad industrial* (1961: doctoral thesis in economics, Univ. de El Salvador), 46. A version of the thesis was published in *Economía Salvadoreña*, Año VIII, No 20 (July–Dec. 1959).

[33] Ramón López Jiménez: *Dr. José Gustavo Guerrero* (1963: Madrid, 12 pp.), 6. Charles Evans Hughes was the Republican candidate for President narrowly defeated by Woodrow Wilson in 1916; he was Secretary of State 1921–25, and later Chief Justice 1930–41. At the time of the dispute with Guerrero in 1928, he was leading the American delegation to the Sixth International Conference of American States in Havana, where the delegation of El Salvador under Guerrero was one of the strongest in objecting to U.S. intervention. Samuel F. Bemis: *The Latin American Policy of the United States: an historical interpretation* (1943: New York, Harcourt, Brace & World), 251–2. This and similar works which mention the part played by El Salvador at the Conference do not mention the dismissal of Guerrero afterwards.

[34] Dalton, op. cit.

[35] See especially his essay *El Mínimum Vital*; also *El Dinero Maldito*, on the problem of alcoholism. He died in 1932. In 1930 he was a deputy in the Legislative Assembly. His works have been published in a number of editions since his death.

[36] He permitted a labour organizer, previously of anarcho-syndicalist affiliation, Felipe Recinos, to operate a section within his party, the section being known as *Partido Proletario*. Luna, 'Un heroico y trágico suceso', 57–8. Other data from Anderson, op. cit., and Julio Contreras Castro: *De cómo fué traicionado el Presidente Ing. Arturo Araujo por Max. Hernández Martínez, el hombre traidor, el vengativo, el demagogo y asesino del pueblo* (1944: San Salvador, Tip. La Unión).

[37] Ramón López Jiménez, article in *Diario de Hoy* (San Salvador), 20 Nov. 1970.

[38] The exchange rate was then ₡2 = $1.

[39] All the details of the plot seem to have been known to only about thirteen or fourteen conspirators, but they sounded out support enough to be confident that 'all the young officers', along with the School of Corporals and Sergeants, were behind the *coup*. One or two majors were the highest-ranking officers directly involved; the degree of participation of the then colonels Joaquín Valdés and Osmín Aguirre y Salinas, who headed the *Directorio Militar* from 3 to 4 December 1931, is unclear, even after the detailed account of the *coup* in Anderson, op. cit., 56–63, who has interviewed Aguirre. My information is also from a taped interview with Colonel Félix Osegueda, then a major and one of the leaders of the *coup*, who denies participation by higher-ranking officers.

[40] At least until shortly before the *coup*. Kenneth Grieb, quoting a report by an American diplomat on a conversation with Araujo soon after the *coup*, states that Araujo had attempted a few days before the *coup* to relieve Martínez of his duties as Minister of War. 'The United States and the Rise of General Maximiliano Hernández Martínez', *Journal of Latin American Studies*, Vol. 3, Pt. 2 (Nov. 1971).

[41] *La Estrella Roja, Órgano del Grupo Marxista de la Universidad y del Grupo de Revolución Universitaria*, in fact of Farabundo Martí's disciples Alfonso Luna and Mario Zapata. A reproduction of the title-page and of some articles is in Ítalo López Vallecillos, *El Periodismo en El Salvador*, 154–60.

[42] For this report, for a piece of writing of Martí's, and an article giving an

idea of his personality, see David Luna: 'Algunas Facetas Sociales en la Vida de Agustín Farabundo Martí', *Revista Salvadoreña de Ciencias Sociales*, No 1 (1965), 89–108. Martí, Luna, and Zapata were shot on 1 February after a brief trial.

[43] This, at any rate, is the version given me by one of the surviving members of the Central Committee of the time. It is possible that the Communist Party could no longer have prevented the rebellion because the rural population was itself so desperate; certainly it would have been difficult. See Luna, 'Un heroico y trágico suceso', 61–2. It is also clear that some of the party leaders were urging the cancellation of the revolt even before the capture of Martí, but that Martí, who was the recognized leader, did not accept their arguments. After the disheartening news of his capture, the Central Committee did accept the arguments, and made the decision, but it was too late. It is possible also that Martínez was using *agents provocateurs* to push the rebels into a showdown he was confident of winning, and before an expected invasion by Araujo could join forces with the communists in a simultaneous action. See also below, p. 166 and 177–8, notes 8 and 9.

[44] It does not appear that there was any plan at all for raising the revolt in Santa Ana, nor anywhere in the east of the country: the rebels did seek support in most of the villages of the west and the environs of the capital. It was the fear of revolt in San Salvador itself which most worried the government and upper classes, who formed voluntary Civic Guard groups, as well as the British and American colonies. Demonstrators attacked police on the same day that the barracks mutiny was forestalled, 18 January, and on the 19th a second barracks was unsuccessfully attacked by an armed group. The officers fought off this attack themselves, not trusting their men, a pattern repeated in Sonsonate during the revolt. These premature outbreaks of the uprising allowed the government to prepare more effectively, rounding up its opponents, and during the main period of the revolt there was comparatively little shooting in the capital. The somewhat panicky British and American colonies caused their respective *chargés d'affaires*, D. J. Rodgers and William McCafferty, to request their governments to send warships to El Salvador. The first to arrive were two Canadian destroyers, *Skeena* and *Vancouver*, which were diverted to Acajutla on 22 January, at the suggestion of the British Foreign Office and on orders from Ottawa. They arrived at noon on 23 January, and on the 24th a platoon was landed, ready to go into action against the rebels. This Canadian landing has not hitherto been publicized. On 4 July 1932 a Foreign Office official wrote on a document in the file 'Thank goodness news of the landing of the platoon was never published'. It would have been embarrassing, because no Salvadorean approval had been obtained for the landing. The policy of silence was so successful that historians writing in 1971 are unaware of it: both Grieb (op. cit., 163) and Anderson (op. cit., 129–30) make erroneous statements implying that no landing took place. The facts are, however, quite clear from the secret report of Commander Brodeur, RCN, to the Naval Secretary, Dept. of National Defence, Ottawa, sent 7 April 1932, a copy of which is in the Foreign Office archives in London. After arriving off Acajutla, Brodeur initially sent his Executive Officer to land at the quay by the *Skeena*'s motor-boat, in whose engine-room two armed men were concealed. After this officer's initial consultations with, among others, the British vice-consul in Acajutla, H. B. Towning ('the only white man' resident there, according to the report), Brodeur went ashore on 24 January, spoke on the phone with the *chargé* in San Salvador, and in response to his request and his alarm at the bad situation in the capital, set off for San Salvador by the British railway line, in an armoured rail vehicle. On arrival at Armenia at 3.30 p.m., he spoke again to Rodgers by phone, and at his urgent request instructed the *Skeena* to land one platoon and 2 Lewis-gun sections. By 4.30 the platoon had landed: it was then re-embarked in response to a message from Rodgers, but landed again at 5 p.m. after a further message, 'and was about to march off the jetty to the Railway Station, when the British Vice Consul at Acajutla informed the Officer in Command that the Salvador Government had issued orders through the local commandant that on no account was a foreign armed party to be allowed to land. The officer in charge demurred at first, stating that he had already received his orders, but agreed to remain on the wharf until he was able to confer with the Commanding Officer over the telephone'. In San Salvador, where he arrived about 5.45, Brodeur found that the request to land the armed

party had been made without reference to the Salvadorean government, though McCafferty had been approached and had raised no objection. Brodeur instructed the platoon to remain on the wharf until he had spoken with President Martínez. An interview was granted at once, at which Martínez adamantly refused Brodeur's and Rodgers's insistent offer of help, saying the situation was well in hand and he saw no reason for foreign intervention. After receiving Martínez's assurances of protection for British interests, Brodeur then went to the railway offices and ordered the platoon to re-embark. (See also below, pp. 177–8, note 9.)

[45] All except Tacuba, furthest away from the centre of the revolt, which fell the next day. Also, there was further resistance a few weeks later in Nahuizalco and Sonzacate. Anderson, op. cit., 129.

[46] This caused Indians to discard their traditional dress and other outside signs of Indian identification, even to the extent, reportedly, in the case of the minority who at that time still spoke Pipil, of turning to an exclusive use of Spanish at least when going to *fincas* to work, and of teaching their children only Spanish. Today, although there is some use of distinctive Indian clothing, even among men (a distinctive style of shirt, *pace* Adams, op. cit., 493), Indian languages have almost disappeared; ibid., 499. However, there has since 1969 been an attempt to revive pride in Pipil culture, centred on the priest and the Indian community at Izalco: an annual festival is held. It appears that after 37 years the trauma caused by the massacre of 1932 began to wear off, and Indians became more confident in asserting themselves as such.

[47] op. cit. See his detailed accounts of the events in the rebel-held towns, and his final assessment. Some of the stories of rebel murders which Anderson *does* accept are denied by surviving rebel leaders.

[48] Men with no official position but accepted as leaders. Today only Izalco has a *cacique*.

[49] The communists were strong in Ilopango and Soyapango, and the most easterly instances of participation in the revolt were in the villages on the western side of Lake Ilopango. Anderson, op. cit., ch. 8. For a detailed description of the building-up of communist support at Ilopango, a difficult but successful task, see Dalton, op. cit.

[50] This explanation was given to me by a medium-sized coffee-plantation owner of Ataco. Like most of his fellow-planters, he is today resident in San Salvador.

[51] There were, it is said, further killings of large numbers of rural workers in the years following the revolt. They were allegedly killed for refusing to work for low wages offered, or for remonstrating when not paid the wages that had been agreed.

[52] Max Brannon: *Las Deudas Privadas en la Crisis Contemporánea* (1937: San Salvador).

[53] Anderson, op. cit., 54.

[54] Browning, op. cit., 280.

[55] Laws were passed under Martínez and again in March 1969, under President Sánchez Hernández, limiting small commerce to persons born in Central America, excluding therefore naturalized Salvadorean citizens as well as foreigners. However, it appears that the better-off Palestinian and Chinese merchants can find ways of being permitted to continue in business. The main effect or perhaps even the main purpose of the laws could be cynically interpreted as providing for a flow of money in bribes from a section of wealthy businessmen to persons with position but not so much wealth. A study of the laws has been carried out in Mexico at the behest of the *Instituto Mexicano de Investigaciones Mercantiles* and published in part as: Adalberto Dagdug Torres: *Documento sobre el ejercicio del comercio en El Salvador*, Tomo I (1969: Mexico, Ed. AESEL). This volume consists largely of reprinting of views expressed by various sections of Salvadorean opinion on the 1969 law. The law did put an end to some foreign businesses, including that of one long-time British resident.

[56] Luna, 'Análisis de una dictadura fascista', 62.

[57] The word was used in El Salvador as the war's aim, in spite of the un-democratic nature of the Martínez régime.

[58] Walter Thurston of Arizona. It is said that those who launched the attempted *coup* of 2 April had expected the diplomatic corps, including the American

ambassador, to intervene in their favour by urging Martínez not to resist. Luna, whose account of the *coup* is detailed, recounts that early on the morning of 3 April, from a telegraph office under the control of the rebels, the ambassador exchanged coded messages with Washington, after which his attitude to the rebels became negative; when in the afternoon of that day their military position crumbled, he refused asylum in the embassy to one of the leaders, Colonel Tito Tomás Calvo, who was shot. His attitude may have begun to change with the execution of Calvo and twelve or thirteen other leaders. The strike, which was in large part provoked by the executions, began to spread from students to workers on 2 May, and by 4 May it had been joined by public employees and by many employers, especially in commerce, who simply did not open their doors. Thus it had been more or less total for four days before Martínez resigned. David Luna, 'Análisis de una dictadura fascista . . .', 106–26.

⁵⁹ Romero's public platform, if not his private position, was to protest his preference for 'democracy' against 'communism'; many saw him as a communist.

⁶⁰ This suggestion is mentioned by Jorge Arias Gómez: 'Informe Verbal', in *Proceso Político Centroamericano*, Seminario de Historia Contemporánea de Centro América (1964: San Salvador, Ed. Universitaria), 72, quoting articles in the daily press of 1963. It is denied by Ítalo López Vallecillos: *El Periodismo en El Salvador* (1964: San Salvador, Ed. Universitaria), 166–9, quoting a detailed account by Menéndez himself.

⁶¹ A partial account can be found in Anon.: 'La Jornada de Ahuachapán, diario de un revolucionario 5/11/44–12/12/44', *La Universidad*, Año LXXXVII (Jan.–Dec. 1962), 103ff.

⁶² There is no adequate translation, since 'Office of the Procurator of the Poor', the literal rendering, does not suggest, for instance, the fleet of buses which were used for such purposes as to take people for outings to the seaside, or its responsibility for the San Salvador orphanage.

⁶³ Adrián Roberto Aldana: *Lo que no se pudo decir: aspectos noticiosos referentes a los sucesos políticos de Septiembre y Octubre de 1960* (n.d. [1960 or 1961?]: San Salvador, Prensa Gráfica). Roque Dalton: *El Salvador* (1965: Havana), 134–7.

⁶⁴ Centred on Major Rosales, one of the three military members of the junta. There were also three civilians, including Dr Fabio Castillo, the most left-wing and the most articulate, whose role as spokesman of the junta gave it a bigger reputation as reformist than some of its members can have deserved or wanted.

⁶⁵ Namely, of Leopoldo Fernando Soto Crespo, organizer of the workers' section of *Partido Acción Renovadora*, who was arrested by the National Guard in March 1966 and never reappeared; and two leaders of the *Federación Unitaria Sindical Salvadoreña*, whose bodies, according to the trade union federation (with horrible photographic evidence of torture), were found after they had been thrown into a river, in early 1968. A horrifying account of these methods is contained in Salvador Cayetano Carpio: 'Secuestro y Capucha en un país del mundo libre', *La Universidad*, Año 92 (May–June 1967), 101–219. Carpio describes scenes witnessed and tortures undergone in a year in which he was – of this there is no doubt – illegally imprisoned in police cells. There is every contrast between the treatment described in these police cells and the humane condition of the prisons under the civilian control of the Ministry of Justice.

⁶⁶ President Méndez Montenegro, the democratic reformist whose efforts to implement reforms during his period of office, 1966–70, had for the most part been frustrated by military opposition and effective veto, had nevertheless been able to extend legal electoral status to the moderate Left. At the 1970 election, therefore, his own party's candidate, Mario Fuentes, was opposed by the rather more leftist Jorge Lucas Caballero, while the right wing was united behind Arana Osorio. The voting was: Arana 234,675 (42.9%); Fuentes 194,798 (35.7%); Caballero 116,865 (21.4%). Arana's minority victory had to be confirmed by the National Assembly choosing between the two leading contenders; here the voting was: Arana 37; Fuentes 17; 1 abstention.

⁶⁷ He 'made efficient use of terrorist bands against purported guerrilla sympathizers', according to Thomas and Marjorie Melville, *Guatemala – Another Vietnam?* (1971: Harmondsworth, Penguin), 277.

# Chapter 4

# The Economic Structure

---

THE WEALTH OF EL SALVADOR, such as it is, still comes primarily from a few commercial crops exported to the industrialized countries, and it would be appropriate to start an examination of economic organization with the main exports.

There is no significant mineral wealth,[1] and there are sound agricultural reasons why coffee should achieve pre-eminence as the cash crop. Most of the country is hilly, and therefore subject to erosion problems with most annual crops, but not with trees. Of the tree crops, the distribution of rainfall and other natural conditions favour coffee, while cocoa, the first great export crop of the sixteenth and seventeenth centuries, is at a natural disadvantage in comparison with producing countries in West Africa. When a substitute for indigo was being sought in the nineteenth century, and the government distributed free young plants of a number of commercial crops, only coffee prospered. It is of course possible that for some plants the wrong varieties were tried, and that El Salvador could successfully grow grapes, for instance, or citrus fruit. At any rate, the climate has proved unsuitable for the varieties so far introduced.

## Coffee

Coffee is grown on properties of widely varying size, from less than a hectare to seventeen estates of over 25 square kilometres, though here coffee is grown on only a small part of the estate's area. The mean size is 3.8 hectares, but this is a deceptively low figure because it takes into account small family plots of coffee where the family also has other sources of income. A more realistic idea can be gained from the fact that half the coffee is produced on estates of 107 hectares (264 acres) or more.[2] But whatever the size, coffee is grown and sold under the direct authority of the owner of the land: there is little renting or sharecropping of coffee land, nor is it owned by public companies. On the smallest plots, the owner and his or her family do all the work themselves and are very poor. On slightly larger holdings, outside labour is hired for the picking only. On larger estates than this, called *fincas*, the owner usually lives in town and leaves day-to-day management of production to an administrator. The absentee owner does not neglect his *finca*, however: he looks after his commerical interests in connection with it, and in town he has better access to information; on the other hand, he is removed from daily contact with his workers, so his sense of obligation to them is likely to be much diminished. Owners do maintain a house on their *finca*, where they may spend many or most weekends, and live for a period during the harvest season. On the large *fincas*, the owner's house is a luxurious mansion. Such mansions are well within the means of the planters, for their share of the income from the estate may well be greater than their total wage bill.

The degree of concentration of coffee land in few hands today is largely a result of the numerous purchases of land from large numbers of smallholders at and after the distribution of individual titles to those who held rights to cultivate the communal land of the Indian communities and *ladino* villages, between 1880 and 1912. The purchases could be made by anyone with medium to large capital, and so included small-town lawyers as well as city professionals, merchants – including those of foreign origin – and men whose wealth stemmed from other forms of agriculture. However, some of the parcels, as they are called, of distributed common land did remain in the hands of their recipients. Thus the pattern of distribution of coffee land was from the start a very wide range in the size of holdings; the effect of the passage of two or three generations has been to multiply the number of tiny holdings by division of the small parcels, but it appears that the large units more often continue to be farmed as a unit, some of the sons turning from agriculture to other sources of income, including the professions.

The coffee tree requires five years' growth before it begins to give any return; since poor farmers with only small plots are necessarily most concerned with what they are going to have to eat this year and next year, they have tended to continue to plant annual food crops rather than coffee trees, except in the areas where these are extremely successful or in the cases where the small farmer has a little more land than he needs merely for subsistence. Coffee has been ideally suited to men with a certain amount of capital, who can afford to wait. At first, the permanent workers needed for coffee cultivation were obtained in the way usual for other export crops: men were offered plots of land for cultivation of food crops for their family to eat, in return for their availability to work on the estate. Under this arrangement the *colono*, as the worker is called, has no security of tenure and does not usually stay permanently on the same estate, but he does have some land to cultivate and so knows that there will be food at the end of the season. However, in the areas where coffee grows well, it is far more productive than any other crop, so there is every reason to turn all the land in such areas over to coffee. This means that the *colono* system, along with sharecropping or other systems of land use which require a variety of crops alongside coffee, have on the whole been eliminated as coffee has spread all over this land, leaving only direct cultivation of coffee by paid wage labour, the labourer buying all his subsistence needs with cash. Until 1965 the estate-owner provided two meals – usually consisting of nothing but the cheapest maize *tortillas*, beans, and coffee – but when in that year the minimum wage law was extended to the rural areas, the provision of meals ceased. The word *colono* has been retained, but it now describes the worker who has a home on the estate and is available when needed for work, but no longer has any plot of land to cultivate. If his home is an isolated wooden or mud hut, it is entirely surrounded by the estate's coffee trees and the shade trees above them; it may on the other hand consist of a room in a building, housing perhaps ten or twenty such *colonos* and their families, located near the residence of the owner and the more humble house of the administrator, in a clearing with a little more open space. Such buildings, called *mesones* like their equivalent in the towns, usually comprise simply a row of rooms facing in one direction and, at the back of these, another row of rooms facing in the opposite direction: each room has a separate door to the outside but no window, nor any other fitting except, in some cases, electric light. Washing, cooking, etc., are done outside. Thus, while better constructed than most rural dwellings which are erected by the occupants with such help as they can engage and out of the materials available to them, these *mesones* are at a minimal standard for officially provided housing.

Nevertheless, even without his own plot to cultivate, the *colono* is in a relatively advantaged position in the coffee areas, by comparison with all except the landowners and administrators. He has his home provided, albeit without any security, and he can expect fairly regular work on the estate paid at the rate established by the minimum wage law, namely ₡2.25 (for adult men): $0.90 or 37½p per day, with Sundays paid if he has worked the six other days of the week (and the same for some of the national holidays). However, if there is no work for him because it is a slack season of the year, then he does not receive any pay either. During the month or so of harvest the piece-work rates, also now established by law and applicable both to *colonos* and to temporarily hired workers, allow considerably higher earnings, particularly since the whole family can take part in the work.

Until the minimum wage law was passed by the Rivera government, women and young persons had done a considerable amount of work on coffee throughout the year; but the minimum wage established for them was ₡1.75, also per 8-hour day, and coffee-planters considered that it was not for most purposes worthwhile employing them at seven-ninths of the man's wages, since they did not do as much as seven-ninths of a man's work, on average, during the day. Apart from the harvest, the only work on the coffee planta-tion now usually given to women is manuring. Another equally fundamental effect of the minimum wage law was that planters now found that it paid to reduce the number of *colonos* to around the number needed at the slackest times of the year, relying on labour hired for specific tasks, and usually for one or two days only, for a considerable portion of the work and not only for the harvest. Since the minimum wage legislation did not cover these piece rates outside the harvest period, they could be kept low, given the chronic unemployment prevailing in the coffee zones.

So the situation of those who are neither *colonos* nor have their own land, but live in the coffee zones with no access to land they can cultivate, and dependent entirely on occasional work on the *fincas*, is obviously precarious. It is clear that the minimum wage legislation was of some advantage at most to some of the *colonos*, although with their womenfolk denied the work they had done previously even that is doubtful: but something like half of the previously regular work-force, of *colonos* and others who were regularly employed although they did not live on the estate, may have lost their regular jobs, and many of them their dwellings, as a result of the law. As for the degree to which the minimum wage decreed exceeded the wages being paid before, it varied from area to area, but a report of 1953[3] contains the calculation that already at that date the real remuneration of adult male *colonos*, including all benefits of meals, dwelling, and incidentals, was ₡2.26 per day on average, although the wage itself was only ₡1.32. When women worked, their total remuneration was calcu-lated at ₡1.67. Meals, on which about 50¢ per day per worker were spent by the planter, have ceased to be provided, so it seems that even the *colonos* who have retained their jobs are only slightly better off. The conclusion seems inescapable that a measure such as a minimum wage law, even though it may be effectively enforced, as it has been on the coffee estates, may well lead to an improvement only for a few of those whom it was intended to benefit, while the use of loopholes and ways to escape the effect of the law may act to the disadvantage of a larger number. The wage-rates previously existing were adapted to the situation of surplus labour and lack of any bargaining power on the part of the workers: the minimum wages established did not alter these fundamental reasons why wages were so low, and they were not so well adapted to the convenience of the provision of accommodation and meals as part of the worker's remuneration. Possibly there was, in the view at least of the Planning Council which recommended the minimum wage law, a 'feudal' element in this form of remuneration, which should be replaced by a 'capitalist' simple wage; but the standard of living of the worker does not depend so much on the form of payment as on the amount, and this is determined by his power position relative to that of the employer: by such questions as whether he can organize a strike, and by the demand for his labour and the number of others ready and willing to supply it.

No agricultural workers' unions or strikes are allowed: the planters have the political strength to prevent them. On the larger estates a pair of National Guards are very often employed to maintain the authority of the owner and administrator, and prevent any form of protest. The owner pays for their maintenance. This is a form of duty to which members of the National Guard are assigned when they have committed some fault or do not have full status, and it does not carry as much prestige as regular service. Any 'agitator' among coffee-workers is of course dismissed and if necessary imprisoned or otherwise dealt with.

During the harvest season, which lasts from November to March but is concentrated in the middle of this period, everyone in the coffee areas has employment and large numbers of others come from other parts of the country, in family groups, to earn their main cash income for the year. These are mainly the subsistence farmers, and the biggest flow is from the northern areas of the country where there are no export crops of any importance. There is some tendency for communities to stay together for this seasonal migration, so that all those from a particular northern village who want to go coffee-picking in a particular year go to the same one or two places where people from the same village have gone in previous years. They sleep mostly out of doors, which is possible because the harvest is in the dry season; but it can be extremely cold at night at the higher altitudes where coffee is grown, and the pickers, from lower altitudes, are often inadequately protected with blankets and suffer from the cold. The money that is earned compensates, however, for the discomfort. Until the 1970–71 harvest the customary rate was 50¢ per *arroba* (25 lb.) of beans picked. The amount picked in a day by an individual varies greatly, of course, but to give a general idea, 10 *arrobas* for an adult, male or female, working at normal speed, might be assumed, and up to three times this amount for an energetic young man extending himself. Since ₡6 equal one pound sterling or $2.40, it can be seen that a family might earn as much as

£2 or $4.80 a day. For the 1970–71 harvest, a minimum rate of 70¢ per *arroba* was decreed, and was fairly effectively enforced, so that there was a real transfer of income from rich to poor. There were undoubtedly instances where the weighing machines were altered, or where the harvest workers were otherwise denied the benefit of the minimum rate,[4] but there were fewer loopholes to affect the minimum piece rate than there had been to affect the minimum wage.

While the large profits made by coffee-planters may have influenced the government to declare these minimum payments, there is no other connection between the price of coffee on the international market and the wages paid to the workers. Normally there is a very wide margin of profit to be made in the business, and shared between planters, processers, and exporters. Not surprisingly, therefore, the larger planters, processers, and exporters do not confine themselves to just one of these spheres of activity, but engage in two or all three, attracting to themselves as large a part of the profit to be made as possible.

A rule of thumb on the profitability of coffee plantations, used for instance by a pressure group of medium-sized estate-owners in their submissions to the government in the mid-1960s,[5] has it that when the export price for green coffee, FOB in Salvadorean port, is 40 dollars (₡100) per quintal (100 lb.), the planter receives ₡70 and ₡30 of this is his profit after tax. ₡40 are his costs of production, including ₡30 for his wage bill. The government takes ₡13.13 in export tax, and the remaining ₡16.87 goes as costs and profits to the processers and exporters. Some other estimates would give the planter a rather lower margin of profit, but a report prepared for the Organization of American States and the Interamerican Development Bank[6] indicates that at the export price mentioned of ₡100, ₡1.62 are accounted for by exporter's costs, ₡8.37 by processer's costs; ₡1.67 by exporter's profit, ₡6.82 by processer's profit. Thus the total taken by downstream activities is ₡18.50, and after tax the corresponding amount received by planters is ₡68.37. The estimate of planters' costs of production given by this source is ₡47. However, this estimate takes into account financial costs including interest on the value of the plantation[7] as well as working capital. Working capital borrowing costs were estimated at ₡2.15, interest on fixed capital at ₡9. Removing this ₡11.15 from costs of production, on the grounds that plantations are usually owned outright and have been acquired by inheritance, and that planters could afford to finance themselves, leaves ₡35.85 as the costs of production and ₡32.52 as profit.

This report was prepared in 1966 and it is true that since then the introduction of minimum rates for pickers has eaten into the profit by about ₡4 or ₡5 per quintal; and costs of some physical inputs such as petrol have risen. But on the other hand, the world price of coffee has risen well above the ₡100 per quintal price. From a low figure of ₡88.17 in July 1969 it rose to ₡136.77 in July 1970, reflecting difficulties in production in Brazil. At the lower price, the profit would be reduced, if one accepts the estimates of the report mentioned, from ₡32.52 to ₡24.80; at the higher, the profit must be in the region of ₡50, after allowing for the larger amounts taken by export tax and the profits of processers and exporters, as well as the increase in rates paid to pickers.

Having established that planters' profits are ₡25–₡50 per 100 lb., fluctuating between these limits according to the movements of world prices, it is possible to say something about the income of the planters. In the following table, the column showing the distribution of income when profits are at ₡33.33, should perhaps be taken as the most typical.

COFFEE PLANTERS: THE DISTRIBUTION OF PRODUCTION BETWEEN LARGE, MEDIUM, AND SMALL-SCALE PLANTERS, AND THEIR PROFITS AFTER TAX[8]

| Number of planters | Production in quintals (100 lb.) yearly | Planters' income when profit is: | | |
|---|---|---|---|---|
| | | ₡25 | ₡33.33 | ₡50 |
| 5 | More than 15,000 | ₡375,000+ | ₡500,000+ | ₡750,000+ |
| 17 | From 10,000 to 15,000 | ₡312,500 | ₡416,667 | ₡625,000 |
| 68 | 5,000 to 10,000 | ₡187,500 | ₡250,000 | ₡375,000 |
| 420 | 1,000 to 5,000 | ₡87,500 | ₡116,667 | ₡175,000 |
| 392 | 500 to 1,000 | ₡18,750 | ₡25,000 | ₡37,500 |
| 1,362 | 100 to 500 | ₡8,750 | ₡11,667 | ₡17,500 |
| 1,034 | 50 to 100 | ₡1,875 | ₡2,500 | ₡3,750 |
| 1,424 | 25 to 50 | ₡833 | ₡1,111 | ₡1,667 |
| 7,872 | 1 to 25 | ₡325 | ₡433 | ₡650 |
| 1,845 | Less than 1 | under ₡25 | under ₡33 | under ₡50 |

*Notes.* The data on the distribution of production between large and small planters were provided by the *Asociación Cafetalera de El Salvador*. They give a total of 14,439 producers. The 1961 Agricultural Census lists 36,538 as the number of properties on which some coffee is grown.[9] The difference is probably accounted for mainly by ownership of more than one property by the same person, but there may also be undercounting of small planters in the above table. The table refers to 1964–65, but it is unlikely that any great change has taken place. The profit figures were calculated for production at the midpoint of the range mentioned in the production column.

This table shows how extremely unequal are the incomes received from coffee production. These inequalities found in association with the cultivation of coffee in El Salvador are not a simple result of the nature of the crop. In African countries the wealth earned from coffee is divided much more equally: on the slopes of Mount Kilimanjaro in Tanzania, for instance, where the Chaga tribe began to grow coffee at the turn of the century, a co-operative was formed in 1925 for the purpose of buying the whole crop and processing and selling it on behalf of the producers (replacing the Indian firms who had dominated the business). Although wealth differences have developed within the tribe, the whole group has clearly benefited together. This may be attributed, more than anything else, to the fact that land rights have been inalienable, so that nobody has been able to build up large estates.

Professor Tricart of the University of Strasbourg has made a direct comparison between coffee-growing in El Salvador and in the Ivory Coast.[10] He finds that in this West African country, known to be one where wealth differences between individuals and regions have developed most strongly in the contemporary period by comparison with the rest of negro Africa, 90 per cent of the coffee production comes from small family growers and coffee, rather than accentuating social differences, has given the peasantry considerable purchasing power. In the 1950s, the coffee-worker in the Ivory Coast earned 20 per cent more in real terms than his counterpart in El Salvador; received much better meals from his employer; and was given a plot of land to cultivate on the side, with a firm work contract concluded for a whole season. All this in spite of the fact that the price of Ivory Coast coffee is considerably lower than that of El Salvador.

The inequality in El Salvador is in fact somewhat underestimated by the table given above, since there is a degree of further monopolization of the profits. It is the large estateowners who are also coffee processers and exporters; and the processers lend working capital to the smaller producers. At the bottom end of the scale, the smallest growers are very often forced by their poverty to sell their future crop before the harvest for a price well below what it will fetch at harvest time, often for as little as half the price.[11] The buyer is usually a larger grower or processer.

The habit of borrowing working capital on the part of the middle-sized producers, in spite of their large profits, stems partly from the ease with which credit is obtainable given the solid backing of a coffee estate; and partly from the fact that payment for the harvested coffee is not received immediately but only in stages over the ensuing year as the coffee is sold on the international market. Most medium-sized planters borrow from the processer to whom they deliver their coffee; they usually borrow ₡40 per quintal of estimated production – as much or more than is needed to finance production costs, especially since additional borrowings can be made for the harvest payments. The money borrowed is used for other purposes, including personal consumption.

These loans of working capital are made by the processers at an interest rate of 10 per cent, using in large part money they obtain from government-controlled institutions (*Compañia Salvadoreña del Cafe*, *Banco Hipotecario*) at 7 per cent; there is no real risk in this relending, since any default will be refinanced on the next harvest or on a mortgage on the valuable coffee land. The planters could borrow direct from the institutional sources, but it would involve a considerable amount of form-filling and time-wasting. The *Compañia Salvadoreña del Café* also buys, processes, and exports coffee, and its prices may regulate the internal market to some extent. However, on this point one must quote from the massive work published under the auspices of the Interamerican Development Bank and the *Banco Hipotecario*, on agricultural credit in El Salvador:

The coffee purchases of the *Compañia* were never of a magnitude sufficient to have a significant influence on prices in the internal market. Only the large producers who were at the same time processers and dealers in the commodity had access to the credit of the *Compañia*. . . . Nevertheless, one positive aspect which must be mentioned with respect to the creation of the *Compañia* [i.e., in 1940] is that its establishment corresponded to a sincere nationalist aspiration. Indeed, it made possible the breaking of the monopoly of coffee exportation which was in the hands of foreigners; Salvadorean nationals were stimulated to engage in this activity. Unfortunately these nationals did not delay in creating another monopoly for themselves . . .[12]

Applying the figures quoted earlier for the profits of processers and exporters when the coffee price is ₡100 per quintal, namely a total of ₡8.49, to the approximately 3 million quintals produced annually in El Salvador, we get ₡25 million, to which we may add another ₡2 million for profits on lending. This sum is divided, by no means equally, among sixty-four processer-exporters and a number of simple processers.[13] At least a quarter of the sixty-four, however, only process and sell their own coffee. In the case of these downstream activities, there is no exemption from income tax.

The planter *is* exempted from income tax: he pays only the export tax on coffee. This arrangement has the virtue of enabling the tax authorities to approach one hundred per cent effective collection, as compared to the 50.2 per cent (*sic!*) which was the officially estimated proportion of personal income tax actually collected in 1963.[14] But coffee export tax, unlike income tax, is not at all progressive. The relation which the coffee export tax bears to the income tax scale is such that when the price of Salvadorean coffee as it leaves El

Salvador is ₡115, a medium figure for recent years, the approximately 450 largest coffee producers with over 150 hectares under coffee pay less than what they would be due to pay under the income tax scale, assuming that coffee-planting were their only source of income. The others, the vast majority who have less than 150 hectares and produce less than about 2,000 quintals, pay more in coffee export tax than they would if it were replaced by income tax. The difference is progressively larger in favour of the grower whose estate substantially exceeds 150 hectares, and against the small producer with much less than that amount of land. It is true that planters are subject also to the tax on capital, but the scale is so low, though progressive, that it does not reach one per cent until the taxable capital exceeds ₡2.2 million.

Although pressure groups of medium-sized producers have from time to time raised their voices to push for the inclusion of coffee producers in the income tax scale, which applies to everyone else, instead of the export tax, they have failed and coffee policy has remained in the hands of the large producers either directly or, particularly since their ejection from control of the *Asociación Cafetalera de El Salvador* in 1960–61 by the short-lived reformist *Junta de Gobierno*, through the complaisance of the President's political appointee who heads both the *Departamento Nacional del Café* and the *Compañía Salvadoreña del Café*. Although one of these two bodies is officially a government department, while the other is a company whose shares are owned by individual planters as well as institutions, they operate closely together from the same building. In fact they constitute virtually a single entity, in charge of coffee to the complete exclusion of the Ministry of Agriculture except in the area of technical research, and much more secretive toward outsiders than most government departments are.

In these circumstances, the attention of smaller planters has turned largely to the problem which unites all the coffee producers, namely the low quota fixed by the International Coffee Organization for El Salvador, for sales to the 'traditional markets' of North America and western Europe. The Salvadorean position is that the present quota reflects the proportion accorded to El Salvador in the Agreement of 1962, and that this was unfair because it used production figures, for the immediately preceding years, which were considerably below the true production totals. The reason why these figures were so low was that El Salvador had been selling quite a large amount of coffee unrecorded in order to dispose of more coffee than an earlier agreement stipulated as the quota for the country. There is also the argument that Salvadorean coffee, of extremely good quality by comparison with Brazilian or most African coffees, should not be restricted. The International Coffee Agreement can be seen, with considerable justification, as a case of the established and wealthier Latin American producing countries saying to the poorer emerging producers 'Keep out of our market'.

The original cause of the low quota may thus have been a short-sighted and not quite honourable Salvadorean policy; but the build-up of excess stocks in recent years, due to the low quota level, seems to have been quite out of proportion with the original sin, and Salvadorean planters claim their country to have been 'the most misused in Latin America' under the Agreement. They blame the fact that at the head of the *Compañia* there sits a political appointee who is not sufficiently motivated to push their case strongly. It is said abroad that Salvadorean exporters have responded to the situation by further clandestine exports, but they do not seem to have been able, in competition with other countries also trying to sell their surpluses to new markets in eastern Europe, Japan, etc., not covered by the Agreement, to place anything like their whole surplus since 1967–68; and stocks have in the following years been building up at the rate of about a fifth of annual production. The delay in sale and therefore in receipt of money for this coffee not legally sold under the Agreement, as well as the low price at which some of it has to be sold, are passed on proportionately to each producer, and in 1970–71 the 'sacrifice quota', or proportion to be sold in new markets for a lower price, was fixed at 20 per cent as against the 5 per cent of preceding years. The price received is in fact only 4 to 6 dollars (₡10–₡15) less per quintal, so the sacrifice is only relative. Another 20 per cent of the coffee delivered by each producer is a 'quota of internal reserve' which it is hoped eventually to sell to traditional markets through additions to the Salvadorean international quota.

The effect of the delayed payment on the producer has been to induce him to borrow further. That proportion of his debt on the working capital loan which he 'cannot' repay within a year because he has still not received payment for that part of his harvest, is converted into a new loan, with new expenses on paperwork chargeable to the borrower.[15]

As a justification for having spent so much time on the details of the structure of coffee production, I should perhaps re-emphasize its importance to El Salvador's economy and social organization. From a position where coffee accounted for 89 per cent of all exports in 1950, it fell below 50 per cent for the first time since 1883 in 1963, and stood at 43.5 per cent in 1969. However, because of the creation of the Central American Common Market, this decline in the proportion of exports accounted for by coffee is in part illusory: of El

Salvador's exports to countries outside Central America in 1969, 69.3 per cent was still contributed by coffee.[16]

Internally, the huge profits made by a few large-scale coffee producers and processer-exporters, subject to especially low taxation, have been the basis for a considerable amount of other investment, first in financial institutions and urban land, and then in nascent industry (besides some other agricultural ventures). And there has been a circular process in which the 'leading coffee families' have maintained the political influence which enables them to keep unchanged the rules of the game, particularly with respect to taxation, which preserve and enhance their wealth and through it their oligarchical position in politics.

And at the other end of the scale there is the fact that a third of the money earned by agricultural labourers is earned in coffee. There is no doubt that coffee-growing areas support a high density of population, as can be observed by walking along any country road in such an area: the number of fellow-pedestrians passed is phenomenal for a rural road, and every now and then there is likely to be a refreshment stall for them, like in a town. This last fact is in itself an indication of underemployment, since the refreshment stalls do not really do very much business. The population, while retained in the countryside by the occasional work available in coffee, or by ownership of a small 'parcel' of coffee land, is extremely poor. If the profits of the medium-sized estate-owners are as large as their production costs and larger than their wage bills, this also means that half or more than half of the coffee income generated in the rural area is siphoned off to the large town, and nowadays mostly to San Salvador. Only the smallest growers do any significant amount of their spending in the rural area. They, and the coffee-workers, cannot support any infrastructure of artisans or service workers in the rural areas. Therefore many of those who do not have a niche as a *colono* on a plantation and do not want to be dependent for a meagre living on the casual work occasionally available in coffee, have to follow the money in its migration to town.[17]

## Cotton

Cotton, the second export crop, contributed ₡49 million to El Salvador's exports in 1969 compared with ₡223 million for coffee. Apart from the fact that both crops call upon a migratory seasonal labour force for the harvest, unfortunately at the same time of year, there is little in common between the way their production is organized. Whereas coffee is a permanent plant, cotton is an annual one. Whereas coffee is grown in the hilly volcanic districts running through the centre of the country from west to east, most advantageously on higher slopes and often on land so steep that it would be subject to serious erosion under any other but a tree crop like coffee, cotton thrives in the flat coastal plain and certain low-lying interior valleys. Whereas the acreage planted to coffee has remained constant in recent years, cotton acreage has been extremely variable from year to year depending on the vicissitudes of profitability. Whereas coffee-planters use their own land, cotton-planters very often rent the land from others on a temporary basis. Whereas coffee consti-tutes the enduring foundation of the wealth of many large planters, cotton is frequently planted, when the short-term profitability looks promising, by men whose main interests lie elsewhere. Whereas the main markets for coffee are in West Germany and the United States, the principal market for cotton is Japan, and this trade link has led to a number of other economic links with the Japanese. Whereas co-operatives for the processing and export of coffee only began in a small way in 1965, the entire cotton crop has, by law, been processed and exported by a co-operative society set up before cotton exports achieved any significant levels, in 1940.[18] Until recently it could have been said that whereas coffee was grown by the most appropriate methods employing large amounts of labour and fertilizer, cotton was cultivated without any care or appreciation of sound agricultural practices. It could now be claimed that the cotton-planters have been taught a lesson and have revised their methods; they remain, however, over-confident in the advantages of machinery over human labour and animal power.[19]

Cotton had been cultivated in the territory of El Salvador since before the Spanish Conquest, as the raw material for locally-made textiles. The first time it achieved much prominence as an export crop was as a result of the American Civil War in the 1860s, but this boom, during which it actually led indigo and coffee briefly in its contribution to export income, was very short-lived, and from 1870 to 1921 it was hardly grown at all.[20]

The second, present, period of cotton cultivation began slowly in the 1930s. It developed through the forties and fifties, in spurts responding immediately to high prices. The first fillip was given by the growth of a local textile industry during and as a direct con-sequence of the Second World War, which interrupted the free flow of manufactures from the United States and Europe.[21] The overall upward trend which followed after the war was based on the export of the fibre, consumption by the domestic textile industry being lower than its wartime peak for all post-war seasons until 1960. The upward trend was probably due in large part to the eradication of the danger of malaria on the hot coastal plain after American and international health agencies began to give substantial help to the

Salvadorean Ministry of Health during and after the war. They used recent medical advances in the control of this scourge, which was the reason for the much lower population density on the fertile plain.[22] The second important change making possible the spread of cotton was the improvement made in the control of the insect pests[23] which attack cotton with particular severity in the humid conditions of El Salvador.

The building of a paved road and feeder roads was a necessary condition for the expansion of cotton acreage. The *Litoral* road through the coastal plain was constructed in the 1950s, largely with this end in view.

In spite of the relatively low population density in the cotton-growing areas, the spread of cotton displaced considerable numbers of *campesinos* from land on which they had been growing staple crops, as renters or squatters or as *colonos* on the cattle *haciendas*.[24] Cotton requires even less labour per acre in permanent employment than does cattle-ranching. Poor people no longer with access to land for growing maize and other food crops now live without work on the margins of roads and in other pockets of public land, in straw huts, waiting for the next cotton harvest when there will again be a demand for their labour. The piece rates for picking, which have necessarily to correspond with those of the coffee harvest taking place at the same time in January and adjacent months, were also raised with the establishment by the government of minimum rates for the 1970–71 season. Cotton, like coffee, attracts migrant workers from areas to the north. The national radio station announces where harvesters can congregate for hire and transport to the plantations.

Profits in cotton-planting grew to a peak about 1957–58,[25] principally because the control of insect pests by blanket-aircraft spraying was reaching maximum effectiveness and the land sown to cotton had not shown many signs of exhaustion. The profits led to an increase in cultivation which reached a peak, in terms of area planted, in 1964. However, by then the insects were becoming more resistant to the constant spraying, yields per acre were falling, and the response was more and more spraying of insecticides, a procedure both expensive and in the long run self-defeating. In 1965–67, the worst years, up to 45 per cent of production costs was accountable to insecticide. Under these circumstances, not aided by a slight further fall in international cotton prices,[26] planters were making substantial losses on their operations. After two or three years of these losses, the area planted in 1967 was reduced to less than 40 per cent of that planted in 1964, and planters were at last forced to heed warnings, made by experts since the mid-1950s,[27] about the short-sightedness of their methods, particularly the indiscriminate spraying. An advisory mission of Israeli experts was invited, and in this new atmosphere an improvement occurred and plantings again showed a profit, albeit a small one, in 1968 or certainly in 1969. Yields per acre have recovered to the best levels,[28] and the acreage planted has begun to grow again. It is not, however, likely to return to the 1964 level unless international prices improve.

There has been some planting of cotton by small cultivators following the example of the large planters, but figures for 1963 show that only 5 per cent of the crop was grown on farms of less than 10 *manzanas*, almost all rented plots, while at the other extreme 55 per cent was grown on estates of over one hundred *manzanas* (173 acres), just half of which were rented and half owned by the cotton-planter. There are also huge operations covering 15,000 acres.[29] Even the small growers use insecticides and fertilizers, though their knowledge of their correct application is reported as very poor.[30] Their expenses are nevertheless considerable and they have difficulty in obtaining credit. There is some lending by government institutions, but it is subject to stringent criteria and insufficient, and the gap is filled by intermediaries who provide all the physical inputs, often including the land, but take at least half and sometimes three-quarters of the difference between the cost of these inputs and the sale price received.[31] This kind of arrangement, under which a person with some capital contributes physical inputs, while a person without resources contributes his labour, and the actual or normal or expected value added is divided equally between the two, is common in many branches of the economy at the non-institutional levels which are not often investigated by economists, both in production and in commerce. The 'half-and-half' division may seem crude, but flexibility to changes in the market situation is probably achieved in many cases by varying the physical inputs: providing or not providing certain working tools or seed for instance. There is another frequent kind of flexibility in the agricultural situation: if the harvest is bad, the creditor may 'consider'[32] his client and take less than his half-share in the interest of a continuing relationship. This kind of flexibility is not offered by more institutional providers of credit, with their much lower interest rates, and is one of the reasons why moneylenders and informal arrangements are sometimes preferred. However, the half-and-half division *does* reflect the very vulnerable market situation of the man without land or capital in a country where labour is abundant.

## Sugar

Much of the territory of El Salvador, particularly in the central belt, lies too low for coffee yet too high for cotton. One of the most successful cash crops grown in this belt,[33] on the undulating land or the interior valleys, is sugar cane. It was introduced by the Spaniards in the sixteenth century, but did not achieve importance as an export crop beyond Central America until recently, particularly since 1966. The international market for sugar is even more fully conditioned by political factors than is the case with other export crops, and this upsurge of sugar exports was to fill the quota assigned to El Salvador on the American market after the Cuban quota was eliminated in 1960. The value of these sugar exports in 1969 was ₡16 million, and sugar became the third export crop. Natural conditions in the areas planted to cane appear to be just as good as those in Cuba. Methods of cultivation are also generally such as to achieve comparable or better though perhaps not so uniform yields.

The internal sugar market in El Salvador is as politically controlled as the international market, in so far as refined sugar is concerned. The government-controlled price to the consumer has remained at ₡0.25 per lb. for over twenty-five years, an artificially high price which appears primarily to benefit the large growers and the owners of the twenty or so sugar-mills grouped in the *Cooperativa Azucarera Salvadoreña*.[34]

Sugar-cane, however, is far more of a small farmer activity than cotton. It is, in fact, particularly associated with ownership of small farms rather than with renting;[35] but there are also some very large estates planted to cane, especially in the western parts of the country. Here it covers huge stretches of land, whereas on the small farms it is grown in fields next to fields of other crops. Processing presents contrasts, too: between the sugar-mills and a modern refinery on the one hand, and the traditional *trapiches*, whether motor-driven or ox-powered, on the other. Some of the cane of the small growers, as well as that of the large landowners, is now sold for refining, but about a third of the whole crop is still processed by the *trapiches*, some of which, the wooden ones, are no different from those of the early colonial period. Oxen pull a long pole in a circle to provide the force to squeeze the juice out of the cane. At least in the area of San Vicente, where small-farm ownership is common and sugar is the main cash crop, the arrangement for processing is that the farmer hires the *trapiche* for a day, or however long he needs, and does the work himself. The product is cones or cakes of coarse brown sugar called *dulce de panela*; the impurities which remain with this process make it nutritionally superior to white refined sugar, but that is not how it is regarded in El Salvador. Being much cheaper, it is considered a poor substitute, and the tendency is towards its disappearance.

Having obtained his *dulce de panela*, the small farmer may take it to market in a town or, more likely, sell it to travelling buyers at a considerably lower price. The reason why he is willing to accept this much lower price is not solely the economic calculation of the cost of transportation; the somewhat lower price he will obtain at the market, compared to that obtained by the trader, because he is not known by the stallholders as a regular supplier and because he is unfamiliar with the market; and the amount of working time he loses by going to the market. Other reasons, from the persuasiveness of the buyers – though he knows that their talk of low prices in town is unreliable – to his dislike of leaving farm animals to be looked after by others; his suspicion that other men will take advantage of his absence for a few days to have affairs with his wife; and his simple distaste for commercial activity, must also be advanced. At all events, large profits can be made by the travelling middlemen.

## Other Primary Exports

The only other primary export product of any importance is prawns, sold mainly to the American market, and contributing ₡13 million to export figures in 1969. The entire industry is in the hands of three or four large companies and a few smaller ones owning both fishing vessels and processing plants, and operating mainly out of a single port, Puerto El Triunfo, which has no other significant economic activity.

With this concentration of such a lucrative export business, one might expect Puerto El Triunfo to be a thriving town. Instead, one finds that many of the fishermen and the workers in the processing factories live in some of the ugliest thatched-hut slums in the country. Some of these huts are built on stilts on the mud flats that are covered by water at high tide. On the low roofs of these huts, fish caught in small boats as a sideline are left to dry in the hot sun, in very dirty conditions. These living conditions are in stark contrast to the housing provided for the workers on the paternalistically-run Hacienda El Jobal[36] just across the Bay of Jiquilisco on the island of Espíritu Santo. It is said that the only prospect of improvement is that the American purchasers of prawns from the fishing companies are demanding that they spend more of their receipts on their labour force, as a condition of continuing to buy from them.

Balsam is still exported, but receipts did not quite reach ₡ one million in 1969. Even indigo is still on the export lists, but shipments – to Peru and Bolivia – were worth only ₡13,000 in 1969. Sesame seed is a new cash crop, with an export value of ₡800,000; it is grown mainly by small cultivators in the east and north of the country, alongside their subsistence crops. The only other crop which needs to be mentioned in connection with exports is *henequen* (a rough fibre), grown in the eastern region on low undulating hills, and used for the manufacture of the sacks in which coffee is shipped. Once again there are some very large plantations, but they account for less than half of the total production. A single factory has a monopolistic position in sack manufacture.

## Subsistence Agriculture and Local Food Crops

In areas which are not particularly suitable for any of the export crops, the pattern of land use has remained similar to that of the colonial period, with the important exception that the increase in population density has led to over-use of much of the land, and to rapid, indeed often catastrophic, depletion of the soil. Most of the country consists of hills and volcanic mountains, susceptible to erosion.[37] The coastal plain, held in very large properties and planted to cotton or left to pasture, is not so exposed, though there has been erosion even on flat cotton land since it has been left with no ground cover during the early part of the rainy season before cotton is sown. Only the areas under coffee are free from the large-scale erosion which is present wherever there are slopes. When the American agronomist William Vogt visited El Salvador in 1946, he warned that unless prompt and large-scale measures were taken, the country was heading quickly for an agricultural disaster;[38] such measures were not taken, but what has happened is that the mass of Salvadorean cultivators, however uneducated, have become aware of soil depletion and use fertilizers as a matter of course. Thus the food crops maintain their yields despite the exhaustion of the soil, or have by 1970 recovered levels lost between 1950 and 1960.[39] The first consignments of maize were exported beyond the Central American area, to Japan, in 1970, a positive change from El Salvador's earlier dependence on Honduras for supplies to make up her deficiency.

The patchwork of maize-growing villages and cattle-raising *haciendas* which emerged during the colonial period can still be discerned over much of the country, though the abolition of community or village landholding has made this pattern less obvious. Only a small minority of the agricultural population, less than 5 per cent, own 10 hectares or more of land,[40] the minimum needed to give sufficient work to a family in Salvadorean conditions.[41] A further 15 to 20 per cent own between one and 10 hectares, while 10 per cent more have plots of less than one hectare.[42] At the other end of the scale, there were in 1961 125 estates of more than a thousand hectares, and nearly half of the land was held in properties exceeding a hundred hectares (47.7 per cent to be exact; as the same person may well own more than one of these properties, it would undoubtedly be true to say that more than half of the land is owned by fewer than 2,148 owners of over a hundred hectares, constituting about 0.5 per cent of agricultural households).[43]

The great majority who do not have their own land, or who have a quite insufficient amount of it, compete with one another to fill the limited needs for labour of the larger landowners (and large-scale renters), or compete for the limited amount of land that these landowners make available for renting or sharecropping. There are a variety of combinations of needs for labour, disposable land, and preference for a cash transaction, and these result in a variety of types of arrangement between landowner (or his administrator) and *campesino*; but they all have in common the fact that they reflect the latter's poor bargaining position.

The older form of arrangement was generally that the *hacendado*, having given regular employment to his administrator and probably a few other men whose loyalty he wished to ensure, would then fill his other labour needs by the *colono* system: he would allow men to live with their families on his property and cultivate a plot for their subsistence needs, in return for the man's labour on his *hacienda*. The *colono* and his family could be called on for any kind of job at any time, but there was nothing to tie him particularly to that *hacendado* unless he established a more personal patron-client relationship with him. It was his freedom to leave which was the *colono*'s only guarantee of reasonable treatment.

If the landowner had unused land, as he usually did, after the requirements of his *hacienda* as an enterprise were met, then he let other *campesinos* not living on the property use it for a season in return for a specified quantity of harvested grain or a proportion, up to half, of the expected or the actual crop.[44] The part of the crop that the sharecropper (*aparcero*) paid to the owner was called the *censo*, and the portion demanded may, at the discretion of the landowner, have been reduced if the crop was poor or the family established special need, or it may have been an amount of grain fixed locally by convention.

Since the 1950s, conditions have changed to the extent that the *censo* has given way more and more to a fixed payment in money, so that the *aparcero* has become a renter; the expansion of cash crops, which had already begun with coffee to occupy all the land in certain areas, has been carried further with cotton and sugar, reducing the area left for subsistence crops. This, and the expansion of population, have led to an increase in the rent charged for land, so that many *campesinos* who could previously afford the *censo*, or the rent, however poor it left them, can do so no longer. Moreover, the minimum wage legislation has led to an increasing conversion of the *colono* system into one of simple paid labour by resident labourers or renting by resident renters. Meanwhile, the passage of time and subdivision of the small farms among heirs is leading toward even more miniaturization of the majority of 'parcels' of land.[45] This process is also aggravated by the selling of medium-sized properties in small plots to cultivators[46] who will have to continue to seek work as labourers, but who wish to own their own plot of land in the hope of covering their requirements for staple foods.

*Campesinos*, then, cannot be neatly classified into categories as owners, sharecroppers, renters, *colonos*, and labourers. They do not remain permanently in the same category, and they often work one piece of land under one arrangement and another under another, within the same season. Indeed many express a preference for variety, at least from time to time, and this is probably part of the reason why much of the workforce is highly mobile, almost 'nomadic'. Thus, after planting their own maize in May, men may go to another area for employment in the planting of rice, sorghum, cotton, or sesame in June and July. After harvesting their maize and perhaps also growing beans in August and September, they may next find employment in the harvests of coffee or cotton in December and January. If they own a plot or decide to rent that year, reckoning that they can cover the ever increasing cost of the rental and the fertilizer, then they must begin preparing the ground for maize (or for maize and sorghum interplanted) in April, ready for the rains which start about the beginning of May and last until late October. On the other hand, they may enter a *colono* arrangement, or simply not plant that year but look for any odd jobs, not necessarily all in agriculture. But since there are fewer jobs than men looking for them at most times of the year, the number of days when they will find work will average less than half the days of the year. 40 per cent of the agricultural labour force is estimated as being superfluous, in the sense that production would not suffer if they were removed, even if there was no investment in machinery to replace men.[47]

In these circumstances, it is obvious that any land over which control is not fully exercised will be occupied by squatters. When the land is national property, the squatters consider that they have every right to use it. In this way, a number of estates which have become government property have been quickly and fully occupied, and the only possible government action has been to consign the plots to their existing occupants as purchasers and charge them an annual instalment for purchase. Squatting occurs on privately owned land too, but only when the owner is not sufficiently interested to prevent it when it takes place. Since most landowners are so interested – and the larger ones employ *guardias nacionales* to patrol their domains, as well as administrators – there is no likelihood whatever that the estates will be broken up by gradual and cumulative incursions of squatters, as one observer has forecast.[48]

A problem which perennially besets small-scale cultivators is their inability to obtain credit from institutional sources and their frequent need, therefore, to rely on moneylenders or to sell their crop before the harvest at a very low price. Banks and credit institutions adopt, as their criterion for lending, the strength of the guarantees offered, so that a large landowner can obtain more credit than he needs for his farm operations and can use the surplus for luxury expenditure. Meanwhile, a small farmer, particularly one who has not got a written title to his land, not to mention the renter, cannot get any credit. If he gets some from the government institutions that exist for this purpose, they will not finance his family's necessary living expenses during the growing season, so he may be forced into the hands of the usurer anyway. No adequate study of moneylending and advance purchase of crops has been carried out (few have been carried out anywhere in the world), but the otherwise exhaustive investigation into agricultural credit carried out in 1966–67 concludes, referring to these forms of credit and to the sector producing basic foods: 'The usual situation in this sector is one of chronic indebtedness without exception'.[49] The picture presented, then, is one of every small cultivator having, in order to eat, to borrow so much and at such a rate of interest during the growing season that he has little or nothing to show for the crop at the end of the harvest and must soon start borrowing again. In fact the situation is probably not as bad as that.

## Cattle-raising

The continued use of large tracts of land for cattle-grazing on natural pasture is an important element increasing demographic pressure on the land left for cultivation, and these cattle *haciendas* are prime targets for agrarian reform. Much of the land grazed could produce more in terms of food and more in terms of cash if it were planted to crops. The preference for cattle is in many cases unresponsive to the recent rise in the value of land resulting from the pressure of population on land and the spread of cash crops; unresponsive because the cattle *haciendas* continue to make some sort of profit even when methods are unimproved, or because the wealthy *hacendado* prefers to finance his cattle-breeding from other income.

A feature of cattle-raising as opposed to the growing of cash crops is the variability in the extent to which new techniques have been adopted, from region to region even within this small country, and from *hacienda* to individual *hacienda*. The more advanced areas tend to be those in the vicinity of the coffee and cotton plantations – the south-west, the coastal plain, and the region around San Miguel; while the north lags behind. It appears that contact with those adopting the most remunerative practices in other kinds of agriculture encourages their adoption in cattle-raising.

The large cattle *hacienda*, even more than the large coffee *finca*, constitutes a miniature autocracy, in which the owner is king and the administrator his viceroy with something approaching absolute powers. Estates vary, however, in the degree to which the despotism is benevolent. There are those where the owner puts obstacles in the way of the school-teacher because he prefers his workforce not to be well educated. The apotheosis of paternalistic autocracy, on the other hand, is found on the island of Espíritu Santo in the Bay of Jiquilisco. The entire island constitutes an *hacienda* and belongs to one of the wealthy families of El Salvador, the Sol Millet family, along with many other properties including coffee *fincas*, finance companies, an urban housing project, and a distributorship for agricultural machinery.

The island, which can be taken as an extreme example of a more progressive type of *hacienda*, is about 6 miles long and 3 miles wide at its widest point, though half of the area is as yet unreclaimed mangrove swamp. It has a population of some 1,200, all of whose daily lives are organized by the administrator. The almost total nature of this control is facilitated by the fact that it is over an island, and all of the links with the outside are under the ownership and control of the estate. These are a private radio telephone system connecting the main estate buildings, where the administrator lives, with the owners' house, used mainly at weekends and on another part of the island, and with the port of Puerto El Triunfo on the other side of the bay; motor boats connecting the island with the port; and the private plane which the owning family use to fly direct to the island from San Salvador. No one is admitted onto the motor boats for the island without the permission of the administrator.

The estate combines a coconut plantation with cattle-raising. It produces between thirty and forty thousand coconuts each day, with just over a thousand head of cattle of very good quality grazing beneath the palms. Each animal is tethered to one palm for four hours, eats up the grass around it and manures the ground, and is then moved on to another palm; thus it grazes around three palms in the course of a day, as well as eating other fodder brought from the mainland. The herd is being improved by artificial insemination from American bulls. Some experimentation is proceeding to determine whether the plants recommended for pasture are the most economical under the local tropical conditions. The collection of coconuts is also efficient: instead of each tree having to be climbed, a high platform is drawn by tractor between each row of the tall palms, so that men working on the platform can reach the fruit. On part of the estate, lemons and cocoa trees are being grown underneath the palms. The overwhelming impression given by the estate, apart from its beautiful surroundings (particularly the view, where there is a break in the mangrove, across the bay with the volcanoes of San Vicente, Usulután, and San Miguel on the other side), is one of order and work.

All the workers are on piece work: their earnings average 50 per cent more than the national minimum wage, on unskilled work like picking coconuts. Skilled workers appear to be no better off than they would be elsewhere in the country, but the estate trains its own skilled workers – one of the points of pride and principle of the island's régime. A number of workers who have come illiterate have been taught to read and write on the estate, and have then learnt the correct methods of animal husbandry from simplified charts, prepared on the estate with illustrations, each showing four of five points to memorize. (There is even a chart showing the five principles of successful estate management.) The estate's school teaches the children to sing not only the national anthem of El Salvador but an anthem of its own as well. The workers are provided with housing that is much better than the usual single room in a *mesón*; the separate houses are constructed of local materials and are more appropriate to the hot environment than the concrete boxes with corrugated aluminium roofs which are often regarded as modern workers' housing in El Salvador. They must be kept neat and tidy; otherwise the administrator would notice and admonish.

In this positivist's paradise, the reaction of the subject population appears to divide into two groups. On the one hand, there are those who take advantage of the opportunity to acquire skills, and who adopt an attitude of unreserved gratefulness and loyalty, entering into the spirit of the enterprise as conceived by the administrator, Don Santiago Méndez, who as a young man had himself been selected by the owner from among other employees on another of the properties, and encouraged to develop his potential for benevolent command. On the other hand, there are those who are resentful in one way or another of the weight of authority over them, and it appears that some would go so far as to perform acts of sabotage against it. They could, of course, leave: and there is a fair turnover of population.

This *hacienda*, however, is by no means typical of the general pattern of cattle-raising. To begin with, only half the cattle are kept on *haciendas*, defined as units at least as large as the *caballería*, the area of land to be granted, in principle, to the Spanish soldier after the Conquest: 64 *manzanas* or about $1\frac{1}{2}$ square miles. There were only 80 estates with more than 500 head of cattle in 1961. The owners of many of the large estates are more interested in the prestige value of owning pedigree cattle, perhaps parading with them at the annual cattle shows, than in such questions as fodder or good land use. Thus wealthy *hacendados* have made use of a credit programme under the Alliance for Progress to import pedigree stock, but the medium and small cattleman has been left on the whole with no benefit from this programme,[50] so that, in general, Salvadorean cattle-breeding is still backward and of low productivity.[51] It bears more resemblance to the food crops for local consumption than to the export crops. With the recent installation of a modern slaughterhouse up to the standards demanded by the United States for meat imports, a quota on the American meat market was obtained in March 1972.[52] The wisdom of developing a branch of production which requires extensive use of land in a country with an intense land shortage is hardly questioned. Of course, there must be regions where it is the most rational use of land, but there seems at the moment to be very little relation between the optimal and the actual location of the herds. If you are well enough off to have cattle, then you have them on your land, wherever that is – unless you can grow an export crop on it.

## Other Aspects of the Rural Economy

It can be seen from the above that there is no such thing as 'the typical Salvadorean village'. The village in itself is not a strong focus of cohesion, and the life led in the countryside varies according to one's holdings – or lack of them – in land, and according to the use made of the land in the area where one lives. In the case of *haciendas*, it may vary considerably according to the philosophy and upbringing of the particular landowner. There are parts of the country[53] where quite large landowners have the reputation of treating their workers and the local population on a level of social equality; but this is very much the exception, and even the feeling of special obligation or responsibility for those who have always worked on one's estate, present in a number of landowners a generation ago, has given way, with improved communications and the increase in absentee land-ownership, to a more instrumental attitude. This instrumental attitude, however, does not preclude, but rather *in*cludes as a constituent element, the existence of special ties of personal acquaintance and usefulness between the *patrón* and some of the workers.

A different consequence of improved communications has been to open rural markets more widely to urban goods, imports and local manufactures, and urban markets more widely to rural products, in

particular perishable foods. The net effect of these changes has
clearly been to increase the inequality in the countryside by removing the market for a number of rural handicrafts – perhaps also to
some extent by putting up the rural prices of meat and eggs, for
example, which the poorer people may not produce, or, if they do,
may be more tempted to sell rather than eat, so losing protein
from their diet. Chickens and their eggs have long been seen as a
source of cash rather than as a usual food item[54] by most poor
people who keep them, but it seems likely that when the price was
very low they may more often have been eaten.

Chickens and pigs have generally been allowed to forage freely
around the house. Recently a number of specialized chicken farms
and a handful of modern pig farms have been started as commercial
operations of a quite different nature. The contrast between the
methods used, the quality and size of the stock, could not be greater
and there is very little production by small farmers using intermediate methods more efficient than the traditional foraging but not
needing a higher capital outlay than is within the scope of the
campesino: few simple henhouses are to be seen. In part this may be
because they would require a new division of labour between the
sexes: small animals are regarded as a sideline for women requiring
very little work, but henhouses would have to be constructed by men,
and would require more work afterwards: it would presumably still
be woman's work.

Women generally have very little to do with the cultivation of the
basic grain crops: even women without husbands would have to
brazen strong local criticism if they were to work on the milpa. They
have, on the other hand, traditionally performed most of the handicraft work, and they take fruit and vegetables – and sometimes the
grains – to market. The decline of handicrafts has left women in a
particularly poor economic position in the countryside, while the
availability of work for them in town has drawn them there.

El Salvador produces only about half of the fruit and vegetables
sold in the urban markets. The other half is imported, now almost
exclusively from Guatemala; before 1969 Honduras supplied about
half of the imported fruit. The specialization is partly a question of
altitude. Guatemala can grow a number of items, like potatoes and
apples, which do not succeed in El Salvador because it is too hot.
Other fruit, such as oranges, are sweeter when grown at higher
altitude in Guatemala, so that the products of that country are
preferred for eating while the local variety is used for making orange
juice. In recent years a number of landowners have begun to plant
orchards of oranges and other citrus fruit experimentally, encouraged
by estimates that the profitability per acre may be even higher than

with coffee. But most fruit is grown in a less organized way, as a few clumps of trees around the house. Large numbers of bananas are grown like this; however, the large cooking banana which was lately so cheap and plentiful has now practically disappeared, having succumbed to a specific disease.

When the figures showing the contribution made by each branch of agricultural production to the gross national product – figures obtained by multiplying the estimates of total production by the prices prevalent at harvest time in the rural areas, and so allowing for subsistence consumption – are compared with estimates of the amount of work put into growing different crops or rearing animals, it becomes clear that much of the cultivation of maize and other basic foods can now be regarded more than anything else as a mere labour-absorbing operation for those excluded from the more remunerative niches in the economy by the concentration in other hands of land and capital. In 1969 – for the most part, before the rise in coffee prices which has accentuated the difference – the contribution of coffee to agricultural production was ₡220 million. The various cattle products were worth ₡91 million; cotton and its various subproducts (cottonseed oil and cake) about ₡60 million. By comparison, the maize crop, the highest in the country's history, was estimated at 6.1 million quintals of 100 lb. At the price of ₡7 per quintal current in rural areas at harvest, its value was only some ₡43 million. Meanwhile, the total labour costs amount for coffee to some ₡62 to 84 million, and the total number of man-days worked must be in the region of 27 to 35 million. It is harder to calculate the average amount of work needed to produce the maize. Alejandro D. Marroquín[55] has estimated the work that goes into obtaining about 25 quintals of maize from one *manzana* of good land in the village of Panchimalco near the capital:

> At least 18 days, working 9 hours a day, to clear the land of the natural vegetation that has sprung up during the rainy season (done in February).
>
> 2 days to prepare for burning this vegetation by clearing a strip of land about a yard wide of all combustible matter all round the periphery of the plot, so that the fire does not spread.
>
> One day for the burning, done in March. (The ashes are a form of fertilizer, but conservationists point out that much of the nutritional value of the vegetable matter to the soil is burnt away. It would be better to dig it in, but this is much more difficult, if not impossible, for the ordinary cultivator with the equipment he has available. Renters and sharecroppers are uninterested anyway in the long-term fertility of the soil.)

8 days for the ploughing, done with a wooden scratch-plough drawn by a pair of oxen, often hired. (Ploughs cannot be used on slopes, and in many parts of the country the poorest cultivators cannot afford to hire the plough;[56] in these cases, recourse is had to the pre-Conquest form of cultivation using only a digging-stick.)

16 days for sowing in May or June, with two other men working behind the ploughman. (This seems excessive, and elsewhere sowing is done after a gap of time after ploughing; it may have to be done more than once if germination fails.)

15 days work done by a boy, scaring birds away from the young plants as they appear above the soil.

3 to 6 days weeding.

16 days bending the stalks over when the maize grows big, to avoid damage from rainwater which cannot run away; more weeding done at the same time.

8 days for harvesting in August–October; at this time, for about three weeks, someone has to sleep out at the *milpa* to prevent theft.

8 days to remove the leaves from the cobs after the maize has been transported to the house (which in Panchimalco costs ₡20 by ox-cart).

2 days to beat off the maize from the cob.

The total is 97 to a hundred days, longer working days on average than those spent in coffee production. It is estimated that 275,000 *manzanas* were planted to maize in 1969, including separately the plantings in August–September and in December when some of the land can be used again for maize. It can therefore be concluded that maize absorbed about 27 million days work, apart from that of the ox-cart driver. Thus maize used about as much labour as coffee, though its product was worth less than a fifth of the value. Even when the other basic grains – sorghum, beans, and rice – are included, the total value of the crops (₡97 million)[57] barely exceeds the *wages* paid in coffee, while they absorb not only far more work but also most of the attention and preoccupation of the vast majority of the rural population. Thus, while economically their production has something of the function of a low-level unemployment benefit, they are accepted readily or even with emotional attachment[58] by the otherwise unemployed, in contrast to a dole which does not require any work.

## Rural Occupations other than Agriculture

Something like 90 per cent of rural men are engaged in agriculture. It is impossible to given an exact figure, because the distinction between a rural village and a small provincial town is often an arbitrary one; but in the Department of Morazán whose administrative centre, Gotera, is the smallest of the fourteen departmental capitals (pop. 3,668 in 1961) 90 per cent of the economically active males in the whole department, including Gotera, were at that date engaged in agriculture. The comparable figures range between 80 and 90 per cent for the other departments without sizeable urban centres, and 70 and 80 per cent for those with large provincial towns.

These figures are considerably higher than for the rural regions of advanced industrial countries, even after discounting the large numbers of people in such countries who live in the countryside but derive their income from urban activities: the commuters, retired city-dwellers, etc. For instance, the island of Yell in the Shetlands, which has no urban centre nor any possibility of commuting to one, and has few retired people other than those who have been resident on the island for most of their lives, nevertheless supports more men engaged in services and professions than in the productive occupations of agriculture, fishing, and machine knitting combined.

Until a generation or two ago, as in pre-industrial Europe, each village or provincial town specialized in some particular craft – known as the 'patrimony' of the place. Sometimes there were two or three, while other places grew a particular crop more intensively instead, or concentrated on some agricultural product. In contrast to what happened in Europe, however, and what is apparently happening in China today, manufacturing has nowhere in El Salvador grown out of local craft production. It has replaced it from the outside, from imports and the factory production concentrated in San Salvador. Most of the specializations have completely disappeared, but there are certain exceptions: cloth, particularly counterpanes, is still produced on the handlooms of San Sebastián near San Vicente; the Ilobasco pottery has survived on the basis of more decorative designs than other regional potteries, so capturing the ornamental market.[59] Other potteries still exist, but they are fighting a losing battle against the metal factory product, not because their products are less efficient or more expensive, but because being 'crude' and cheap they are considered inferior.[60]

A few specialities can still compete. Bricks can still be produced fairly effectively by traditional methods. The sausages of Cojutepeque can rival the factory sausage; and cheese continues to be produced in the villages of the north, though only because the distance from the capital makes the transport of fresh milk uneconomic.[61] Specialized markets like that of Apastepeque for indigo have vanished, but cattle markets remain, spaced out at distances of one day's droving, between the main areas of production in the north-east and the centres of consumption.[62]

There are some artisan activities which have to be carried out in the area where the consumer lives and are more difficult to replace by factory production. Activities ranging from house-building to practical dentistry – still performed after an apprenticeship rather than a formal training – are the main alternatives to agricultural work.

For women the situation is different because they are excluded from work in the fields. Until ten or fifteen years ago a huge amount of women's time went into the grinding of maize by hand, both in the home before making *tortillas* for the family, and as an occupation on *fincas* or *haciendas* where meals were provided for the workers. Now, however, small electric mills have become ubiquitous, and women in towns and villages send their children each day with the maize to be ground. The continued trade in new grinding stones though, identical to those used before the Conquest, testifies to the fact that there are still many women who are either too poor or too far from a mill to make use of this service. Since the grinding-women on the estates usually had to work a 12- to 14-hour day, starting well before dawn, the disappearance of this occupation must presumably be seen as an improvement in women's conditions; but it has meant that there is less demand for their work, a situation reinforced by the effects of the minimum wage legislation of 1965.

In areas where suitable canes are to be found women still make basketry and mats. Like the undecorated or crudely-decorated pottery, also made largely by women, this craft is suffering from the competition of the factory-made alternative and particularly from the fact that, since entry to it is open, requires no capital, and can be combined with household tasks, its potential popularity reduces the market price of the product to a very low level. The general problem of the economy, from the point of view of the majority of the population, is here encountered in a particularly severe form. When people would otherwise have no income at all, they are willing to work for a very low return; but the more who do so in the relatively few occupations available to them, the more competition they make for one another and the lower the return for each becomes.

## Migration out of the Salvadorean Countryside

Until 1969 the underemployed people of the Salvadorean countryside had two alternatives to remaining there: they could go to the towns, or they could cross the border into relatively un-populated Honduras. The manner in which the second alternative has been closed to them will be discussed in chapter 6, along with the

1 Officers' Club Room, Military Polytechnic School, San Salvador,
  c. 1910. On the wall, portrait of President Fernando Figueroa

2 A street in San Salvador, c. 1920

3 General Carlos Ezeta (1852–1903), President 1890–94

4 Arturo Araujo (1878–1968), President 1931

5 General Maximiliano Hernández Martínez (1882–1966), President 1931–44

6 Colonel Arturo Armando Moli► (b. 1927), President 1972–

7  President Lyndon B. Johnson's meeting with all five Central
   American Presidents took place on 5–7 July 1968. *Front row, left
   to right:* President and Mrs Johnson; President Fidel Sánchez
   Hernández, Sra Marina Uriarte de Sánchez Hernández;
   President José Joaquín Trejos Fernández of Costa Rica, Sra
   Clara Fonseca de Trejos Fernández; President Oswaldo López
   Arellano of Honduras. Not shown in the photograph, but also
   present, were Presidents Julio César Méndez Montenegro of
   Guatemala and Anastasio Somoza Debayle of Nicaragua
8  Archbishop Luis Chávez y González and President Sánchez
   Hernández outside the new (unfinished) cathedral of San
   Salvador after a special Mass to celebrate the end of the war
   with Honduras in 1969

9 The Presidential Palace, San Salvador, entrance

10 The view from the entrance of the Presidential Palace: the barracks of El Zapote, headquarters of the Artillery Regiment. On 25 March 197? the regiment's commander, Col. Benjamín Mejía, launche a *coup* in the early hours of the morning and was easily able t take President Sánchez Hernández prisoner. But the *coup* failed later in the day

11 Salvadorean refugees bringing their belongings across the international bridge from Honduras just before the war of July 1969. The expulsion of Salvadorean settlers from Honduras was the main cause of the war

12 The refugees from Honduras were housed in temporary camps, but they were quickly reabsorbed into the general population

13 One of the largest of the pyramids at the Maya site of El Tazumal, Chalchuapa. Built many centuries before the Spanish conquest, perhaps as much as 2,000 years ago

14 The church of Metapán in northern Santa Ana department, completed in 1743

15  Performances of historical plays representing battles of Spanish
history are part of religious festivities in small towns and villages.
This is at the *fiesta* of San Lucas in Cuisnahuat, Sonsonate
department, November 1970

16  Drying coffee at a *beneficio*

17 Seasonal coffee pickers being picked up at the town of Berlín, where they have slept out overnight on the public square, for the day's work at a *finca*

18 Coffee pickers who have slept out in the chilly air of Berlín rouse themselves slowly. It is Sunday and they have nothing to do

19 Cotton growing at the foot of the (active) volcano of San
Miguel, January 1971

20 Sugar cane in its beautiful flowering season, with the volcano of
San Vicente in the background, January 1967

22  Cattle on flat land; henequen on infertile slopes—in southern San Miguel department, January 1971

21  Henequen (sisal) growing in southern San Miguel department

23 Ploughing. This is the more advanced method of agriculture introduced by the Spaniards, possible only on flat land and by farmers who own or can hire a plough. Elsewhere the digging-stick is used

24  Colonia Morazán, San Salvador, 1966. The rural aspect is
largely because this new group of about a hundred dwellings
had not yet been connected to the rest of the city by a road
bridge over the small Acelhuate river

25  A typical rural family and dwelling

26  Husking sorghum (Indian millet)

27 El Coro, San Salvador, 1966. The aluminium-roofed huts were erected for victims of the May 1965 earthquake. Above them, an older row of shacks form part of a squatter settlement

28 Shopping street near the centre of San Salvador. Shop names show the admiration for things American

29 Plaza Libertad, the central square of San Salvador

30 Slogans painted on the monument to Liberty in Plaza Libertad.
   'Camilo Torres and Sandino live on. Glory to the guerrillas.'

31  The headquarters of the Organization of Central American
    States, San Salvador

32  Medical faculty building, University of El Salvador, completed
    1970

history of that migration. The internal movement is even larger in scale, and the economic activities of the towns and cities should be seen in the context of the flow of people seeking work.

Natural population growth in El Salvador is one of the highest rates in the world. Official statistics for 1968 show 43.2 births per thousand population, against 9.1 deaths, so the rate of natural increase was 3.4 per cent. El Salvador is, then, a typical example of a country in which advances in medicine introduced in the last thirty years in particular have cut the death-rate and the infant mortality rate by half – the latter from 120 to 60 registered deaths per thousand live births – but the birth-rate remains almost as high as ever. The birth-rate figures have begun to drop a little too now: from a level of 49 per thousand population, which held during the 1950s, they have been falling by about one per thousand each year since 1963.[63] El Salvador appears to be conforming well to a general rule that the first effect of medical improvements is slightly to increase the number of successful pregnancies, and that the birth-rate only begins to fall when a significant section of the population has to choose between an extra child and more material possessions. For the majority of the population of El Salvador, more children will not significantly reduce their standard of living because it is very low anyway, and the children are a rather erratic equivalent of a social security system for old age. Besides, children are one of the few sources of pleasure and entertainment available to the women. For the very rich, more children will not affect the standard of living either. The recent reduction in the birth-rate reflects, no doubt, the growth of an inter-mediate class attracted by material goods which compete with children, as well as an increased availability of contraceptives.[64]

Whatever the cause, this latest demographic trend has barely begun to reduce the rate of population growth, particularly in the rural areas. Since there is practically no work available in these areas other than in agriculture or in occupations directly dependent on agriculture, and since it is impossible for land to expand, the only chance for the rural areas to absorb the extra population is by more labour-intensive cultivation. It has already been shown above, however, that such intensification as does exist is not primarily in the more productive directions of irrigation or the turning-over of extensive *hacienda* pastures to cultivation, but in the over-use of existing cultivated land and the over-grazing of small pastures, leading to erosion and soil depletion. It is evident that people eventually have to leave the land. Rural-urban migration in El Salvador should probably not be seen so much in terms of push factors from the land and pull factors into the towns, as in terms of the number of attractions of rural life which keep more people there than would be expected purely on the basis of comparing the income they can earn there with the income they could earn in town.

Rather than thinking simply in terms of rural and urban life, however, one should consider at least three levels: rural, provincial town, and San Salvador; if not more, because most of the migrants to the capital come from provincial towns, while those who leave these towns are being replaced by others who come in from smaller places or from the countryside itself. It is only for the villages in its immediate vicinity that San Salvador is the first pole of attraction for the truly rural population.

The indications are that over a ten-year period about 4 per cent of the rural population leaves for the towns. This is a net figure: more likely, what happens is that about 6 per cent leave but about 2 per cent return. In any case, the movement is by no means enough to offset the rate of natural growth of population in the countryside. Also in a ten-year period, about one per cent net of the population of all provincial towns leaves for the capital. However, this is very much a net figure: what is happening is that the great majority of those who leave the countryside go to the small towns, and while some move on to San Salvador later, the greatest part of the movement into the capital is of persons born in the provincial towns. A survey which I carried out in San Salvador shows that only a quarter of the people coming into the capital come directly from rural areas, and more than two-thirds were born in provincial towns, defined as places of over a thousand population.[65]

The capital, then, is receiving each ten years in net internal migration about 5 per cent of the population of the rest of the country, or 50 per cent of its own population at the beginning of the ten years. Apart from this, its own natural increase is greater than that of all other regions – about 4 per cent per annum. This greater natural increase is entirely because the majority of migrants coming in from the provincial towns are young women, so that over a quarter of the population of the capital consists of women of child-bearing age, while only a fifth of the rural population does. The actual number of children born per thousand women aged 15 to 44 is slightly lower in the capital, at 198 per year compared with 222 in the rural areas (in 1964). Provincial towns show intermediate figures.

The fact that women form a majority of the migrants is not surprising, seeing that they are debarred from most agricultural work, that the handicrafts on which they used to be occupied have declined, and that there is more work of the labour-absorbing kind for them in the towns, as domestic servants and in petty sales, particularly around markets. Men, on the other hand, formed the great majority of the emigrants to other countries, particularly Honduras.

There is no set pattern of leaving home to seek one's fortune at a particular age, but naturally the great majority of both males and females do so fairly soon after they become capable of earning their own living. This is as early as twelve or thirteen for girls who go into domestic service, or even earlier in some cases. After reaching the age of twenty-five or twenty-six, very few of those who have not migrated to the city will ever do so. Less than a quarter of those who come to the capital are married when they come, and there is no tradition of one member of a married couple staying at home while the other goes to the city, unless they are separating for good; though this is quite common, and one in twenty of the women who come to the city do so in order to get away from their husbands.

The overwhelming reason for the net flow of migration to the capital is economic. But the individuals who go, relieving the others who remain of some of the economic pressure on them by reducing the competition for land and work, do not always move for purely economic reasons. An analysis of the replies to a detailed series of questions about reasons for coming to San Salvador, which I put to a sample of some 270 migrants in my survey, shows that about 40 per cent of the motivation[66] among men for coming to the capital is not directly economic in nature, while the same is true for 50 per cent of the women's motivation. The main other reason for men is to continue their education (9 per cent), but only half of those who come with this intention in fact ever fulfil it. Next in importance are the hope that city life will be more enjoyable or entertaining (6 per cent) and dislike of agricultural labour (4 per cent of the motivation); next, if we are to believe the replies, some dislike of flies and mosquitoes, the hope that relations with girls are easier in town, and the cases of those who were not intending to stay in the city when they arrived (3 per cent each). Among women, 12 per cent of the motivation is to accompany a husband or to join a man already met. This is different from saying that 12 per cent of the women are accompanying or joining husbands: many of them have other reasons for coming to town as well, and a few say that they joined up with a man merely as a way of coming to the capital. Getting away from certain people is another important reason for women: 5 per cent from a husband, 4 per cent from a parent, and 3 per cent from a step-parent. 6 per cent of the motivation is the seeking of medical treatment, 4 per cent to get education, and 4 per cent for reasons of enjoyment or entertainment – the proverbial 'bright lights'; 3 per cent are motivated by dislike of flies and mosquitoes, and 3 per cent move to feel freer in the city. Large numbers of both men and women also mention the education of their children; it is a stock, respectable, answer.[67]

One popular misconception is that the shanty towns of all Latin

American cities are filled with migrants freshly arrived from the
countryside, who may later improve their situation and move to a
more solidly-built part of town. In fact, in San Salvador at least, the
great majority of migrants go first either to stay with relatives in
whatever part of the city they may live, or else make for the inner
*barrios* around the centre. Later, some may go to the shanty towns,
but the proportion of adults in the shanty towns who were born outside the city is only slightly higher than in San Salvador as a whole.[68]
Shanty towns are a way of solving the housing problem for any of the
poor of the city, especially the more enterprising, but not particularly the migrants.

Another misconception is that migrants have great difficulty in
adjusting to urban life. In fact since most of them come from other
towns, and since the kind of work done in the capital is not on the
whole so very different from that done in the smaller towns – a very
small proportion are employed in large factories – they do not feel
they are in an unfamiliar environment. After five or six years in San
Salvador, only a quarter of the migrants would like to return to
their place of origin even if they were offered employment there.
(Many who do not like the city will have returned home sooner than
that.) Although it seems that in some respects migrants do retain
attitudes and some habits – not going out so much for entertainment,
for example – different from city people, they are not on the whole
more dissatisfied with their lot or more emotionally disturbed. While
I have no evidence about the migrants from rural areas to provincial
towns, I am sure the same would be found for them also.

## The Urban Economy: Commerce

Throughout the country, the surplus of population over existing
opportunities for productive employment has inevitably led to an
excess of people engaged in commerce. Thus, if 40 per cent of the
rural people engaged in agriculture are superfluous, the same or an
even higher proportion of those engaged in selling in the towns are
superfluous to the efficient and convenient handling and distribution
of the goods sold. The surplus consists mainly of self-employed
traders competing against one another and so reducing the volume of
trade done by each. It does not seem that the competition between
petty traders reduces their profit margins to benefit producers or
consumers. What happens is rather that the large number of traders
reduces the volume of trade done by each, and this encourages or
(at the pettier level) obliges them to keep their customary margins
high in order to maintain their level of return.

Monopolistic practices on a grand scale – hoarding by merchants
of basic foods, forcing their prices up even to several times the value

in some cases – are remembered as particularly characteristic of the Presidency of Castaneda Castro (1945–48). Although these practices have been greatly reduced through measures taken by his successors, nevertheless incomplete information, lack of storage capacity, transport, etc., still lead to many small-scale situations of monopoly which can be exploited by astute traders. The sphere of commerce, in spite of its overcrowding, is one in which some individuals rapidly amass considerable fortunes.

At the top of the ladder are the importers and exporters. The wealth of this group, often of foreign origin – German, Italian, Spanish, Palestinian, Chinese; and notably some Jews, a fact which is noticed – rivals that of the families identified primarily with coffee-planting. Not that the two groups are altogether separate and distinct; many of the planter families are themselves engaged in the export of their coffee, and there are other cases of combining the two types of activity. The merchants, however, have generally been readier to go into industry, while the planters have confined themselves more, though by no means exclusively, to agriculture, finance, and urban land- and property-holding.

The import-export merchants operate with an efficiency not to be found in many aspects of internal commerce; but they take advantage of an oligopsonistic position in the domestic purchase of some export products, notably sugar, and they tend particularly to charge very high unit prices for imported vehicles, machinery, and other durable goods and their spare parts. The philosophy of small profits but quick returns is, in fact, very little followed in El Salvador, except by a few street traders, and although certain stores have a reputation of leading in this direction.

At the level of internal commerce, the bulking of agricultural products generally goes through at least two stages: owners of lorries visit rural market places and tour the producing areas, buying the products from the producer; from someone who has bought the crop in advance of the harvest at a very low price; or from a local bulker and transporter who has collected the goods. To give an example of mark-ups at each stage, in January 1971 the price paid for maize at the local market of San Vicente by lorry-owners was ₡7 per 100 lb., while that for sorghum was ₡5.50. The lorry-owner transports the product, very likely to the main market in the capital, and delivers it to a wholesale merchant with premises in the streets around the market place. In January 1971 the wholesale merchants of San Salvador were paying the transporter-bulkers ₡7.75 or ₡8 for maize, and ₡6.75 or ₡7 for sorghum. At this stage maximum bulking has occurred. The wholesaler then sells to market stallholders and shopkeepers, who are often women. The price was ₡8.25 for

maize, ₡7.25 or ₡7.50 for sorghum. The final price for sale to th
public was ₡0.10 per lb. for both maize and sorghum. This roundin
of prices for sales at small values is very characteristic, and makes
big difference to retail mark-ups. Sometimes, but not always, th
retailer is more generous with the measure when the mark-up work
out larger. But although the one cent coin exists, and circulates t
some extent because it is used by the government (internal postag
is 6¢), the next lower price usually quoted in San Salvador is '2 fc
15¢' and the next higher '2 for 25¢'. Since the sorghum could not b
sold at a profit at 2 lb. for 15¢, it had to be as expensive as maize, a
10¢ per lb.

Often, the stallholder or shopkeeper does not sell all her good
direct to the public but sells to a smaller-scale vendor. The latte
cannot usually go below the price at the stall or in the shop, but ha
to squeeze her profit out of a lower price offered by the shopkeeper c
stallholder. A typical arrangement is that the latter makes the good
available on credit, and takes half the mark-up, so that in the abov
case the ₡1.75 for maize or the ₡2.50 for sorghum would be divide
equally between the two. This is done mainly with fruit and vege
tables, and other things which people buy on impulse when they se
them. The whole of the rest of the cycle of bulking and breakin
bulk applies, though, to maize, sorghum, and beans usually, an
often to fruit and vegetables too. These, when imported fron
Guatemala, are delivered to the same wholesalers. Fruit and vege
tables locally produced may reach the urban market places mor
directly, either being brought in to the stallholders by the producer
themselves (or rather their wives, since this kind of trading i
woman's work); or else the stallholders or market women buy ther
in the local markets of the rural areas around the capital. Unt
quite recently they used to meet the producers on the roads int
town, and press them into selling there. The product may g
through a variety of hands. What is apparently rarest is for th
urban consumer to buy it directly from the producer or his wife.

Thus the urban public market is not so much a meeting-place c
buyers and sellers as an empire of intermediaries. Each person wh
brings goods to the market to sell knows certain stallholders to whor
he regularly sells. For example, the independent fishermen of E
Tamarindo, on the Bay of Fonseca, deliver their fish to the loca
departmental capital of La Unión, paying lorry-owners of La Unió:
for the transport. However, they sell the fish not in the market plac
of La Unión but to the fishermen's co-operative in that port. Th
co-operative, to which they do not belong, then sells to the marke
stallholders: it is large enough to assure them regular supplies all th
year round, which the men of El Tamarindo could not do. A con

trasting case where regularity is also demanded is that of the charcoal-burners who bring their product, the most widely used domestic fuel for cooking,[69] into the markets of the capital. They work individually or in pairs and hire a lorry to bring in a load when they have made one. They know a number of stallholders in various markets, but they do not like to sell the whole lorryload to one woman, because if one charcoal-burner did that and then another arrived, the woman would buy from him too, but would not be able to pay immediately: she would ask him to allow her to pay after a few days. Thus each charcoal-burner sells ₡15 to ₡50 worth of charcoal to each market woman; that way they pay cash.

Marketing of small imported consumer goods, and of products manufactured in the factories of El Salvador, typically goes through a chain starting with a distributor, but proceeds thereafter through all the same stages of breaking bulk as with the local agricultural products. The existence of these numerous stages responds to the surplus of labour and the concentration of capital. People with little capital combine their labour with it in as great a concentration as possible: they will wait long hours for a low return.

## The Urban Economy: Manufacturing

Since about 1930 a manufacturing industry has grown up, centred almost exclusively in and around the capital, and consisting of factories whose processes generally have nothing in common with those of the handicrafts they displace. This sector of the economy has been growing in recent years at a rate of about 6 or 7 per cent per annum, with the help of the Central American Common Market. The Common Market has made possible a geographical extension of the largely middle-class market for the kind of manufactured goods produced. In 1969 the contribution of 'manufacturing' to gross national product was ₡470 million, but this total includes artisan production, as well as the processing of coffee, cotton, etc. It also includes such processes as the mixing of imported chemicals and the refining of oil, where the real contribution to the Salvadorean economy is only a fraction of the nominal contribution to GNP.

Official statistics list the number of workers employed in 'manufacturing' as 34,712 in 1968 (not including owners who work, family members who work without pay, administrative staff, or technicians). Their pay was ₡47 million. These totals exclude coffee-processing, but they include sugar, and sugar alone accounts for 10,000 of the workers, mostly in the *trapiches* described earlier. It is, in fact, difficult to isolate figures which apply to the modern manufacturing sector alone, but it is clear that while it constitutes an important, and ever more important, part of the economy from the point of view of its product's value, it gives employment to a comparatively small number of people.

## Other Aspects of the Urban Economy

San Salvador is the centre of administration and of most kinds of services. As with most other Latin American countries (neighbouring Honduras is one of the two or three exceptions), the concentration of all activities except agriculture at the capital is very strong, and provincial towns seem to sink progressively deeper into provinciality, at least by comparison. A numerical illustration of this imbalance is the fact that 80 per cent of the gross income declared by persons and companies for income tax purposes is reported in the Department of San Salvador. The main reason is that the capital is preferred as a place of residence by all the people with money and social position, and there are no overriding geographical reasons making it cheaper to carry out any activities – except agriculture, shipping, etc. – anywhere else. In the first decades of the century, before communications were as good as they are now, Santa Ana in the west enjoyed a period of progress based on coffee and the efforts of its local upper class; but it is now stagnant. The third city, San Miguel in the east, is twice as far away from San Salvador and, correspondingly, somewhat more effort has been made even of late to preserve its dynamism. But outside the area of San Salvador, the only real growth-points are the ports, and they are only growing from a very small base: the port facilities offered until 1961, when a new quay was brought into service at Acajutla, were primitive.

Transport, which serves primarily to link the capital with the rest of the country rather than provincial town with provincial town,[70] is predominantly by road. The small area and dense population have made possible the development of a fuller network of paved and other roads than most underdeveloped countries possess; and transport by bus is accessible to most of the population. At slightly higher fares there are smaller 'micro-buses', seating some eight to twenty people, which ply the main routes between towns as a rapid service. Goods also travel mainly by road, although there are railway lines connecting the capital to the ports of Acajutla and La Unión, and to Puerto Barrios in Guatemala. The decline of the railways partly concerns such geographical factors as the relatively short distances involved compared to larger countries. It is also partly a result of the fact that the contracts signed between the Salvadorean government and two foreign firms – one American (International Railways of Central America), the other British (The Salvador Railway Company) – for the construction of the railways and their subsequent operation, provided that at a specific date they were to become state property. The result was that few or no improvements have been made after about 1940 to the rolling stock and equipment. The British line, to Acajutla, did not possess the same advantage, *vis-à-vis* road transport, of controlling the port facilities and denying access to lorries, as was practised by the American company at La Unión; and in view of its unprofitability, in 1962 it was transferred by agreement, to the government before the date specified in the contract. Since then, however, the railways have continued to lose business. A far cry from the time, in the 1920s and 1930s, when the railways were regarded as the main agents of progress, bringing life to the towns through which they ran. A single event marks the decisive step in the transition from rail to road: the completion of the first road bridge over the Lempa River, the Puente Cuscatlán, in 1940.

Internal air traffic has also declined in importance since the 1930s, with the improvement in the road network. Now there is virtually no internal movement of goods by air, and only such passengers as go in the private planes of the rich. There are, nevertheless, more than a hundred airstrips[71] serving these planes and, more important, the planes which spray insecticide on cotton fields. All international traffic is concentrated at the single airport of San Salvador at Ilopango, though there are plans to construct a second for luxury tourist purposes at El Tamarindo on the Gulf of Fonseca. The Gulf is indeed an attractive one; at present there is no international tourism, only a few holiday villas of wealthy Salvadoreans. After the 1969 war with Honduras, the Gulf of Fonseca is being used for surface transit of Salvadoreans and Salvadorean goods, taken in launches to Nicaragua, since the land route through Honduras is closed to them.

The government began to take a direct part in the provision of electricity, in 1948–54, rather earlier than of transport. This involved not the takeover of an existing company, as with the railway line to Acajutla, but an important addition to existing installations with the construction of a dam across the Lempa as it flows between the Departments of Chalatenango and Cabañas in the north. Since 1954, the government institution has opened other smaller generating plants as well as amplified the capacity of the main hydro-electric station on the Lempa. One programme now in operation is to tap the geothermal energy associated with sulphur springs near Ahuachapán, a natural feature which has attracted the curiosity of visitors since the sixteenth century.

The government sells electricity to the existing companies, notably a Canadian-owned firm which supplies San Salvador, and also undertakes some direct distribution to consumers in population centres to which electricity has been newly extended. The private companies have in the past been reluctant to provide electricity to smaller towns on grounds of unprofitability.[72] The government organization aims, either by itself or through the companies, to bring electricity to all the towns, though most rural areas are still excluded, on the grounds that the standard of living outside the towns is not high enough to justify the introduction of electricity. It is noticeable that most domestic consumers use their electricity for lighting purposes very sparingly and are satisfied with a light little better than that provided by candles. This is not entirely to be explained by low income relative to electricity tariffs, which are government-controlled and tend to favour the domestic consumer. It is, perhaps, more related to the absence of a habit of reading. There are, however, many people in the towns served with electricity who cannot afford to have it in their homes. Thus, in 1962, 35.2 per cent of the whole population lived in population centres to which electricity was supplied, but only 15.5 per cent[73] had their own measured supply, rather than perhaps a single bulb on an extension line by arrangement with a neighbour, or none at all.

Other services can be divided into three groups. First, those provided by the government or with which the government is closely connected, such as education and health. Secondly, those which require a considerable amount of capital, such as hotels, cinemas, and advertising agencies. These do not differ enough from those of other countries to need special mention here, except to point out the enormous range in the level of luxury offered, from, for example, the totally unhygienic eating stall in the dark corner of the covered market, to the Intercontinental Hotel, corresponding to the range in the level of income. Thirdly, those which require little capital but can absorb labour in large amounts, particularly female labour: domestic service, washing and ironing, dressmaking; for men, the construction industry absorbs a considerable amount of labour. The very high proportion of population employed in services in Latin America, as shown in official statistics of many countries, does not indicate high levels of production and a growing demand for services, as a similarly high proportion does in the most advanced industrial countries. On the contrary, it shows the inability of the existing economic structure usefully to employ large numbers of potential producers. This in turn, I think, is due to the combination of a liberal policy toward imports and the concentration of income, so that the consumption of the rich is largely of imports, while the poor have very little capacity to consume more than the most basic necessities.

# NOTES

[1] There is now no mineral production: only quarries.

[2] *2º Censo Agropecuario 1961* (1967: San Salvador, Dirección General de Estadística y Censos), 17, 238–9.

[3] J. Ambrossini: *Informe al Gobierno de El Salvador sobre los asalariados agrícolas* (1953: International Labour Organization OIT/TAP/Salvador/RI).

[4] See for instance *El Independiente* newspaper, 15 Dec. 1970.

[5] *Movimiento Gremial Cafetero*, now disbanded. They also assumed ₡2,500 was the price of a *manzana* of land producing 10 quintals per year, and on this basis claimed that the profit rate was reasonable, just over 10 per cent. But the problem of inequality is precisely the existing concentration of the good coffee land in few hands.

[6] *La Tributación del Café en El Salvador* (1966: OEA/BID). Mimeo.

[7] Taken in this source as only ₡1,800 per *manzana* producing 12 quintals. A third source gives a 'conservative' estimate of ₡3,500 (*La Asociación Cafetalera de El Salvador Impugna la Meta de Producción Fijada al País por la OIC*; 5 May 1969: Asoc. Caf. de ES, mimeo, 6).

[8] Except for the tax on capital, the maximum rate of which is ₡19,120 for the first ₡2 million and 1.4 per cent on the excess over ₡2 million (*Bolsi-guía*: 1969: San Salvador, 237).

[9] *2º Censo Agropecuario 1961*, 17, Cuadro 13.

[10] Jean Tricart: 'Le Géographe et le Développement Économique et Social: lère partie, Origine des Déséquilibres Régionaux', *Développement et Civilisations*, No 10 (March–June 1962), 90.

[11] Grupo Permanente de Trabajo: *El Crédito Agrícola en El Salvador* (1967; 1970: Banco Hipotecario de El Salvador), Vol. II, 463. Confirmed by interviewing persons who say they have had to sell at as little as ₡30 per quintal in August a crop which will be worth ₡70 in December.

[12] ibid., Vol. I, 281–2.

[13] There were 91 processing plants (*beneficios*) in 1961. Plantations frequently have drying yards which are no longer used; now most Salvadorean coffee is processed by the wet method which requires a considerable amount of equipment, for pulping, fermentation, washing and drying to remove the outer pulp completely, then thrashing to remove the inner parchment skin. The processing plants only work during the picking season.

[14] Consejo Nacional de Planificación y Coordinación Económica (CONA-PLAN): *Plan de la Nación para el Desarrollo Económico y Social 1965–1969*, Vol. I (1964: San Salvador).

[15] *El Crédito Agrícola*, Vol. I, 516–18. One of the reasons why the processer is willing to give credit is in order to ensure that the grower delivers his harvest to him and not to another. This may be made a condition of the loan.

[16] The destination of Salvadorean coffee (excluding the small quantities of instant coffee exported), and the average price received, can be seen in the following table calculated from figures for 1969 (*Anuario Estadístico 1969*, Vol. I, 2a. sección, 22–3):

| | | | |
|---|---|---|---|
| West Germany | 48.3% at ₡2.03 per kg. | (Germans prefer a better |
| United States | 34.9% | 1.89 | quality) |
| Netherlands | 4.1% | 1.97 | |
| Poland | 3.1% | 1.56 | (New markets not covered |
| South Africa | 2.9% | 1.64 | by agreement) |
| etc. | | | |

[17] The following extract from a speech made in 1954 was included in a eulogistic biography of the speaker, one of the wealthiest coffee-growers, speaking in the United States as vice-president of the *Federación Cafetalera Centro América–México*. It may strike the reader, as it did me, somewhat wryly:

American housewives have been led to believe that the price we charge is high, and that we are making substantial profits, and what is worse they have been led to think that all this money is hoarded up by a few coffee millionaires who do nothing but have a royal old time at home in their own countries and on frequent visits to Europe, where they spend a good part of the dollars which come from the United States.

Those who have produced this propaganda against the coffee countries are very mistaken, because if there is one product that deserves the price that is paid for it, that product is coffee. Just imagine for yourselves for a moment the work done by our workers who start on the job at 6 in the morning and go on till 2 in the afternoon, under a burning sun, twice as strong as you have here in Miami in summer. Imagine the human wear and tear involved in a day's work. Our *campesinos* do not use gloves or machines to help them in their work, but with their hands calloused by the effort, and working in a stooping position most of the time, they have to do this work to offer the magnificent product which you sell. A cup of coffee represents many hours of work by one of our workers.

Retranslated from the Spanish in José Salvador Guandique: *Roberto Edmundo Canessa* (1962: San Salvador, Ed. Ungo), 6–7. Canessa was Foreign Minister in an Osorio Cabinet.

[18] The cotton co-operative, dominated by the larger planters, has concerned itself with processing and marketing, and with political pressure for government financial help; it also has service departments for spraying, etc., but it has no enforced observance of good farming practices. The coffee co-operatives, on the other hand, were set up by medium and small growers who pressured the *Compañía Salvadoreña del Café* into giving them some financial aid. *El Crédito Agrícola*, Vol. II 450.

[19] Costs of production, as of 1966, were estimated as ₡829 per *manzana* for plantations using mechanized traction, but only ₡721 for those – mostly the smaller ones, accounting for less than a third of total production – using draught animals. The figures quoted include ₡137.50 as annual land rent, and they also include ₡47 and ₡41 for interest on working capital for the mechanized and un-mechanized operations respectively. *El Crédito Agrícola*, Vol. II, 488.

[20] Lauer, op. cit. See Browning, op. cit., for a good detailed discussion of cotton 226–48. For another interesting view see Tricart: 'Un exemple du déséquilibre ville-campagne: le cas du Salvador', *Développement et Civilisations*, No 11 (1962; 2nd part of report cited above, p. 123, note 10), 84–7. He stresses the pointlessness of the capital-intensive cultivation of cotton, the exacerbation of inequality, and a demographic effect of migration to cotton-growing areas: the predominance of males there. This demographic effect he may have exaggerated.

[21] Browning, op. cit., 230.

[22] Help from the United States government began in 1942 with the creation by President Roosevelt of the Institute for Inter-American Affairs and, within each Central American country, of an Inter-American Co-operative Service of Public Health; these were phased out after 1960, after United Nations agencies had arisen to take over their function. Yellow fever was also beaten, while malaria was very much reduced. Juan Allwood Paredes: *Los Recursos de la Salud Pública en Centro América* (1967; 1969: San Salvador, ODECA), 33, 78.

[23] Browning, op. cit., 230.

[24] ibid., 236, 238–9, 247–8.

[25] From year-by-year figures on sales income per *manzana*, derived from data in the annual reports (*Memorias*) of the *Cooperativa Algodonera Salvadoreña* on the area planted, the total crop after processing, and the average price received in international sales. On this basis the gross income per *manzana* in 1958 reaches ₡936. We can assume that the additional profit from the sale of the seed for oil was just equal to the costs of processing and other expenses of the *Cooperativa*, as of 1958; recently the seed has increased its contribution. The acreage reported as planted may have been overestimated for reasons connected with the obtaining of credit. Bearing such uncertainties in mind, the gross income fell to ₡625 in 1966, but recovered to ₡871 in 1969: compare with the costs given above (note 19). Insecticide costs, an important element, are now being reduced under a programme of the Ministry of Agriculture (Min. de Agr. y Ganadería: *Informe Anual de Labores 1969–70*, 85, where the claim is made that this reduces insecticide expenditures from ₡260 to ₡176 per *manzana*).

[26] From a high point due to Korean War stockpiling, of ₡122 per quintal of processed cotton fibre in 1951, the price fell to about ₡68 in 1958–64, then to about ₡64 in 1966, with no substantial change since. These are rough figures of average price received for Salvadorean exports, not corrected for slight deterioration in average quality.

[27] Fritz Loenholdt: *The Agricultural Economy of El Salvador*, report of the U.N. Technical Assistance Mission to El Salvador (1953: San Salvador).

[28] 12.5 or 13 quintals of fibre per *manzana* (*c.* 840 kg. per hectare). It had been about 9.5 in 1965–67. These high yields are hailed as being second only to those achieved in Israel itself. Jo Beresford: 'Cotton saved by strict programme', *Financial Times* survey of El Salvador (27 April 1970: London).

[29] Browning, op. cit., 237–8, 246.

[30] Jesús Avilio Cutié Tula: *Determinación de la Situación Comunitaria de los Cantones Havilla y Tecomatal del Departamento de San Miguel* (1968: thesis, Faculty of Agronomic Science, Univ. de El Salvador), 46–7.

[31] *El Crédito Agrícola*, Vol. II, 500.

[32] See above, p. 54, note 76.

[33] Between 500 and 1000 metres altitude.

[34] *El Crédito Agrícola*, Vol. I, 461; Vol. II, 521.

[35] This is clearly in large part a result of the fact that sugar takes more than a year to grow and is a semi-permanent plant that can be cropped a number of times before being replaced.

[36] See below, p. 137.

[37] This is particularly the case in the north, as can readily be seen from lower figures of agricultural production in the three departments located entirely in that zone: Chalatenango, Cabañas, and Morazán. The zone produced considerable quantities of indigo, but ever since the extinction of that crop it has been decadent.

[38] William Vogt: *The Population of El Salvador and its Natural Resources* (1946: Washington, Pan-American Union, a report).

[39] Yields in kilograms per hectare:

| | 1950: | | 1961: | | 1970: | |
|---|---|---|---|---|---|---|
| Maize | | 1,295 | | 1,027 | | 1,463 |
| Sorghum | | 1,156 | | 989 | | 1,120 |
| Beans | | 1,063 | | 636 | | 780 |
| Rice | | 1,320 | | 1,320 | | 2,071 |

*Sources.* Figures calculated from 1950 and 1961 Agricultural Census tables listing acreage planted and total production; for 1970, from xeroxed data provided by Ministry of Agriculture, converted from quintals per *manzana*. Beans are commonly planted together with maize in May, and then planted again alone in September; all these yield figures refer to total acreage, counting all the land each time it is planted with each crop.

[40] 1961 censuses of agriculture and population: 19,597 properties over 10 hectares; 406,464 men in agricultural occupations excluding dependants working within the family.

[41] According to Ambrossini, op. cit., El Salvador's agricultural activities absorb 41.28 man-days of work per *manzana* per year on average. At this rate, 10 hectares would require 590 man-days. Since we can assume, with Rafael Menjívar, that the average family can contribute 2 man-days of work per day, counting the work of wife and children as equivalent to that of a man, 590 man-days per year is about what the average family can work. Rafael Menjívar: *Formas de Tenencia de la Tierra y Algunos Otros Aspectos de la Actividad Agropecuaria* (1962: San Salvador, Ed. Univ.), 10.

[42] *2° Censo Agropecuario 1961*, XXII.

[43] The true degree of concentration of landownership depends also on the quality of the land held in large estates compared with that held in small plots. There are no systematic data on this question, but at least for one region, the northern, Tricart reports ('Un exemple du déséquilibre', 90) that the estates have monopolized the valley land which is under-used, while the subsistence farmers are confined to the slopes which they work to exhaustion.

[44] Adams, op. cit., 434–5, says that the specified *censo* in a number of places was usually one *fanega* (400 lb.) per *manzana*; this would be less than half the crop, though he does not give yield figures for these places. Strangely enough, however,

at La Venta across the border in Honduras, a country with far more spare land, where land rents are usually correspondingly lower, Adams reports that one-third or one-half the crop was paid.

[45] The area held in owner-cultivated properties of less than one hectare was 5 per cent greater at the 1961 census than that of 1950, the area of properties of 1 to 2 hectares was 29 per cent greater. There were decreases in the total area held in the more family-sized farms of 5 to 10 and 10 to 20 hectares.

[46] Usually on extended payment systems, renting with promise to sell.

[47] CONAPLAN: *Plan de la Nación*, Vol. I.

[48] Browning, op. cit., 261ff., 300. Dr Browning was kind enough to lend me his manuscript before publication, and intrigued by his thesis about the break-up of estates, I was able to make enquiries on the subject on my visit to El Salvador in 1970–71. As a result, I am convinced that Dr Browning has over-generalized from what has occurred on some estates where ownership has become confused or inheritance or which have become national property. I was universally told that landowners would have no difficulty in calling upon agents of the law to evict squatters unless they had established customary rights by many years occupation by law, 20 years unhindered. In urban areas, where squatting is merely for habitation not cultivation, the situation is somewhat different; but see below p. 244.

[49] *El Crédito Agrícola*, Vol. II, 68. See also p. 60, and in Vol. I, 528, where the interesting observation is added: 'It is a notorious fact that many of these money-lenders have enriched themselves in a very short space of time. Cases are known of some families who have begun with this type of business and have achieved position of dominance in the upper economic and social strata'.

[50] *El Crédito Agrícola*, Vol. II, 574, 583, 603.

[51] ibid., 573.

[52] *Informe Anual de Labores 1969–70*, 239–41. Cattle are exported to Guatemala for the meat market there: about 20,000 head in 1969 (ibid., vi).

[53] e.g. Jayaque. Adams writes, however, that in the Chinameca-Jucuapa area 'the relationship was clearly one of extreme superordination and subordination. The laboring group was of a completely distinct social class and practised divergent customs (separations and shifting of spouses was common). In Jayaque, however, the landholding class, while distinct, did not seem to retain itself in such a superordinate position. There was no question that there was a distinction in practice between the groups, but the landholders themselves were a local population and were more of a local upper class'. op. cit., 431.

[54] David E. W. Holden: *Central American Villages* (unpubl. ms.), 69. This author says that at Joya de Cerén, a village about 20 miles west of San Salvador, chickens are a means for the women to obtain small amounts of cash at irregular intervals 'They did not see the chickens as providing either meat or eggs for consumption except at very rare intervals on special occasions'. At a second village, El Pilón in La Unión department, the same author found by questionnaire survey of 15 families that 33 per cent of the families ate meat less than once a week, and another 41 per cent just once a week; 22 per cent ate eggs less than once a week, another 11 per cent just once a week; less than one per cent had meat every day, but 2 per cent had eggs (ibid., 155). Beans are probably the primary source of protein for many Salvadoreans, though cheese is fairly often eaten also.

[55] Marroquín, *Panchimalco, Investigación Sociológica*, 191–4.

[56] Holden, op. cit., 60; Adams, op. cit., 436–40. Usually, the poorer are also those whose land, whether their own or rented, etc., is located on the slopes of rocky terrain where ploughs cannot be used anyway. Adams says that at Izalco the Indians still use digging-sticks even in association with their ploughs, because it is an element of their traditional culture.

[57] CONAPLAN: *Indicadores Económicos y Sociales*, Mayo-Agosto 1970, 52.

[58] Browning, op. cit., emphasizes this attachment, 5–6, 270.

[59] i.e., a market for small decorations for mantelpieces and nativity scenes at Christmas, and a tourist market for ornamental plates, vases, etc., artistically decorated with designs inspired by those of the Maya.

[60] For a description of a number of crafts as of 1952–55, see Adams, op. cit., 441–4; it is not exhaustive. Although there has been a decline in crafts, they are

still more evident in El Salvador than in some neighbouring countries, particularly Honduras.

[61] *Noticias de Mercadeo Agrícola*, Año 3, No 10, Oct. 1970, 22. (San Salvador, Min. de Agr. y Gan., Depto. de Comercialización).

[62] For instance, the markets at Sensuntepeque, a centre of production in the north; San Rafael Cedros, halfway in to San Salvador; and Soyapango, just outside the capital. There is a map showing the cattle markets, with indications of price differences between them, in *Informe Anual de Labores*, *1969–70*, 44.

[63] CONAPLAN, *Indicadores Económicos y Sociales*, 18.

[64] My impression is that the official Catholic Church attitude to birth control has very little effect on behaviour in El Salvador, except possibly where the local priest emphasizes it. Having heard of the discussions within the international hierarchy of the Catholic Church which preceded Paul VI's Encyclical *De Humanae Vitae* of 1968, and particularly of some of the opinions expressed at Vatican II in favour of revising the Church's opposition to birth control, many people appear now to be under the impression that the official church attitude has been modified, anyway. Contraceptives are available for purchase, and there is a limited amount of subsidized distribution. In this respect the situation has changed radically since about 1960, particularly with the founding in 1962 of the very active organization favouring birth control, the *Asociación Demográfica Salvadoreña*, which maintains a clinic in the capital.

[65] Survey of 270 migrants; sample was random within 7 areas of San Salvador, chosen to represent different types and qualities of housing but not including élite or upper-middle class. Alastair White: *The Social Structure of the Lower Classes in San Salvador, Central America, a case study of the social consequences of economic change* (1969: Ph.D. dissertation, Univ. of Cambridge), ch. 3.

[66] References to a 'percentage of the motivation' mean not that that percentage of the respondents mentioned the motive concerned, for many respondents mentioned various motives, or rather, when I read a list of some 30 possible motives which I had prepared after preliminary enquiries, picked them out as factors in their own cases. The 'percentage of motivation' was arrived at taking into account the number of other motives present in each individual case; thus, if a man named 4 motives, each naming counted with only a quarter the weight which, had he named only one, that one would have had. Each migrant's case, then, made the same total contribution to the percentages of motivation, irrespective of the number of motives into which it was divided.

[67] These two paragraphs are based on my survey.

[68] ibid., ch. 4, on the adjustment of migrants.

[69] Others are wood, paraffin, propane gas, and electricity.

[70] This is clearly seen in a map showing the volume of traffic on roads. CONAPLAN: *Plan de la Nación*, Vol. II, after 380. Thus the daily volume of vehicular traffic between San Salvador and Santa Ana or Sonsonate is ten times greater than that between these two towns in the west.

[71] CONAPLAN: *Plan de la Nación*, Vol. II, 385.

[72] ibid., 321.

[73] ibid., 301, 325. The figures rose to 20 per cent by 1968 (*Anuario Estadístico 1968*, Vol. III, 109).

# Chapter 5

# The International Position of El Salvador

HER GEOGRAPHICAL POSITION as a small densely-populated country between the much larger but relatively empty territories of Guatemala and Honduras, and without her own Atlantic seaboard, has meant, ever since 1820, that her relations with the rest of Central America have been of considerably greater importance to El Salvador than is the case for any of the other four countries. Their importance has been re-emphasized in recent years by the growth of the Central American Common Market and by the 1969 war with Honduras and continued hostility, particularly on the part of Honduras toward El Salvador. Relations with the other Central American countries are in practically every way very different from relations with other countries. It is a relationship of equality or, in the case of Honduras, of economic superiority; a relationship, for the ordinary Salvadorean, of familiarity (Guatemala City and Tegucigalpa, and even Managua, can be reached in one day by bus).

However, her relations with the advanced industrial countries have been the most important in shaping the pattern of El Salvador's development since independence, and the effect of these relations, in all their aspects, will be discussed first. The burning question which must be borne in mind in considering each aspect of these relations is whether it tends to reinforce the existing situation of El Salvador's relative poverty and relative inequality within the country, or whether it tends to alleviate them. No certain answer can ever be given to this question, since one can only guess at what might have happened under other circumstances.

## Trade

In her trade with countries beyond Central America, El Salvador is still virtually exclusively an exporter of primary agricultural products and raw materials. In this respect, nothing has changed since the first years after the Spanish Conquest. It is true, however, that during the Presidency of Sánchez Hernández the possibility of sending the products of El Salvador's factories to markets in advanced countries has been mooted, and the first tentative steps were taken

160

with consignments of bathroom towels sold in Holland in 1968.

Instead of importing practically all of her manufactured goods directly from the advanced industrial countries, however, as she used to, El Salvador now produces a wide range of products herself. The pattern of her trade today, expressed approximately in millions of colones, is that she exports a few primary products to the advanced countries, to the value of some 350 million, and imports from them some 150 million worth of consumer goods per year, but also imports another 150 million worth of raw materials and semi-finished goods for the factories which have been established; and finally, she imports the equipment for these factories, and other machinery, to the value of about 70 million.[1]

She then exports a total of 190 million worth of goods to the other four countries of Central America (or three, since the war with Honduras[2]), almost all of which are industrial products; and imports a total of 150 million worth from these countries, of which some 40 million is for raw materials and unprocessed food, while the other hundred or 110 million are industrial products roughly comparable with those which El Salvador exports to the same countries. This Central American interchange, as far as manufactures are concerned, would hardly exist at all if it were not for the Common Market set up in 1959-62.

The former concentration on the export of primary products was clearly harmful to the interests of the great majority of Salvadoreans. It consigned them to the status of a reserve of workers, called upon for the most part only in the coffee-picking season, whose large numbers kept the price of labour down to minimal subsistence level. Denied remunerative employment in production by the free inflow of mass-produced imports from advanced countries, they had to fend for themselves most of the year and produce those goods whose mass production elsewhere presented the least relative advantage: items which, in comparison with others, could not be produced at so very much lower a cost in industrialized countries using mass production and advanced techniques; and those which were too heavy, bulky, or perishable to be cheaply transported the distance from those countries.

This, and not the inheritance of a tradition, is the reason why the Salvadorean population devoted itself to the growing of maize, millet, beans, and rice; meat, eggs, and fish, which are perishable; and a few other products whose weight gives the advantage to local production and not to mass production in advanced countries: bricks and cement; soft drinks, beer, and ice; candles and soap. Such were the 'industries' existing before about 1930, and between that date and about 1950 textiles were the only important addition.[3]

Mass production is the cheapest way to produce goods; but mos
Salvadoreans could only have benefited from the freedom of trade i
they had all been engaged all the year round in the production o
the export crops, and then only if the income from these crops ha
been distributed more evenly. It is necessary to say this becaus
there are still those who argue that the interests of all are best serve
if each country concentrates on those lines of production in which i
has a 'comparative advantage'.

Some Salvadoreans, however, did benefit from this form of trade
the coffee-planters had very cheap labour available to them
provided they did not allow that labour to form powerful union
which would demand a bigger share of the proceeds; and all the
better-off tenth of the population benefited from the cheapness o
domestic servants and from the possibility of buying the products o
the advanced industrial countries, which were superior in quality t
what could have been produced locally at the time. They did no
necessarily buy these imports at very much lower prices, however
since the other main group to benefit from this form of trade was the
traders themselves, and their prices for imports reflected the ability o
the rich to pay. Broadly, the interests of all the rich and powerfu
groups and individuals coincided with those of the leading industria
countries, first Britain and then the United States. So it is not surprising that there was neither any attempt by the rich to develop
local handicrafts into an industrial structure, nor any attempt on the
part of Britain and the United States to draw El Salvador into any
formal colonial empire or intervene directly in her internal affairs.

The change from this situation to the present one was gradual,
beginning with the first small textile factory by 1912[4] and taking some
impetus from the scarcity of imported goods during the Second
World War, but only really gathering speed after the *coup* of 1948
and, particularly, after the agreements for free trade within Centra.
America early in the 1960s. Among the reasons for the change were
the pressure or potential pressure from below, and the realization
that only industrialization could provide a growing basis for wealth
in the future. Moreover, the increasing numbers of semi-professional
and office employees were beginning to form a sizeable new middle
class, which could provide the best market for local industrial
products since they could afford them in fair quantity, but would
prefer a cheaper local product to a higher-quality import. International influences, in the post-war period as before, have been
important in heightening awareness of the situation within El
Salvador and spurring members of the civilian and military élites
into appropriate action: much of local industry has been established
with local capital and initiative.

Now, therefore, only about two-thirds of all exports and one-third of all imports are of the traditional type. However, this does not mean that El Salvador has gone half-way to redressing the ills of the traditional pattern of trade. First, virtually all exports of manufactures go to Central America, and, together with the manufactures of the other countries of the area, have by now practically exhausted the possibilities of import substitution in those five countries. There is not a big enough market in the area, which has a population of 17 million but a much smaller number of people who can afford industrial products in any quantity, to allow profitable production of the larger consumer durables such as motor-cars. Secondly and more important, a large part of existing industry in El Salvador, especially the industry set up under laws favouring such investment in the 1950s and 1960s, uses not only expensive imported machinery but also imported raw materials which have already undergone a major part of their processing in the more advanced countries. To a considerable extent, the plant established in El Salvador exists in order to take advantage of these laws. The tariff barrier is evaded and the final stage of manufacture is performed within the country.

If these two weaknesses in the pattern of trade and industrial development were to be overcome, and El Salvador were to find a market in Europe, North America, and Japan for her manufactures of consumer goods, thus developing industries which made more use of local manpower and raw materials, she would still be in a position of economic dependence for capital equipment and expertise *vis-à-vis* the more advanced countries. She would also still have a lower standard of living. But that standard would not be so disproportionately low, and should the gap narrow, El Salvador would be able to buy more from those countries as well as sell to them. The extent to which the gap could be bridged would depend on the proportion of the reserve army of underemployed labour that could find jobs in the developing industries.

If this were to happen significantly in El Salvador (but only there and not in all the other coffee-producing countries), then El Salvador would cease to be a profitable place to grow coffee. The opposition to industrial development by a number of planters is quite logical, though the attempt sometimes made from this quarter to identify the course followed since 1948 with a communist conspiracy is certainly not. Coffee demands much labour, which does not have to be as cheap as it is in El Salvador, but, under present world conditions, has to be fairly cheap. If the coffee-workers in any one country were to win any great wage increases, then they would price that country out of the market. Increases would have to be more or less parallel in all such countries for the price to be forced up. The same is true of other commodities. Even in El Salvador present wages are too high for the profitable planting of coconuts for the international copra market, although geographical conditions are good. It could be argued that the main reason for the deteriorating terms of trade for countries producing primary products is that whereas in the industrial countries the wage increases won by the workers *were* more or less parallel in all these countries (except Japan, where they came later, allowing a phenomenal growth-rate there), in the countries producing primary goods, even when a higher rate was won in one place, production merely tended to shift to those other places where wages remained low. In the case of minerals, differing government demands for royalties as well as greater differences in physical costs of extraction would also have to be taken into account.

Commodity agreements such as those that have existed for coffee since 1940 (continuously only since the late 1950s) can make no difference to these facts in the long run. Such agreements, with their quotas for the various producing countries, do introduce a new political element into trade, however. Differences have developed, now of about 10 to 20 per cent for coffee, between the price on the controlled market covered by the Agreement, and the price outside the Agreement, which is principally the market of eastern Europe and the Soviet Union. This means that the amount of the Salvadorean quota depends on the political goodwill of the other members of the Agreement. Of the first Agreement, the Inter-American Coffee Agreement of 1940, Vernon D. Wickizer wrote in 1943:

> The net advantages of the Agreement to the United States are less easily appraised. The cost of coffee to the American consumer was markedly increased, certainly by more than would have occurred without the Agreement. Against this, however, must be set a number of imponderables in the political sphere. In operation, the Agreement has been highly successful in assuring Latin American adherence to United States political objectives.[5]

## Political Alignment

The present Coffee Agreement, unlike the first and unlike the quota for sugar, is a multilateral affair involving West European as well as North American consuming countries, and its political implications are therefore by no means so clear-cut as those of the first Agreement or those applying to sugar. To some extent this situation reflects a small but detectable move away from United States hegemony over El Salvador, which was at its zenith from the outbreak of the Second World War until the 1950s. El Salvador has been firmly within the American 'sphere of influence', in the sense that American power in the region had the last word in any conflict, ever since Britain gave up any thoughts of competing for this informal political control about 1860.

However, until the late 1920s and even until the Second World War, El Salvador maintained a certain political distance from the United States and there were periods of what, if the two countries had been on more equal terms, might be described as tension. The main reason for this was the series of American interventions and even armed occupations throughout the Caribbean area but in particular in Nicaragua. These the Salvadorean upper class saw, not unreasonably, as a threat to their own autonomy. Apart from the colonies and former colonies of Britain, France, and the Netherlands, El Salvador and Costa Rica are the only countries in Middle America and the Caribbean which have *not* experienced an American intervention at one time or another. Salvadorean opposition to American activities in Nicaragua began with the expeditionary force sent to oppose William Walker in the late 1850s. It continued with strong resentment at the possibility, envisaged in a treaty signed between Nicaragua and the United States – the Bryan-Chamorro Treaty of 1916 – that an American naval base might be established in the Gulf of Fonseca.[6] When in the early 1900s the long-projected Canal was finally built in Panamá and not across Nicaragua, the United States might have been expected to lose interest in that country, but in fact 1909–33 was the period of her most active involvement there. When in the late 1920s Augusto César Sandino led Nicaraguan nationalists in a guerrilla struggle against the American forces and their local allies, he received considerable support in El Salvador.

Unlike other countries in the region, El Salvador did not break off diplomatic relations with Germany in the First World War, but maintained neutrality. In 1922, strong opposition was voiced when the government of Jorge Meléndez, under the terms of an arrangement for consolidating the country's foreign loan with an American financial group, allowed an American agent to supervise the collection of customs duties, 70 per cent of which were to be used to repay the loan.

When Hernández Martínez became President after the December 1931 *coup*, the United States refused to recognize him[7] – the first real test of an unwise declaration made in 1923 that the United States would not recognize any government in the region which came to power by non-constitutional means. The ambassador on the spot, Charles Curtis, who was inexperienced and acted on the assumption that only American interests in El Salvador should be considered, and not the principle of the declaration, reported that

Hernández Martínez enjoyed the confidence of the best circles in El Salvador and implied that he deserved support. Thereupon the State Department sent a special envoy of higher rank, Jefferson Caffery, who tried to persuade the young officers who had installed Martínez to remove him. They replied that they had chosen Martínez precisely because he was the constitutional successor. However, it appears that Caffery, and after his departure on 8 January the *chargé* William McCafferty, were making some progress when the uprising of January 1932 supervened. Martínez may have deliberately helped to precipitate the rising in order to consolidate his own position,[8] though this would have required an extraordinary degree of *sang-froid*, given that he could have had no confidence in the loyalty of the common soldiers of his army – only in their officers and in the National Guard. Six warships made their way to Salvadorean waters: the British cruiser *Dragon*, two Canadian destroyers, the United States cruiser *Rochester*, and two United States destroyers. It was the British who then insistently offered to land troops to aid in the suppression of the rebellion. They were indignantly rebuffed, however, both by the commander on the spot and by Martínez, who received the Canadian officer. The reply might have been different, if the revolt had not already been near to defeat.[9] American recognition of Martínez was withheld for a further two years, while unsuccessful diplomatic efforts were made to persuade other countries to refrain from recognition.

In Latin America, the nationality of foreign officers employed to train a country's armed forces has often proved a good indicator of the external political sympathies of the government. It has implications too for the future inclinations of the officers trained, some of whom will themselves occupy top political positions. It is therefore worthy of note that during the first century after independence the foreigners who played a major role in training and organizing the Salvadorean army tended to be from Latin countries with no important political role in Central America: from France, Colombia, Chile, and later on from Spain. It is also symptomatic that in the 1930s the officer appointed to command the *Escuela Militar* was German, and that a number of young Salvadorean officers were sent to Italy for training, among them the future President Osorio.[10]

And yet, in spite of Martínez's personal preferences and style of government, von Bonster, director of the military academy, was dismissed in late 1939, and El Salvador was one of the first Latin American countries to declare war on the side of the United States, immediately after Pearl Harbor. Nor was this because of any pressure from within El Salvador, where the upper classes were divided in their sympathies and much of the populace, whose contact with individual Germans had often been rewarding and whose knowledge of alternative political systems was nil, tended in a vague way to favour Germany. Perhaps the Inter-American Coffee Agreement played its part, but at bottom it was the now indisputable hegemony of the United States over the small countries of the Caribbean region which pulled El Salvador into line so smartly in the Second World War where it had failed to do in the First. El Salvador was not a particularly valuable ally nor a very active one. What the war meant more than anything else, at least in the memories of many Salvadoreans today, was that the German and Italian settlers had to be interned in the United States.[11] Their estates were returned to them after the war, however, unlike in Guatemala (where the Germans had been a far more numerous and important section of the coffee-planters).

One of the rewards for participation in the war began to appear in El Salvador, along with other neighbouring countries, before it ended: the kind of aid familiar in the last quarter-century, and which in the 1960s was called the 'Alliance for Progress'. Help was given first for a road programme, to complete the Salvadorean section of a road to the Panamá Canal which had strategic significance; for a big improvement in the provision for public health; and for military training. (Since the war the foreign training of Salvadorean officers has been mainly in the hands of Americans: President General Sánchez Hernández, for instance, attended a military academy in the United States and witnessed the Korean War as an observer with the American and South Korean forces.)

El Salvador's place in the post-war political world was as one of the most loyal friends and followers of the United States. If, for instance, the Americans have wanted a resolution proposed in the United Nations but have not wanted to put it forward themselves, they might prefer to get it proposed by one of the more important but more independent-minded countries of the Western camp. If this has failed, it has been possible to fall back on countries like El Salvador. El Salvador led the indictment of China for her suppression of the Tibetan revolt of 1959.

Within this framework there have been minor themes pursued by particular Presidents. Among them Osorio stands out, though perhaps only because his period of office, 1950–56, happened to coincide with the left-wing government of Jacobo Arbenz in Guatemala and its overthrow. Oscar Osorio, even more than the other recent Presidents of El Salvador, was an admirer of the system of government of the *Partido Revolucionario Institucional*, the official party in Mexico, and he made an attempt to model his official party, the *Partido Revolucionario de Unión Democrática*, upon it.[12] Osorio's attitude toward events in Guatemala had more in common with that of Mexico than with that of the United States, and in 1952 he met Arbenz to work out a basis for co-existence. This presumably meant that Guatemala would discourage the 'export of revolution' to El Salvador while the latter would respect Guatemalan autonomy. At any rate, El Salvador did not take any part in the American-organized invasion of Guatemala from Honduras in 1954 which overthrew Arbenz.

## Foreign Involvement in the Economy

In contrast to neighbouring countries and Honduras in particular, El Salvador has never had large tracts of her territory owned by foreign companies, and she could never have been called a 'banana republic'. Coffee land has been and is owned by foreigners, but these foreigners have tended both to take up permanent residence in the country and to become assimilated with the Salvadorean upper classes. The main reason why El Salvador is exceptional in this respect is that she has no sparsely-populated zone nor any area distant from the capital and suitable for development by foreigners as a separate enclave, like the Atlantic coastal regions of the other Central American republics or the Alta Verapaz coffee-producing region of Guatemala. The only important possession of the famous United Fruit Company in El Salvador concerned its dominant role in transport from the Atlantic coast of Guatemala to the United States – the railway line from San Salvador to its ports of Puerto Barrios and La Unión. Later, after the Second World War, when this and the other fruit companies started to decline as powers in the region, it was compelled under the American anti-trust legislation to sell its shares[13] in the railway company.

Apart from trade, therefore, foreign interest in the economy of El Salvador has been centred on loans, on the undertaking of engineering projects and recently the provision of other forms of expertise, and on investments which do not create enclaves, but are integrated with the rest of the economy.

The direction of trade outside Central America has followed closely the rise and decline of the various industrial powers, with the obvious exceptions imposed by the fear of communism: contacts even with eastern Europe, including Yugoslavia, are few and far between. The relative decline in trade with Britain has more than reflected the relative decline in Britain's general share in world trade, since the time in 1852 when the Prussian ambassador in El Salvador reported that two-thirds of her exports went to Britain and two-thirds of her imports came from there.[14]

The United States overtook Britain in trade with El Salvador about 1900, and by the end of the Second World War almost all Salvadorean trade was with America. But in recent years West Germany has bought more Salvadorean coffee than America. The Germans prefer the quality of Central American and Colombian coffees, while the Americans drink mainly the milder coffees which come from Brazil and are slightly cheaper. Since cotton goes almost exclusively to Japan, while the Americans take the prawns and sugar, the total result is that by 1968 and 1969 the value of El Salvador's exports to West Germany was marginally greater than to the United States. As for imports, the United States is still by far the greatest single seller. However, in recent years, the combined total value of the goods sent from Japan and from western Europe has exceeded that of goods from the United States. The figures for individual countries in 1969, omitting Central America, were: United States ₡152 million; Japan ₡45 m.; West Germany ₡37 m.; Holland ₡22 m.; Belgium with Luxembourg ₡17 m.; Great Britain ₡14 m.; Canada ₡11 m., etc. Venezuela also appears with a figure of ₡17 million, since Salvadorean oil imports are from Venezuela.[15]

The history of the loans made in the nineteenth century to the governments first of the Central American Federation and then of El Salvador, which also assumed its share of the Federation's debt, is a sad story for the Salvadoreans and one that has not yet been fully unravelled. The loans were negotiated by intermediaries on the London and other financial markets. While the interest rates may not in themselves have been exorbitant, the commission and other charges were, for some of the early loans at least, so large that only a small part of the original sum was actually at the disposition of the receiving government. The interest rate, if recalculated on this sum, was very high indeed. What was then received was not often used for purposes which gave lasting or even immediate advantage to the country as a whole, but for the financing of the frequent wars, or later for repaying old debts and so maintaining the country's further credit-worthiness.

Having seen that in other countries of the area the governments' failure to repay a loan might lead to occupation, of the customs house if not of the whole country, by troops of the power whose financiers had made the loan, and having suffered the indignity of American control over their own customs house in 1922, the Salvadorean élite turned against foreign loans. President Martínez went so far as to place a marble plaque in the chamber of the National Assembly on which it was inscribed that El Salvador would never again seek or accept any such loan.[16]

A few years later, however, Martínez had to remove his own

plaque. A new style of loan, conceived as foreign aid, was becoming popular. Tied to particular projects which are supervised by the lending government or international institution, it is supposed to avoid all the pitfalls of the older kind of loan, such as unwise use for uneconomic purposes. During the 1960s, the total of such loans made to El Salvador was 179 million U.S. dollars (amount authorized). Of this sum, 27 per cent was lent by the American government (A.I.D.); $25\frac{1}{2}$ per cent by the Inter-American Development Bank; $18\frac{1}{2}$ per cent by the Central American Bank for Economic Integration, set up in 1961 under the arrangements associated with the Common Market, and whose funds are themselves provided largely by A.I.D. and the Development Bank; 15 per cent by the World Bank; 7 per cent by the United States Export–Import Bank; 5 per cent by the International Development Association and the International Finance Corporation; and $1\frac{1}{2}$ per cent by the West German government.[17]

What are the effects of these loans? First, their political implications must be noted. They tend to tie the country to the United States where the great majority of the funds originate. This happens at two levels. The Salvadorean government becomes accustomed to foreign loans as an essential element in the strategy of economic development, so it would be disinclined to adopt any policy displeasing to the Americans which might jeopardize the free flow of further loans. El Salvador cannot, like some larger underdeveloped countries, play off one donor country against another, or at least take a more independent line on the basis of firm internal support, without losing the co-operation of the United States and the aid agencies. At the second level, the publicity given to the loans tends to create a popular impression of unstinted United States generosity, particularly since the 'funds' or 'resources' received are usually mentioned, but not the fact that they have to be paid back. Thus not only a vague goodwill for the Americans is created, but also a feeling that everything is getting better under the existing political system and that therefore nothing should be done to change it, even by voting for an opposition party which would in fact, if in office, continue to receive the loans.

Secondly, there is the build-up of the obligation to repay – just as with the nineteenth-century loans. The nineteenth-century burden (strangely enough) has been finally cleared off, with the last payment made in 1970 on the 1922 loan which consolidated it. But the volume of the new debts is beginning to reach the point where a new dimension is given to the question of repayment. (Apart from $179 million mentioned above, it includes also $10 million outstanding on loans, mainly from the World Bank, made before 1960.)

Many of the loans made in the 1960s involved periods of five to ten years grace before repayment; but these periods are running out. Moreover, the loans carry interest, at various rates ranging from less than one to about 6 per cent. So the question arises whether the state can afford to make the repayments or whether it will be contracting new loans or renegotiating the old ones in order to do so. If this course is taken, then El Salvador assumes a position very similar to that of debt peonage on the colonial *hacienda*.[18] The government, in its Five-Year Plan for 1968-72, envisaged that in 1972 the total outstanding foreign debt would have risen by nearly 80 per cent and from 9 to 12 per cent of gross national product.[19] It appears, however, that the A.I.D. and international banks were reluctant to see this happen, since at least until June 1970 the negotiation and disbursement of loans showed no signs of increasing at the rhythm required.

The question of the purposes and uses of the loans also arises. These vary and it is hard to generalize. Some, such as the programme to combat malaria by spraying all dwellings, are wholly laudable from any point of view. But it is reasonable to say that most of the projects financed will have the effect of expanding and benefiting a middle stratum of people who have a niche in the modern sector of the economy, rather than contributing to ameliorate the lot of the masses. Only 11 per cent of the funds went to agriculture, although it is intended to increase the amount in the 1970s. Moreover, an examination of some of the agricultural programmes in operation has shown that the funds (at least in these cases) have tended to concentrate in the hands of landowners for whom they were not designed under the terms of the loans. These larger landowners were in a position to obtain credit from their banks on a normal commercial basis, but made use of the programme funds because of the low rate of interest. For instance, a majority of the pre-1967 beneficiaries of the Programme for Land Improvement, sponsored by A.I.D., farmed more than the 75 hectares fixed as the maximum for the programme.[20] Those in charge of distributing the funds may not necessarily have favourites. It may have been easier and cheaper for them to disburse the money in larger sums to those who had prepared projects for irrigation and drainage, rather than in smaller amounts, with more technical assistance, for soil conservation on small farms – the principal purpose of the programme.[21]

20 per cent of the foreign loans of the 1960s were made for the improvement of the international airport and the ports, and for road construction. The main road system is now modern. Some stretches, such as that through a gorge between Santa Tecla and Colón, are spectacularly so and very convenient for those who have motor-cars.

This construction has often been carried out by a foreign firm, using specially imported heavy earth-moving and other equipment, and therefore providing relatively few jobs for the large numbers of Salvadoreans who are always on the look-out for this kind of work.

12 per cent of the loans were for housing, which in practice means the housing of the urban middle classes; 11 per cent for education, including a big experimental project on the use of instructional television, loans for which were authorized by A.I.D. in 1968 and 1969, and which got under way in 1970–71; 5 per cent each for electricity and for piped water and sewage provision, both of which will benefit most of the urban population; 7 per cent for telecommunications, which, apart from the imposing marble-faced buildings which are now the hallmark of the telegraph offices and telephone exchanges in the cities, means that the government and private subscribers have an improved service, including in particular access to many more of the small towns and villages. 4 per cent is intended for a new market complex for San Salvador, not yet built. A slightly smaller sum was provided for public health projects, principally the anti-malaria campaign and an impressive new children's hospital in the capital. 4 per cent has gone to a profit-making development bank, the *Financiera de Desarrollo e Inversión*, which almost exclusively finances industry. The remaining 17 per cent was directly provided for industrial development, contributing to the kind of industrial development which will be discussed below.

Apart from loans, a far smaller number of grants are made by the United States government to El Salvador. Running very approximately at the rate of $2 million per year,[22] they include, for instance, the payment to an American planning firm to draw up an urban plan for San Salvador and its suburbs. It is no accident that the western section of the capital, the upper- and middle-class residential area, is taking on more and more the appearance of an American town. Such matters as the width of the highways; the wide strip at the side of the highway on which building is not allowed; the fact that the regulation forbidding this effectively discourages private house ownership on the main road, leaving it for commercial use; and finally the free proliferation of signs and advertisements along the strip in front of the buildings – all these are typified by the new *Boulevard de los Héroes* (the heroes of the 1969 war against Honduras).[23] This road serves as a good visual illustration of the tendency that adoption of American expertise implies. One sector of the country becomes the image of the United States, but a bigger sector, in both a geographical and social sense, remains unaffected.

In the case of the urban plan, the employees of the relevant Salvadorean government department say they could have done the job themselves. This is also the complaint of engineers in some other fields where foreign firms are engaged to plan or carry out public projects, in particular a Chicago firm of hydraulic engineers which has fulfilled a number of such contracts since the early 1950s.[24] Whether or not this kind of foreign involvement is now superfluous, it is already much less prominent an element of public spending than in the past, particularly in the days of railway-building.

Foreign investment, however, is not declining in importance. For the early 1950s, the American economist Bert Hoselitz estimated the amount of direct foreign investments in El Salvador as 25 million dollars.[25] The data for the end of 1965 show that at that time $35 million was invested in the form of the foreign share in the capital of mixed enterprises alone, an element which formed only 14½ million of Hoselitz's total.[26] By the end of 1968, a list of foreign investments, including private loans, comes to a total of $131 million.[27]

This increase responds very largely to a desire to produce locally for the Central American market industrial products, often of brands well known to consumers throughout the Western world. Advantage is taken of the absence of import tariffs within Central America and the concessions offered for industrial investment (periods of exemption from all tariffs and taxes). To obtain these concessions the foreign investor must accept the partnership of local businessmen contributing 50 per cent of the capital: such partnerships naturally tend to link Salvadorean industrialists with international capital in a political sense too.

The investment is international rather than exclusively American. Twenty countries, from Japan to Luxembourg, the Bahamas, and Curaçao are on the list showing the origin of share capital, though the most frequent mentions of the United States and of Panamá illustrate the predominance of American and multi-national corporations. The largest single factory in terms of employment, a textile plant with some 2,000 workers, is mainly Japanese-owned, while Britain is represented, in the industrial field, by the single cigarette factory.

## International Cultural Links and Influences

The Americanization of Salvadorean life and culture has probably not been carried quite so deep as in the case of pre-revolutionary Cuba, for instance; or of Nicaragua, if one is to judge by the fact that Salvadoreans play soccer, while Nicaragua shares with Cuba the distinctiveness of having adopted baseball as the national game. But it has gone quite far. It is probably inevitable, given the kind of commercial links with America and the fact that what is modern or new is generally American, so that the modern and the American become associated in the popular consciousness. Reaction against this process is recent, and its voicing is as yet confined to the university. (Opposition to American imperialism is much older; but it is only since about 1969 that attention has been paid to ideological penetration as a part of it.)

In the early 1900s El Salvador was a country of overwhelmingly Spanish culture, particularly at the upper levels. At the lower level she is best described as simply Spanish American, with no strong features unique to El Salvador. The bourgeois life of each town revolved around the bandstand in the central *plaza*, close to which were to be found the residences of upper-class citizens, who paraded on the square when the band played on Sundays or holidays. Festive occasions in San Salvador called for a bullfight, while in smaller, more 'Indian', towns the dance-play of the fight between Moors and Christians by the members of a church fraternity was performed.

At that time it was to Europe and especially to France that the upper classes looked for a literary and artistic culture which was a much more central part of their social life than it is today. In San Salvador in the early years of the century a fine theatre (the *Teatro de Bellas Artes*) was erected, classical music and Romantic poetry were heard, read, discussed, and written. Paris was the main destination to which the rich headed on their trips abroad, with Madrid in second place.

All this has changed, or rather been diminished and superseded and become a very minor and decaying pattern. Bullfights are no longer held, and the bandstands are silent; there is no elegant *paseo* around the square, as there still is in Spain and some other parts of Latin America; in fact there is no longer a proper central square in San Salvador at all, but three or four squares, none of which is focal. The rich have moved their residence to the western outskirts of the city, and the main destination for trips abroad is Miami. Although a French cultural centre caters for a minority who still want to read French books (there are also German and American centres, but no British Council), there is in fact very little interest in literature or the fine arts generally. An interesting datum can confirm this impression: in 1970, of all the Spanish-speaking countries, El Salvador was in bottom place for the value of purchases of books from Spain.[2] She was below Honduras which has both a lower population and a lower *per capita* income, and in proportion to her population she took less than a quarter of the value of books taken by Mexico, a seventh of those taken by Colombia, and an eleventh of those taken by Argentina. The fine theatre has become a dilapidated cinema. For live performances given by singers or other visiting international entertainers the rich are more likely to go to the Intercontinental Hotel. The conclusion is that the European cultural orientation was linked to the bourgeois-town style of life and that both have been rejected by the new generations, particularly since the 1940s.

The new middle classes which have come up through economic changes mainly since that decade never really assimilated European culture, though of course they will have had some contact with it, and this intermediate stratum is probably the most Americanized. Perhaps one can overgeneralize about a social group which is not even clearly demarcated (does it include the lucky manual workers who have jobs in the modern factories?). But they have pulled themselves up from the masses below under an economic system in which the American influence is paramount; and they have tended to associate their individual success, and social progress, with the American style. Middle-class cinema-goers usually prefer American films; whereas at lower economic levels it is the Mexican film which is preferred by most of those who go to the cinema at all.

Popular entertainment in general shows a fairly even balance between what is American and what is Latin American in origin. In music, the Liverpool sound had its influence in the 1960s. The more sedate European dances, once popular, are no longer to be heard. There has also been a decline, though not so complete, in playing the *marimba*, a large xylophone and its associated music which are a valuable contribution of Guatemala and the surrounding area to the world's musical traditions.[29] They have succumbed as the transistor radio (as cheap as ₡7) has penetrated all sections of the population, and as record-players have become more available to provide music for dancing. One of the many commercial radio stations specializes in broadcasting the Mexican *ranchera*; but the others include a heavy proportion of American pop songs or Latin American songs heavily influenced by the American, in their programmes of continuous music interspersed with advertisements.

The commercial barrage is a ubiquitous aspect of Americanization, producing a consumer-oriented culture where only a minority can afford to be consumers. One of the few widely-advertised products which most people can consume on a large scale are headache pills and those which promise a remedy for nervous ills. These have a big sale. Another aspect is the wide circulation of American popular magazines in Spanish, imported in far greater numbers than magazines from Latin American countries. They occupy a role in education second only to that of the formal school system. The way they, and some of their Latin American imitators, perform this role can perhaps be illustrated by an example. In the course of a survey I asked a boilerman whether or not, to make a good wife, a woman should refrain from sexual relations before marriage. His reply was 'It depends on the temperature of the blood. The hormones are in command. I read it in *Lux* magazines'. There is, it must also be said, an American contribution to education, outside the formal system, which is more useful. American correspondence schools have a large number of home pupils in El Salvador, learning in particular technical subjects such as motor- or radio-repairing. There is also an American School in San Salvador, mainly for the children of Americans on assignments in the country; but it also takes wealthy Salvadoreans: in 1966, the children of both the President and Vice President were pupils.

Salvadoreans are also emigrating to the United States. Some tens of thousands have gone there to work, with San Francisco the main destination, though by no means the only one. A very frequent element of this emigration is that the Salvadorean takes a job in America which is of a social status or degree of skill lower, sometimes considerably lower, than that of the work he was doing in El Salvador. For only a small part of this migration resembles that of the Mexican *braceros* of rural origin, unskilled except in traditional farmwork. It is rather a continuation of the pattern of migration by stages: the country people migrate to the small towns; those from the small towns migrate to the cities; and those from the cities are beginning to migrate to the United States. The people with at least a modicum of skills and education are those who go. At the top, there is something of a brain-drain of some of the more gifted products of the educational system. They may go to America for purposes of specialization, perhaps on scholarships, and not return. (A corollary of the migration of young Salvadoreans to the United States is that a sizeable number of them have fought in the United States forces in the Vietnam War.)

The main criticism being voiced in the University of El Salvador about the scholarships to the United States is not that scholarship-winners do not always return. Rather, so the critics say, they return with a new mentality more in keeping with the system of American economic and political domination. The financial aid which provides for these scholarships and that which provides for projects within Latin American universities are seen as aiming to convert these universities into technological centres of a secondary order for the better consumption of the technological products of the United States. It is certainly true that a rather automatic imitation of the American patterns of teaching, particularly in scientific and technological subjects, has led to the creation of experts in methods appropriate for solving American scientific and technological problems, but inappropriate for a creative approach to the very different real problems of El Salvador. They have tended to apply the methods without asking themselves how much impression they are making on the real problems. However, this is hardly the result of foreign aid, except as a very peripheral factor. It has come about not so much because of the deliberate development of dependent science, technology, and economics in Latin America, as because of the slow rate of development of independent ones, despite the talk of a need for them.

The revolutionary atmosphere at the University of El Salvador helps to persuade a number of wealthy parents to send their children – their sons in particular – to other countries for their higher education. Many go to the United States; but there are still a large number who go to Spain, which is often seen as offering a pleasanter student life for those who are not academically ambitious. Of Latin American countries, Chile and Mexico receive most Salvadorean students. With Chile, as with nearby Mexico, there is something of a tradition of intellectual contact – and today it is worth mentioning that the Chilean poet Pablo Neruda is probably the biggest single influence in young university literary circles in El Salvador. Although there is widespread interest in Cuba and her revolution, the government has reduced contact virtually to zero.

## NOTES

[1] Figures based on a detailed breakdown in *Anuario Estadístico 1968*, Vol. I. The classification system used there is not followed, since it groups together some consumer and capital goods, and is inadequate for the purpose.

[2] The war of 1969: see below, pp. 183–90.

[3] In 1950 there were 39 factories with annual production valued at more than ₡1 million, 22 of which manufactured drinks. There were a further 50 establishments with production valued at ₡500,000–₡1 m., and 132 with production between ₡100,000 and ₡500,000, including enterprises such as printers. 15 of the total were textile plants, including a factory producing *henequen* (sisal) sacks for exporting coffee. Data from Leonilo Armando Alas: *El Comercio Exterior y la Inflación en El Salvador 1931–1952* (1954: thesis, Fac. of Economics, Univ. de El Salvador).

[4] Percy M. Feltham: *La Industria Textil en El Salvador* (1952: U.N.).

[5] *The World Coffee Economy* (1943: Stanford, Food Research Institute), 192.

[6] See, for instance, Mario Rodríguez: *Central America* (1965: Englewood Cliffs, Prentice-Hall), 116–26.

[7] Under the Washington treaty signed with the Central American states in 1923, the United States was committed not to recognize governments arising from *coups*. The principle was at stake. The irony was that Martínez had been given power because it was assumed he would gain this recognition.

[8] Grieb, op. cit. Martínez was also threatened by an imminent invasion from Guatemala and Honduras by supporters of Araujo, which was put off and then abandoned when the communist-led uprising broke out. So Martínez had an additional reason to provoke the uprising: he could label *Araujista* resistance as 'communist'. Julio Contreras Castro, op. cit., 38.

[9] The details of the Canadian landing and the circumstances of Martínez's interview with the Canadian commander are given above, p. 113, note 44. As for

the military significance of the presence of the ships and the landing of troops, Brodeur may or may not have been exaggerating when he stated in his report: 'The arrival of ships created a very strong moral support to all concerned . . . No steps had been taken by the Salvador government to protect anything or offer serious defence to revolutionary forces, for fear that the Army would revolt. So all troops were kept in the capital where a serious attack was expected at any moment. Army officers and the National Guard were the only ones that could be really depended upon in case of a serious uprising . . . There is no doubt that the presence of the ships on the coast strengthened the president's stand considerably as he immediately started sending troops out of town when he found we were prepared to act in case of emergency. The landing of the platoon had a wonderful moral effect on his troops'. The first American ships, the two destroyers, arrived in Acajutla on 25 January. After a meeting with Brodeur, who had returned to the port that morning, they sailed on the next day to La Libertad. On 29 January the *Rochester* arrived, and then the general in charge of operations in the west, José Tomás Calderón, informed both the American and British commanders that order had been fully restored and 'four thousand eight hundred Communists liquidated' – a figure which he chose in order to give a better impression that he was in command of the situation. (The figure was reported to the press, and the following day there were demonstrations at the Salvadorean legation in Mexico protesting the bloodbath, whereupon Calderón 'explained' that he had only meant that 4,800 had been dislocated, not killed. Calderón, who had only a few weeks before led military resistance to the *coup* against the constitutional régime of Araujo, was in 1942 to be dismissed from Martínez's government, in which he held a ministerial post, for supposed pro-Nazi sympathies.) Brodeur went ashore to verify the statement, and was effusively greeted by Calderón. The next day, 30 January, General Faustino Choto Rivas, commander of Sonsonate, took Brodeur and three of his officers on a tour of the areas of the revolt, with lunch in Sonsonate and an invitation (declined) to witness 'a few executions'. A Salvadorean account (Martínez Vargas, op. cit., 44–5) has it that both Calderón's message and this tour were necessary to persuade the Canadian commander to desist from his intention to land troops. But this cannot be the case: by 29 January Brodeur already knew that cause for alarm was over, and at this stage the primary concern which he voices in his report is over the appalling conditions of the workers at plantations (he visited one American-owned, another British-owned estate), to which he attributes the uprising. The Canadian ships left on 31 January, after Brodeur had paid a third visit to the capital. On 1 February the *Dragon* was ordered from Panamá to La Libertad, but the order was reversed soon afterward, following reassuring telegrams from Rodgers, and she returned to Caribbean waters. (She had been summoned from Trinidad on 22 January, and could have reached El Salvador by the 27th, but had been held standing by at the Pacific end of the Panamá Canal). Foreign Office files 15812–15, Public Records Office, London.

[10] Martínez's government also distinguished itself internationally by being among the first to recognize both the Japanese puppet régime in Manchuria in 1934 and Franco's régime in Spain in 1936.

[11] The Salvadorean *marimba* band *Atlacatl* was stranded by the war in Axis-occupied Europe. Interned in Germany, the band was nevertheless allowed to continue giving concerts in German towns.

[12] It is said that the Mexicans have also helped the PCN in the 1960s to establish itself on the lines of the Mexican *Partido Revolucionario Institucional*.

[13] 42.6 per cent of the shares, a controlling interest.

[14] David Luna: *Manual de Historia Económica de El Salvador*, 203–4, quoting Ambassador Hugo Hesse.

[15] *Boletín Estadístico* No 84 for Oct.–Dec. 1969 (Mar. 1970: San Salvador, Min. de Economía), 127–8.

[16] Ricardo Gallardo: *Las Constituciones de El Salvador* (1961: Madrid), Vol. II, 727–8.

[17] Information from United States A.I.D. office in El Salvador.

[18] See above, pp. 41–2. This parallel is made by Cheryl Payer: 'The Perpetuation

of Dependence: the IMF and the Third World', *Monthly Review*, Vol. 23, No 4 (New York, Sept. 1971), 40.

[19] CONAPLAN: *Plan de Desarrollo Económico y Social 1968–1972*, Parte general, 114.

[20] *El Crédito Agrícola*, Vol. I, 540, 544.

[21] ibid., 531–67, esp. 563.

[22] This does not include the United States surplus foods distributed by Catholic Relief Services, which as of 30 September 1964 claimed to be feeding 581,000 people in El Salvador, or a fifth of the whole population. 'Summary of Programs of Catholic Relief Services' (March 1965: booklet, Catholic Bishops' Fund for the Needy Overseas). The programme, which was locally administered by people connected with the Church, tended to increase the Church's influence on the poorer sections of the population. It has been reduced in scale since 1965. Grants also come from other sources, both governmental and private, including, for instance, British government aid for a technological institute. A figure is given for the total value of donations in the year 1967, in CONAPLAN: *Plan de Desarrollo*, 124: ₡29.8 million.

[23] The road was originally to be named after Juan Lindo, the Chief of State in 1841, but Lindo was a Honduran.

[24] In a newspaper article, 'Consorcios de ingenieros negativos para el país', *El Mundo*, 11 Dec. 1970, Ing. Rafael Colindres Silva says: 'But my generation is disposed to struggle so that at least our children do not work under the unnecessary tutelage of the already superfluous foreign experts'.

[25] Bert Hoselitz: 'Desarrollo Industrial de El Salvador', *Revista de Economía de El Salvador*, Vol. VIII, No 23–28 (1956), 859.

[26] Jacobo Waiselfisz, 'El Comercio exterior, el mercado común y la industrialización en relación al conflicto', in Facultad de Humanidades: *Contribución al Estudio del Conflicto Hondureño-Salvadoreño* (July 1969: San Salvador, Asociación de Estudiantes de Humanidades, Universidad; mimeo), 74, quoting another source.

[27] Min. de Economía, mimeo. Some types of investment, such as wholly-owned subsidiaries or banks and insurance companies, seem to be excluded from these totals. Hoselitz's report estimated these at about $10 or 12 million. There is also a flow of capital in the other direction, of unknown proportions. Salvadorean newspapers advertise real estate in places like Miami. Esther Alonso and Daniel Slutzky, in 'La Estructura agraria de El Salvador y Honduras, sus consecuencias sociales y el conflicto actual', in *Contribución . . .*, 31, report that in 1960 the U.S. Federal Reserve Bank stated that the amount deposited in its system and originating from El Salvador was $800 million, a sum well in excess of Salvadorean GNP for that year.

[28] *ABC*, Madrid, 2 Feb. 1971, 51. Spain is still the leading publishing country for books in Spanish. It is possible, however, that more books were imported indirectly through other countries and did not enter the statistics quoted.

[29] The Mexican *mariachi* seems, on the other hand, to have increased in popularity in the last 15 years or so, and there are a number of professional groups.

# Chapter 6

# El Salvador in Central America

---

OF THE FIVE COUNTRIES of present-day Central America, Costa Rica stands apart both geographically and in her more equitable distribution of land and wealth. Her general educational level is correspondingly higher; her political system more democratic. Power has changed hands twice at elections there since the last revolution in 1948. The root cause of this difference is the fact that in Costa Rica the Spanish conquerors found fewer Indians. Those whom they did find had not made the same advances in agricultural civilization, so they were not so suited for agricultural labour. As there was no great mineral wealth either, there was no incentive to bring in large numbers of slaves, and not much incentive to settle in the area at all. Thus it was settled more slowly by the Spaniards, who became independent farmers, much as the English and other settlers did at first in similar circumstances in North America. Costa Rica still has a population of only about 1.7 or 1.8 million. Nicaragua, though Costa Rica's geographical neighbour, is a complete contrast in most other respects, notably in the continuing concentration of political and economic power in the hands of the Somoza family. Some economic indicators put Nicaragua on the same level as El Salvador, but the ratio of trade in manufactured goods between the two countries – about 2 or $2\frac{1}{2}$ to 1 in favour of El Salvador – shows that in this important area at least Nicaragua is behind. Nicaragua now has a population of about 2 million, almost all living on the Pacific side of the country. Honduras is reckoned on most counts to be the poorest of the five countries, and certainly has the least development in manufacturing, but her rural population is probably no worse off – in fact it may well be better off, with more land available – than that of any of her three neighbours. Correspondingly, there has been less migration to towns, and the capital, Tegucigalpa, has remained very much smaller than the other capitals. In contrast with Nicaragua, the Honduran Atlantic coast has been populated at least in its western section, and the town of San Pedro Sula has grown to rival Tegucigalpa in size and exceed it in the development of manufacturing. A feature of Honduras is the predominance in commerce and to a large extent in industry of people who are not Honduran by origin, principally Palestinians at the higher levels, Chinese and – at least until the war of 1969 – Salvadoreans at the lower. The two population centres differ strongly in atmosphere, the Atlantic being much more ethnically hetero-geneous, more Caribbean. The population of Honduras is now about 2.7 million. Guatemala stands out still as the most populous country in Central America, with about 5½ million inhabitants, and as the country where the distinction between *ladinos* and Indians is still strong. The political polarization and repression have already been mentioned, as well as the existence of guerrilla movements, who have been active continuously since 1960. Guatemala has developed a manufacturing industry similar in size and kind to that of El Salvador. All the Central American countries other than El Salvador have an English-speaking black (there are some whites on the Honduran Bay Islands) minority population concentrated on their Atlantic coasts, but also in the capitals. In general the range of 'racial' somatic features such as skin colour is greater in each of these countries. Only El Salvador has developed a *mestizo* homogeneity. Despite this, or perhaps in compensation for it, a strong sense of national identity has been fostered in each of the other countries, and there is relatively less emphasis on the goal of Central American unity than there is, at least among the upper and middle classes and in the educational system, in El Salvador.

Interestingly enough, there was no great gap of discontinuity between the last of the old-style attempts at political union of Central America and the beginning of the present economic integration movement whose reality, paradoxically enough, has shown up the unreality of the ideas of political federation. Although the last time a 'Republic of Central America' was actually proclaimed was in 1921 (it embraced three of the states,[1] had little real effect, and formally lasted for only four months), discussions for a similar type of federa-tion were being held in 1948. The *economic* integration movement could be said to have begun in 1950, when the five countries asked the United Nations Economic Commission for Latin America (ECLA) to examine the possibilities for development of the region; in 1951, when they signed the 'Charter of San Salvador' setting up the Organization of Central American States (ODECA) with a secretariat in San Salvador; or in 1952, when a Central American Economic Co-operation Committee was established. A good deal of the initiative for economic integration at this time came from ECLA, whose economists were concerned with the fact that if there were to be any general free trade area in Latin America as a whole, then the Central American countries would be at a disadvantage unless they had developed an industry of their own, capable of competing in such an area. It was judged that they could only do this if they first set up their own Common Market which would be as large as the markets of most individual Latin American countries. The scale of production and its technological level would then be similar. Given that ECLA's advice would have some effect in this direction, while it was impossible for the Commission to persuade the countries to change their internal income distribution and create a bigger home market that way, the judgement was logical within ECLA's basic premise: that development based on technology and methods imported from advanced countries like the United States should be encouraged.

In line with this orientation, the next Central American organizations to be set up were the Central American School of Public Administration (ESAPAC) in 1954 and the Central American Institute of Research and Industrial Technology (ICAITI) in 1956. The first provisions for free trade within the area were signed in 1958 and began to become effective in 1959. The freeing of internal trade had been carried out for most items by 1963. In this period Costa Rica showed most caution, doubtless worried that her much higher average income would be pulled down by competition from countries where labour was so much cheaper.

The 'free trade area' became a 'Common Market' with the approval of a common external tariff schedule in 1964 and some provisions for the free mobility of capital and labour at about the same time. Mobility of labour, which especially concerns El Salvador with her dense population, has never been entirely free in practice.

It is impossible to know what would have happened if there had been no Common Market, but it is at least reasonable to contend that the industrial development which has followed its creation has been a superficial palliative. It has retarded the development of pressures which would force the governments, particularly in El Salvador where alternatives are limited,[2] toward much more far-reaching social reforms. If there were no Common Market, industrialization could only have taken place on the basis of an expanded internal market, and that could only have been achieved by a redistribution of existing wealth and income. The pressure of numbers of underemployed and the pressure of international example and ideological influence in favour of industrialization could have combined to pull at least part of the military and civilian élites in this direction. Such pressures, however, would probably have been resisted, which would have meant a more repressive and more polarized political situation. Or perhaps both these alternative scenarios attribute too much significance to the industrialization process which, while it has multiplied trade between the Central American countries several times over and has given a huge stimulus to one kind of industrial development, has in fact resulted in the creation of relatively few jobs and has not had much effect on the majority.

However this may be, in the later 1960s it became apparent that at the level where the Common Market was having an effect, this effect was more favourable to El Salvador, in particular, and to Guatemala and Costa Rica, than to Nicaragua or especially to Honduras. The former countries were developing industries faster, largely because they had a better base from which to start off at the beginning of the exercise. In the case of El Salvador there were other reasons: the comparative lack of opportunities for investing in agriculture, making industry a relatively more attractive field for the Salvadorean wealthy class; her central location, good development of roads and other infrastructure (electricity supply had doubled during the 1950s) – even perhaps the greater dynamism of the government's development bank – encouraging foreign investors.[3]

## Relations with Honduras and the 1969 War

This growing economic disparity was one of the causes of dissatisfaction in Honduras. El Salvador was beginning to take on, *vis-à-vis* Honduras, the relationship typical of an advanced country with its underdeveloped satellite. Almost all El Salvador's exports to Honduras were manufactured goods, while by far the greater part of imports from Honduras was of food and raw materials. Honduran manufacturing, most of which did not have the scale or technology of the new Salvadorean industry, may well have been on balance more hindered by competition in its development to cover the home market than helped by the availability of the Central American Market. Some sectors were almost certainly hindered while others were favoured. This was not all, however. A good many of the exports sent from El Salvador to Honduras consisted of goods to which only a final manufacturing process had been added in El Salvador after importation from outside the area. If they had been imported direct from their original source by Honduras, they would not only have been cheaper, but the Honduran government's funds would have benefited from the tariff which would have been levied on them.[4]

Furthermore, in the late 1960s El Salvador was becoming rapidly more self-sufficient in basic foods, so that her imports from Honduras were in sharp decline, and there was nothing to compensate Honduras for the rapid and continuous growth in her imports from El Salvador. The balance of trade between the two countries shifted from being highly favourable to Honduras in 1962, just after free trade began, to equal in 1965, and to being highly favourable to El Salvador in 1967 and 1968, with no end to the trend in sight. Hondurans have also voiced the fear that Salvadorean capital was beginning to penetrate Honduras in a way dangerous for Honduran business autonomy; but this may have been no more than a rumour.

There were, at any rate, powerful economic reasons for at least a section of Honduran society to oppose free trade with El Salvador (with Guatemala and Costa Rica too, to some extent; but El Salvador alone accounted for half of Honduras's trade within Central America, in both directions). The campaign within Honduras to buy *national* products, which had existed at least since 1966, could not have much effect. Recourse was also had to a 'consumption tax' on goods from the other Central American countries, a tariff in all but name applied also by Nicaragua for similar reasons. But Honduras's trade balance continued to worsen.

Within Honduras, there were also the traditional political reasons for focusing discontent on foreigners. President López Arellano, who had come to power by a military *coup* in 1963, was coming to the end of the period for which he had had himself elected (1965–70) and the pressure was on him not to push through his own re-election or impose a stooge. His principal power base, in a political system of an older Latin American vintage, more *caudillista* than El Salvador's, was the army. It was generally thought that López Arellano wished to continue in power, and anything that increased the role of the army would help him to do so. Moreover, and probably more significant, there was a series of political strikes starting in September 1968 which showed a considerable degree of effective union organ- ization against the government. (There was first a general strike in September 1968, centred on San Pedro Sula, but spreading also to the rest of the north coast region and also to Tegucigalpa; it was immediately declared illegal and was repressed after a few days, with the imprisonment of its leaders. The immediate motive for this strike was the imposition of the 'consumption tax'.) [5]

It can be assumed that these political and economic considera- tions played an important part in the decision taken by López Arellano's government early in 1969 to dispossess and expel large numbers of the Salvadoreans who had settled in the Honduran countryside. This decision did most to precipitate the war.

Salvadoreans had been settling in fair numbers in Honduras since the first decades of this century. The migration began at the time when the fruit companies, the famous American-owned United Fruit Company and Standard Fruit Company, were opening up their plantations, mainly of bananas, on the north coast of Honduras. This region was at that time, like the rest of the Atlantic lowlands of Central America, very sparsely populated. The pressure of people on land was already being felt in El Salvador, but not in the southerly parts of Honduras. So it was natural that a very high proportion of the fruit companies' workers were Salvadoreans; the percentage was still estimated as about 30 in the 1960s.[6] But the fruit plantations gradually declined as a point of attraction for the migration, and Salvadoreans began more and more to cross the border simply to find land to cultivate, mostly by the traditional methods and mostly for their own consumption. In this movement the border Departments of Chalatenango and Cabañas, with their more exhausted soils, contributed most, and migration to Honduras was for the rural population of El Salvador, particularly from these northern departments, an alternative to migration to the towns and to San Salvador. In 1969, probably between 60 and 70 per cent of the Salvadoreans in Honduras were small-scale cultivators of this type, including those who had settled on unclaimed national land, those who rented or sharecropped, and a few who bought land. In 1952, 88.6 per cent of Honduran territory was still national land, so that all that was required for settlement was willingness to bring new land under cultivation in a remote area with poor or non-existent communications with the outside. There was always uncertainty about whether, once this effort had been made and perhaps a road had been extended to the area, a more powerful person might be able to claim successfully the now improved land. With more pressure on land to the south, however, reflected in higher annual rates for renting land, increasing numbers of both Salvadoreans and Hondurans took the risk and made the effort to occupy new areas, forming a mixed population in each such area rather than exclusive communities.[7]

A third type of migration consisted of those engaged in commerce and urban workers, and by 1969 there were considerable numbers of Salvadoreans in Tegucigalpa, San Pedro Sula, and the other towns of Honduras as well as in the countryside. The total number of migrants is difficult to estimate, because most of them crossed the border without documentation, and for this reason avoided registration in the Honduran census of 1960. This census gives a figure of 38,000; for 1961, a demographer's estimate puts it at 63,000.[8] However, the figure usually quoted at the time of the war and since has been 300,000. These two latter figures are not so discrepant as they seem, since the former does not include children born in Honduras of Salvadorean parents, whereas the last presumably does, at least the young ones still with their parents.

The Salvadorean migrants tended to have rather higher levels of education and skill in the various branches of commerce and other work which they undertook than the Hondurans who were engaged in similar work. This applied especially to urban activities, for urban skills were more highly developed in El Salvador, a result no doubt of the earlier pressure on land and migration to towns; and also perhaps to a better public education system. In 1963, the Honduran government spent only $7.3 million on education. In El Salvador the equivalent figure was $15.6 million (in 1964).[9]

These relatively higher levels of skill led to the Salvadoreans doing that much better in Honduras. They achieved more than they could have done at home and earned the envy of many Hondurans. This is probably the most explosive kind of minority group situation, one which has often given rise to pogroms of Jews and in the 1960s to the slaughter of Ibos in northern Nigeria. The minority group competes over a wide range of occupations rather than finds a special niche in the economy, and competes with a success that the majority group cannot reconcile with its own ideas of equality or superiority. In the case of the Salvadoreans in Honduras, the situation was softened in that there are no religious and very few cultural differences between the two nations, let alone any physical distinctions or differences of dress. The degree of closeness can be shown by the fact that while many of the migrants married (or entered an irregular union) with Honduran spouses, many again found a Salvadorean spouse or remained unmarried. Unfortunately there are no data which permit one to be more exact on this point, but it is clear that there is some preference for a companion of the same nationality.

In the 1950s the fruit companies reduced their workforce, first because a banana disease had devastated the plantations and made advisable a reduction in acreage, secondly because it was becoming more profitable to mechanize many operations, and thirdly because ever more militant unionism made the companies decide, wherever feasible, to go over to a new system under which they would turn over the land to the workers as smallholders and then buy the crop from them. The fact that the plantations ceased to absorb labour led to the growth of underemployment in Honduras with obvious consequences for the hitherto friendly relations between Hondurans and Salvadorean immigrants. A returned migrant interviewed in San Salvador in January 1967 (before the events which culminated in the war) had come back from Honduras in 1958 after twenty-one years there, during which he worked as an ironsmith for the *Yunai* (United Fruit Company) in Puerto Cortés. He gave as his reason for returning: 'They did not want us there any longer: they said that we were taking work away from the Hondurans. They dismissed me for being Salvadorean'.

The potential tension, however, appears only to have reached public expression, and then only gradually, in 1965–67, with items in the Honduran press and radio alleging first that a *part* of the Salvadorean immigration consisted of criminals. For a long time, of course, those who have committed crimes in one Central American country have fled to a neighbouring one where it is very unlikely they will be pursued. The tone became more strident in 1968. Whether the campaign reflected an undercurrent of opinion which had already grown to strong proportions, or whether, as Salvadorean sources[10] say, it was fostered by a group close to President López Arellano, is difficult to say. At the same time Honduran authorities at local level were making it difficult in practice for Salvadoreans to regularize their documentation as residents, in spite of agreements providing for this, and by 1967 there was no doubt of the hostility between López Arellano's régime and the army officers of El Salvador. In May 1967, forty-five Salvadorean soldiers were apprehended in the Honduran border town of Nueva Ocotepeque, in two lorries carrying arms. It was thought that they were possibly on a mission to supply arms to rebels against the López Arellano government, but that the conspiracy was discovered before the arms arrived. Tension between the two governments mounted, and did not noticeably slacken even when, in June 1968, the soldiers were exchanged for a Honduran, reputed to be on close personal terms with López Arellano, who had been arrested in El Salvador shortly before the Nueva Ocotepeque incident on ordinary criminal charges[11]; nor in July, when López Arellano came to San Salvador for a meeting of all Central American Presidents with President Lyndon Johnson.

An agrarian reform law had been passed in Honduras in July 1968 partly under American influence[12] and also in response to signs of a peasants' movement which might threaten to invade private properties, as occurred in 1969.[13] (El Salvador was almost alone among Latin American countries in not having passed such a law, even a token one, in the decade of the Alliance for Progress.) Under the terms of the law, national land was to be preferentially distributed, private estates only being purchased where necessary and by prior payment. Only native-born Honduran citizens were to benefit from the law.

It was probably only in the early months of 1969, however, that the decision was finally taken to use the agrarian reform law to expel Salvadorean settlers or, looked at in another way, to use the land settled (and usually improved or brought into cultivation) by

Salvadoreans as the land to be distributed. On 30 April Salvadorean settlers received letters from the government's agrarian reform agency giving them thirty days to 'return' the land. It is not clear how many letters were received, but it seems that expulsions had already begun in one area before 30 April, and that they took place in May and the first week of June on the scale of several hundred families in the Yoro region. Two demonstrations against the government took place in May in Tegucigalpa, for apparently unconnected political reasons. One student was killed.[14]

The first of the World Cup football matches which were to give the war its reputation abroad as the 'football war' took place in Tegucigalpa on 8 June. Honduras beat El Salvador by one goal to nil. On the same day the first sixty-three dispossessed Salvadoreans are reported to have arrived at the border as refugees. By now feelings were strong on both sides; but there is no doubt that the tone of a section of the Honduran press and radio was far more inflammatory than that of their counterparts in El Salvador. The Honduran government appeared to encourage these broadsides. One theme was that Salvadoreans should not look to Honduras to solve their problems, but should overthrow the oligarchy in El Salvador. The second match took place in San Salvador on 15 June (won 3:0 by El Salvador). What was said to have happened in connection with this match was the main theme of Honduras's case in the ensuing international publicity. More important, it was instrumental in arousing Honduran hatred against Salvadoreans. Honduran supporters attending the match were alleged to have been stoned, women raped, etc. There seems no doubt that these stories were wildly exaggerated or fabricated. Suspicion had it that the exaggeration or fabrication was at least abetted by the Honduran government.[15] According to Salvadorean sources, there followed three days of atrocities against Salvadoreans in Tegucigalpa committed by a Honduran organization of political thugs and anti-Salvadorean extremists known as the *Mancha Brava*, which had links with members of the government. Hondurans claim that this story, in turn, is wildly exaggerated or fabricated and that the only actual incidents took place in Olancho, a rural area. Whatever may be the truth about the accusations of 'genocide' made by El Salvador on 25 June, refugees streamed back in much larger numbers after the 15th, to the official number of 10,000 by the 25th. (It appears that altogether the number of refugees reached between 20,000 and 50,000.)

After a period of fruitless diplomatic activity in which El Salvador attempted to obtain guarantees for Salvadoreans in Honduras, the Salvadorean army invaded Honduras on 14 July. It did so with overwhelming popular support. The atmosphere for any organized opposition to the war, perhaps emphasizing that land and jobs should be made available for all Salvadoreans in El Salvador, did not exist, although individuals in the university and the trade unions continued to hold this opinion. Given public approval all political parties supported the war, although some of them may have done so without conviction. An opposition leader later declared that one of the reasons why the Salvadorean army wanted to contribute to the tension with Honduras, and go to war, was to get political backing to purchase new weapons.[16] New arms had certainly been bought in 1968, but this seems unlikely to have been an important reason. It is possible, however, that the army was simply determined to inflict a defeat on its Honduran rival, or wanted to remove President López Arellano from office, partly for personal reasons. There was certainly no question on the government's part of wishing to alter frontiers.

The Salvadorean army quickly showed its great military superiority, destroying much of the Honduran air force on the ground by aerial bombing, and advancing to cut off the roads from Honduras to Guatemala and to Nicaragua. The war, in fact, had a resemblance to the Israeli–Arab six-day war. It lasted for five days, ended in the occupation of territory but not the overthrow of any government, and demonstrated a greater degree of military superiority, based on human abilities rather than armaments, than had been thought to exist before the battle. The war was stopped, by the formal intercession of the Organization of American States, but in fact by pressure from the United States upon El Salvador. By the end, the Salvadorean army could have advanced on both fronts toward both Tegucigalpa and San Pedro Sula. Although the Honduran accounts of Salvadorean atrocities before the war appear to have had no foundation, while Salvadorean accounts of Honduran atrocities did have at least some basis in fact, the actions of Salvadorean troops in the areas they conquered may unfortunately have restored the balance. At any rate, the ideal of unionist brotherhood suffered a big reverse in this conflict, although it is still maintained in El Salvador.

Under further international pressure, Salvadorean forces withdrew from the occupied territory in August. Considerable tension continued between the two countries, although the hostility appeared to be maintained much more strongly in Honduras than in El Salvador. A feature of the conflict was the disparity between the relatively measured tone of official and private press and radio in El Salvador and the intemperate tone of the Honduran media. Honduran radio went so far as to urge 'Honduran, pick up a plank and kill a Salvadorean'.[17]

Curiously perhaps, the Common Market survived the war, in the

short term at least, with the only exception that Honduras and El
Salvador completely barred entry of one another's goods, and
Honduras closed to Salvadorean goods the overland route to
Nicaragua and Costa Rica. However, at the end of 1970 there was a
crisis in which Honduras imposed a wide range of tariffs and threatened in effect to leave the Market if she did not receive a certain
increase in the special finance made available to her as the least
developed partner. This complicated question was also the main
issue in the Honduran elections which were in fact held in February
1971, and it was not resolved before those elections. López Arellano
handed over to the declared winner of the elections, Ramón Ernesto
Cruz. Although he is of the same party, the change might have made
it possible for relations with El Salvador to become less frozen.[18]

Meanwhile, with the Common Market looking much less solid
and permanent, El Salvador has turned attention for the first time
to the idea of selling manufactured goods beyond the area. Moreover,
to limit what is still seen as a surplus population, more attention has
been turned to programmes of birth control, while some arrangements have been made to send Salvadoreans to work in the
Dominican Republic.

It seems that unorganized migration has increased in the direction of Guatemala. Indeed, a few isolated but ominous instances
have occurred of expulsions of Salvadoreans without documents from
Guatemalan rural areas. In November 1970 there was a tense
moment when Guatemalan air force planes attacked a fleet of
Salvadorean fishing vessels and the two countries issued contradic-
tory statements as to whether the incident, in which several Salvadorean fishermen were killed, had occurred in Guatemalan waters.
The affair was, however, closed when the Guatemalan President,
Arana Osorio, apologized with the explanation that the air force had
mistaken the fishing fleet for a rebel force coming to reinforce the
guerrillas in the mountains. If such a mistake was in fact made, then
one must conclude that the Guatemalan air force pilots were
extremely nervous about rebels. It would appear, anyway, that the
present Guatemalan government wishes to have friendly relations
with that of El Salvador. When there is a need to arouse anti-foreign
sentiment in Guatemala, it can be turned on the British for continued
occupation of Belize. On that question, and perhaps only on that
question, all Central America can be united.

# NOTES

[1] El Salvador, Guatemala, and Honduras. There is an account in Alberto
Herrarte: *La Unión de Centro América, tragedia y esperanza* (1953; 1963: Guatemala,

Min. de Educación), 187–93; another in Ricardo Gallardo: *Las Constituciones de la República Federal de Centro-América* (1958: Madrid, Instituto de Estudios Políticos, Vol. I, 535–49).

[2] In all the other countries there is, for instance, more opportunity for the further increase of production of primary products for export, because there is more unused land and greater mineral potential.

[3] David R. Raynolds, who served in the American embassy in El Salvador from 1958 to about 1964, appears to attribute the faster growth of industry in El Salvador to the vigour of Salvadorean entrepreneurs and the close relations between industrialists, bankers, and 'government leaders' engaged in the common enterprise of industrialization. Raynolds: *Rapid Development in Small Economies: the example of El Salvador* (1967: New York, Praeger), esp. 56–8, 78–9.

[4] Waiselfisz, op. cit., a well-reasoned 84-page article on the economic background to the war, 24–7.

[5] ibid., 28–36.

[6] Edelberto Torres Rivas: *Familia y juventud en El Salvador* (1969: Santiago de Chile, Instituto Latinoamericano de Planificación Económica y Social), quoted Alonso and Slutzky, op. cit., 2.

[7] ibid., 5–13.

[8] CELADE, Santiago de Chile. Quoted Alonso and Slutzky, op. cit., 2.

[9] The Honduran population at the 1961 census was registered as 1,884,765, i.e. three-quarters the size of that of El Salvador (with a similar rate of growth). Thus *per capita* Honduran expenditure on education is about two-thirds that of El Salvador. It is possible that the figure for Honduras does not include some educational expenditure which in Honduras is collected in local taxes and spent on the local school. Adams, op. cit., 582, mentions such expenditure.

[10] 'The Truth about the Conflict between El Salvador and Honduras – The United States Residents of El Salvador interpret the origins of the El Salvador–Honduras Conflict', statement of 22 July 1969, distributed as booklet by the government of El Salvador; Abel Salazar Rodezno: *Derecho de Legítima Defensa, conflicto El Salvador–Honduras* (August 1969: San Salvador, La Prensa Gráfica); David R. Calderón: *Origen de la Mancha Brava* (Sept. 1970: San Salvador, Imp. López).

[11] The doubt, apparently, was whether he was arrested in Salvadorean territory.

[12] This aspect is emphasized in Orlando Fernández: 'Honduras–Salvador: días y años de una guerra', *Tricontinental*, No 19–20 (Havana, July–Oct. 1970, published also in an English edition), 51–82, on 65. An agrarian reform law had been first passed in Honduras under the previous, Liberal, régime of Villeda Morales in 1962, but it had not been implemented by Lopez Arellano's government after the *coup* of 1963, by which he came to power. F. D. Parker, article on El Salvador, section History, *Encyclopaedia Britannica*, 1971 ed., Vol. 8, 302c.

[13] Alonso and Slutzky, op. cit., 49–50.

[14] Salazar Rodezno, op. cit., 20, 24.

[15] The allegation is made with great detail by Calderón, op. cit., 39–40, 51–55.

[16] Statement to the author. He may have been overestimating the power of the opposition deputies in the Legislative Assembly, although in 1969 they had more influence than usual; see below, pp. 211–12.

[17] 'Hondureño, coge un leño, y mata un salvadoreño'. Reported by Orlando Fernández, op. cit., 71. Fernández, a Guatemalan, takes a neutral position between the two sides in the conflict, condemning both governments; but he confirms the impression that the Honduran domestic press and radio campaign was very much cruder and more inflammatory than the Salvadorean.

[18] This was not to be. On 4 December 1972 López Arellano staged a new *coup* against Cruz and reassumed power.

# Chapter 7

# The Political Process

UNFORTUNATELY THE MOST IMPORTANT question in Salvadorean politics is closed to investigation: namely the nature of the relationship between the military officers in direct control of the state, and the civilian élite. During and immediately after the war with Honduras the army enjoyed an unprecedented degree of popular support. At the end of the war opposition leaders in effect asked President Sánchez Hernández and his military colleagues if they did not now for once have sufficient political strength to end their dependence or interdependence on the small rich oligarchy. This point arose, according to opposition leaders, at a meeting of the 'National Unity' front, comprising the representatives of all the legal parties[1] and formed just before the 1969 war. But it did not get a positive response, and government actions since that time have shown that the informal alliance is as strong as it was before. What is difficult or impossible for an outsider to know is whether this relationship is simply voluntary on the part of the officer group, corresponding to a similarity of ideas; whether the wealth of the civilian élite plays any part, direct or indirect, in ensuring that the officers do not stray very far from the interests of the élite in the formulation and execution of government policy; or whether there are other pressures it can bring to bear. It is not without significance that many military officers build up substantial property holdings as their military careers progress. Some are medium entrepreneurs, one or two large-scale operators.[2]

It is probably not sensible to ask how many officers play a role in the formulation of policy. As with many hierarchical organizations, the President of the day normally makes the decisions, but has to take into account the likelihood of a *coup* against him if his policies do not reflect the trend of general desires among the officers, in the first place his senior colleagues. In 1948 there had developed a rift in opinions between the older officers and a younger generation, and the *coup* by the latter was in part the result. But there is no sign of a similar rift having developed again. Conceivably the example of Peru's present military régime is attractive for some officers who would wish to imitate it at least in part, but no military group is publicly known as espousing this position. One thing which a President would certainly not be able to do under present circumstances would be to perpetuate himself in office beyond his term, reduced from six to five years in 1962.

## The 'Official' Party

The *Partido de Conciliación Nacional* (PCN) is the vehicle through which the continuity of the régime is translated into the terms of formal democracy. It was founded after the *coup* of 1961, but inherits the tradition of official parties which dates from the nineteenth century or, in at least something like the present form, since the *Liga Roja* of the Meléndez-Quiñónez period (1917–27) – since before the military domination of the Presidency began. The only régimes which have not made use of the institution were those of 1927–31, May to October 1944, and October 1960 to January 1961. The PCN is the successor of the *Partido Revolucionario de Unificación Democrática* (PRUD) of Osorio and Lemus, and inherited not only the forms of organization but a good many of the personnel. The leaders of the Christian Democratic Party say, and there is no reason to doubt them, that before forming the PCN the officers who had carried out the 1961 *coup* approached the Christian Democrats, then a very recent foundation, and offered to make them the official party – with, of course, a colonel as President.

The fact that this offer could have been made illustrates the lack of civilian influence within the official party on the policies of the government. At the top the party is firmly controlled by the President (who is its 'General Co-ordinator') and the army officers who form his immediate entourage and support. At the next higher levels it provides a means for the personal advancement of a number of civilians, particularly from the professional classes in the capital. It might be described as a kind of labour exchange, a meeting-place where the military can find civilians willing to work with them loyally. The latter can get jobs in control of government institutions, up to the position of minister and down to that of head of a department within a ministry or semi-autonomous institution. Such positions are also a springboard or a basis for the acquisition of other advantages, since official patronage will be recompensed in one form or another. Some occupants of such positions do little or no work in them. Their contribution may be in the form of helping to organize the official party's election campaigns. On the other hand, there are certainly some professionals, members of the official party, whose motivation is not entirely opportunist, but who believe that they can make a contribution to social justice by ensuring that a part of the administrative structure has this aim.

There is a gap between these upper levels of the official party and the lower levels composed of people with much less education – manual workers, peasants, some clerical workers – who generally have long-standing connections with the army or some part of the administrative apparatus or both, as well as with the official party. Indeed, it is particularly at this level that these three organizations merge into a unity, a triad, the members of which are only formally separated from one another. Those connected with the triad are interchangeably known as *gobiernistas* or *oficialistas*; their connection is often also a personal one with one or two army officers or prominent civilian members of the party or government. Some branches of the government, such as the Ministry of the Interior, are much more closely connected with party and army than others, such as the Planning Council. The Ministry of the Interior controls those municipal councils which have been won by the official party – currently the overwhelming majority of provincial authorities. They have comparatively little contact with the central offices of the party.

Although at the level of manual work anyone who works for the government in any capacity is likely to be identified as a *gobiernista*, it is in fact possible to work for the government without having any connection with the army or the official party, especially in semi-professional jobs. But this can entail disadvantages, especially in the way of blocking promotion prospects. It is presumably possible to be an army officer without taking any interest in the official party or the government; individual officers have on occasion taken a prominent part in setting up other parties, particularly right-wing parties; but such action is clearly disapproved of by fellow-officers, and participation by officers in left-of-centre opposition parties is effectively prevented. Informal social control within the army is normally enough to ensure that divergent views are expressed only within the army. This can in part be explained by the smallness of the country – few enough army officers are involved and they are on personal terms with one another. It is also, however, in part a result of General Martínez's conscious policy of separating the military from the civilians by offering them a distinct social life, with their own clubs and bars, and discouraging army officers from their previous patronage of civilian social centres. For Martínez, this may have been no more than a tactic to prevent the formation of conspiracies against him and to isolate the military from civilian discontent with his régime; but the social separation was largely maintained after Martínez's downfall and leads some people in El Salvador to refer to the military as a caste, likening it to the officer castes of pre-war Japan or Germany.

The army, for those with some talents and with loyalty to the unwritten rules of the caste, is an avenue of upward social mobility. Even if the statement that 'the officers in El Salvador today owe their positions to plantation owners who knew them as cadets and recommended them to the military as trustworthy potential officers'[3] is only true in a few cases, it is certainly true that they come from backgrounds ranging from middle-class down; that the army provides for advanced education of those officers who wish to pursue professional training in such fields as engineering; and that at the end of an active career there is not only the prospect of a high position within the army, or excellent contacts for making money as an entrepreneur, but also the prospect of an important administrative post. Under the military Presidents a high proportion of these posts are always given to officers. Since young officers will have had these expectations throughout their military lives, it is fairly clear that they would be more likely to welcome a more Egyptian- or Peruvian-type change in the military's role than a 'return to barracks' and purely civilian rule.

Although, then, the military cannot be expected to give up their hold on the Presidency except under very strong general pressure, nevertheless it would be almost as naïve to think of the situation as one of simple 'military rule', as it would be to accept the official version according to which the army is completely apolitical while the PCN has been elected to political power. The military reserves for itself many government positions, including the Presidency, but the policies pursued cannot be said to be a shaping of the country's social system according to the ideas of the army leaders.

The political system cannot be seen simply in terms of certain groups – the army, the oligarchy, the American embassy – holding the power or a certain proportion of the power; such a view of power is suitable only for situations where politics is merely a struggle between rival coalitions over the spoils of office. In nineteenth-century El Salvador it was perhaps appropriate enough to think in these terms, since changes in régime resulted in no economic or social changes; no changes in the terms of the transactions between people outside the political arena; and no changes in the type of relationships even within the political arena, merely of the personnel. Although I have tried to show that some differences in ideology can be detected between pragmatist and idealist liberals as well as between liberals and conservatives, it is true that to a great extent the parties were simply groups vying to form the government. The winning group would reap the ensuing advantages. Around 1852, all the government employees were changed when there was a change of régime.[4] By the time of General Martínez things were greatly altered, but the suppression of the 1932 uprising and thereafter of all opposition could still be interpreted as the determination of a *caudillo* to keep all political power in his own and his loyal followers' hands, with the blessing of a second group, the oligarchy, enjoying the benefits of an economic system left essentially untouched by the political sphere.

But the element of *caudillismo*[5] almost completely disappeared from the political system with Martínez's resignation. Later political leaders have built up different kinds of popularity, a less contractual link between leader and follower, on the basis of paternalist demagogy, the promise of real democracy and reform, or a reputation for uncorrupt, sympathetic, and solid work in a public office. But the personal popularity of certain leaders is a minor element of the political situation, an extra resource adding to the likelihood of the achievement of that leader's goals, including both his personal goal of high position, and, more important for almost everyone else, his policy goals. His popularity is not the major source of strength of these policy goals.

What, then, is this major factor determining which political goals will prevail, how the economic and social system will be changed or whether it will remain the same? In El Salvador as in other complex modern societies, the goal's potential is determined by the degree of support effectively organized around it, the lengths to which its supporters will go in the expression of their support, and the strategic position of those who express it. At a secondary level, other factors undoubtedly enter in, such as the tactical expertise of those engaged in conflict or bargaining to achieve the goal, and all manner of other resources which can be brought to bear by supporters of the declared policy. All this, of course, in relation to the organization of opposition.

In this context, the President is merely the most strategically placed individual, the one whose desires are likely to have the greatest weight when he pursues them energetically. But he cannot do exactly as he likes while in office. Even if the whole military caste were united on policy goals, it would have to seek some civilian support too. Martínez was forced out of office when civilians united in a strike against him, and this could happen again to a military régime whose policies were universally rejected by civilians of all social classes. Thus 'military rule' and 'the military as tools of the oligarchy' are both oversimplifications; but the latter is closer to reality than the former. The military maintains a political system under which the organization of support behind substantial economic reform policies is carefully circumscribed and severely limited. At the same time the wealthy are able to exploit to the utmost the advantages which their wealth provides in their campaigns against economic change, and the military itself organizes the rural population in an anti-revolutionary movement. When the bias of this political system is relaxed, as it was briefly in 1944 and 1960, the Left gains strength very rapidly; but even in more normal times the amount of organization permitted to the Left is enough to produce some countervailing power to that of the extreme Right (which wants no state intervention at all in the economy). The outcome of this heavily weighted balance of forces is an ineffective degree of reform and such a stimulation of industry as will not damage the vested interests of the rich, but will rather provide them with new opportunities.

The Right organizes its support and pressure through informal contact, through virtually complete domination of the press, through pressure groups, and through representatives on the boards of directors of a number of governmental and semi-governmental institutions. It does not organize to any important extent through the political parties, though one small party stands on the extreme Right and the PCN, while most of its members, including those who sit in the legislature, are always ready simply to take the government line, includes at least one deputy on the far Right.

The role of the PCN as such in the formation of policy is very minor. But it might have a slight net reformist rather than conservative influence, particularly since the party, to appear representative, includes some trade union members among its deputies in the Legislative Assembly. An interesting innovation in the role of the PCN appeared to be introduced before the 1967 Presidential election: instead of its Presidential nomination vote being a pure formality, the names of eight 'pre-candidates' for the Presidency and Vice Presidency were circulated for discussion within the party. Although it was not explicitly so stated, the military officers on the list were the only acceptable candidates for the Presidential nomination, while the civilians were potential occupants of the Vice President's purely honorific role. The discussion took place, at provincial as well as national level, and it appeared as if the party was choosing the President freely from among the colonels whose names were submitted, in effect, by the outgoing President and the army. However, when the party's nomination convention took place in October 1966, President Rivera made a speech in which he unexpectedly said that he hoped that Colonel Sánchez Hernández would get a unanimous vote. Some of the departmental delegations did, in fact, vote for other military candidates, but the final effect would seem to have been more a designation by the outgoing President than a choice of the PCN. After Rivera's speech Sánchez Hernández got a large majority.

## Opposition Political Parties

There seems to be a natural place in the political system for two well-defined reformist parties: one standing well to the left but pitching its personnel, programme, and activities in such a way as just to remain within the limits permitted at the time for the party to be recognized and to take part in elections; and another including a fairly wide spectrum of opinion in the centre and centre-left or 'moderate left', taking a vague and general enough stance to pick up support over the widest possible range of opinion. There is also a place for a small party to the right of the government, and for one or two other small parties of a personalist character and relatively undefined political position. Finally, the number of unrecognized parties, movements, or groups on the left has no particular limit other than the number of conceivable differing political lines, since when electoral politics is denied them, there is no advantage in aggregating into large parties.

There is a 'natural' place for these parties because, since 1963, a system of proportional representation to the Legislative Assembly has been operative, and conditions have existed for the development of regular party organizations. There are 52 seats in the Legislative Assembly, and they are allocated by department: nine to San Salvador department and smaller numbers to each of the other thirteen departments, according to their population. Voters vote for parties not individuals, and the resulting selection of the parties follows the usual formula for proportional representation. This procedure does not give as great an advantage to the largest parties as does the single-constituency system of Britain, let alone the system which applied in El Salvador before 1963, under which the party which got the most votes in a department took the whole representation of that department. The practical effect of the latter system was to ensure that there was very rarely any opposition at all in the legislature. However, proportional representation by department is not the same as proportional representation according to votes cast throughout the country. When the number of deputies from a department is small, it gives an advantage to the largest two parties, and effectively ensures that small parties are excluded unless they have their strength concentrated in one or two particular departments.

All this is important because the chance of having seats in the legislature has been a great spur to the formation of regular parties with some continuous activity, rather than mere groups congregating around an individual of some popularity and advancing his candidature for the Presidency, then breaking up and subsiding into inactivity after the Presidential election is over. It has also had the effect of channelling opposition activity into the legislature and away from organizations which are, for the military and civilian élite, less controllable, more disruptive, and more disturbing. Deputies receive a salary, which means that they are almost the only full-time opposition politicians, and may mean in some cases that they acquire a vested interest in electoral politics as a means of opposition.

The party which has established itself in a vague centre-left position is the *Partido Demócrata Cristiano*, formed in 1960 as part of the loosely-connected movement covering most of Latin America and with links to the Christian Democrats of Europe, particularly West Germany, and of course to the Catholic Church. It would be quite mistaken to identify the PDC of El Salvador with the conservative position of some of these organizations, however. The affinity is perhaps closest with the Christian Democrats of Chile and the radical movement within the Catholic Church. Since the party does not wish to alienate any potential support from those who only wish tentatively to move away from *oficialismo*, its policy statements and public position tend to be vague. On the other hand, there are not many potential supporters who could be won over from the Left by a more radical stance. Thus, for instance, the manifesto or programme of government issued by the party for the Presidential elections of 1967 gives a more prominent place for proposals to 'strengthen the family' than to agrarian policy, and agrarian reform, although envisaged, is proposed only as a gradual process, subject to availability of funds to pay for the land expropriated and for a full programme of infrastructure development, agricultural credits, and technical assistance. Such an agrarian policy could only succeed in making a small minority of selected *campesinos* into modern farmers, leaving the great majority no better off. The most radical proposals of the programme are to legalize rural unionization, subject coffee production to income tax, enforce a reintroduction of the former system of provision of meals to rural workers, now as part of minimum wage provisions, and to reorient the policy of acceptance of foreign aid loans so as to maximize the use of local labour rather than accept loans tied to the purchase of expensive machinery. Apart from these proposals, there are promises to spend more on health, on education, and to introduce social security for government employees. Mention is also made of pursuing the political union of Central America. The programme is, then, only mildly reformist; but it is clear that many of the party's leaders would wish to go further than this, and also that the party has shown a certain tendency to move to the left. This carries a growing conviction that a considerable amount of state intervention is necessary in a country like El Salvador in order to achieve the Christian Democrat ideals of a moral community freely associating in pursuit of the general good, allowing each man to satisfy his needs and respecting his dignity. The shift to the left responds in part to international influences such as the movement of opinion in the Latin American Church, and in part to a more general movement in the climate of opinion in El Salvador, with a decrease in the ability of the official party and right-wing press to maintain the credibility of their anti-communist scare campaign.

The Christian Democrats, given their association with the Church, have a special advantage over other opposition parties in being relatively immune from this scare. This could well be an important and perhaps decisive factor enabling the party to become the strongest opposition group, displacing others which might otherwise have competed for support from at least a segment of the wide part of the political spectrum which the PDC represents.

The PDC does not have a single outstanding leader, but rather its top rank consists of a dozen or so urban professionals. Its most popular figure, however, is undoubtedly Napoleón Duarte, who achieved this position during his years of office as mayor of San Salvador in the mid-1960s. He was the first Christian Democrat to occupy this office, undoubtedly the most visible and probably the most important office which an opposition politician can occupy under the existing political system. The PDC has held the municipality of San Salvador continuously since 1964.

The second 'natural place' for an opposition party is the position on the left, but just within the limits tolerated by the government of the day for a party to be recognized as legal and able to take part in elections. Since these limits do not remain stable, but tend to relax or harden as the political situation changes and the government comes under more or less pressure from the Right to proscribe the party of the Left, it is not surprising that several parties occupying this position have succeeded one another as one has been proscribed or as organization on the left has come to be more tolerated.

Thus the news that the *Partido Revolucionario Abril y Mayo* (PRAM), whose title refers to the months in 1944 when popular pressure forced Martínez's resignation, was to be legalized, was in 1961 probably the last straw which led to the overthrow of the junta which contemplated this move. The next party to occupy the position was the *Partido Reformador Nacional* (PRN), recognized in 1961 but outlawed in 1963 when its orientation began to emerge more clearly. It had never achieved much popularity, however, and unlike PRAM did not continue in existence as an unrecognized party.

Then came the turn of *Partido Acción Renovadora* (PAR). The party had been in existence for twenty years, a unique record, but it

had been without a defined policy except as an alternative to the
official party. It had contested the 1950 Presidential election with a
colonel as candidate, but a colonel, Asencio Menéndez, who was
associated with the idealist liberal tradition, who had tried to organize a *coup* against General Martínez in the 1930s.[6] It has been
claimed that he was deprived of the Presidency on this occasion only
by direct electoral fraud. Later, the PAR won San Salvador municipality with organizational support from the Left,[7] but until 1965 it
continued to be dominated at the top by a political line without any
significant element of social reform. In that year a 'new line' won
control of the party after an acrimonious internal struggle and a
physical occupation of the headquarters. The men of the new line
took the party to the left of the permitted spectrum, and away from
ineffective competition with the role of the PDC. Thus the PAR
programme for the 1967 elections proposed an agrarian reform to be
completed within two years. It was to consist of the expropriation of
land in excess of 150 *manzanas* held by an individual, with payment
either in cash or in bonds to mature over at most twenty years, the
land to be distributed in lots of at most 6 *manzanas*[8] to those cultivating it or persons cultivating other land not belonging to themselves
but not expropriated; the coffee, cotton, and sugar lands to be
farmed by 'economic associations' which could be set up by private
individuals or by the state, so that production units would not be
broken up. Other measures proposed included a vast scheme of
government construction work to absorb unemployment; the
organization of a national co-operative for the marketing and
storage of agricultural products; obligatory renting of idle land at
fixed rents; a 40 per cent reduction on rents for dwellings; price
controls and a reduction in particular on medicines; a more progressive tax scale; and, apart from promises to spend more on housing, a programme to improve the standard of shanty towns,
granting the land to the people who had built themselves dwellings
on it.

The party also proposed setting up diplomatic relations with 'all
states' (a neutral way of referring to their intention of establishing
relations with socialist countries such as the Soviet Union, not of
opening legations in every capital of the world). In public speeches
PAR leaders laid emphasis on their advocacy of a 'revolution in
freedom' and condemned

> a certain type of revolution, that revolution urged by the false
> prophets of the extreme Left, a revolution that comes with blood,
> that comes with dictatorship, with submission to a new imperial-
> ism, Sino-Soviet imperialism.[9]

Such pleading, however, did not save the PAR from the campaign of the PCN who presented it as a communist group which would make of El Salvador another slave camp like Cuba, as Cuba is presented in the Salvadorean press.

There were persistent rumours of the likelihood of a *coup* from the Right because the government refused to proscribe the PAR before the 1967 elections. It was permitted to fight the election because the government knew that its own control of the rural vote was an absolute guarantee against a PAR victory. The conviction prevailed that it was better to allow the PAR to compete but to reduce its vote to a minimum by putting obstacles in the way of its campaign, than to proscribe the party and risk it being thought that the PAR had majority support. Another consideration may have been that the official party of Guatemala had most probably brought defeat on itself in 1966 by proscribing all the parties of the Left except the very moderate *Partido Revolucionario*, thus allowing that party to win the election with a united vote of the Centre and the Left, while the right-wing vote was split. In El Salvador, the PDC had gained 32 per cent of the votes in the legislative elections of 1966, and the PAR about 8 per cent. The prime danger, therefore, to the continuation of *oficialismo* was in consolidating the opposition vote in the hands of the PDC candidate.

PAR strength was in fact greater than the 8 per cent figure would indicate, for three reasons. First, the 1966 elections had been held at a time (in March) when the old guard of PAR was still very active in its denunciation of the new leadership. Secondly, the 1966 legislative elections were simultaneous with municipal elections, and in the capital the PDC campaign had gained greatly from the popularity of its candidate as mayor, the incumbent Napoleón Duarte; whereas in the Presidential election the PDC was running its much less well-known secretary-general Abraham Rodríguez. Thirdly, in the legislative elections the PAR campaign was not associated with the name of the university rector Fabio Castillo, their Presidential candidate in 1967. Fabio Castillo was, and is, the best-known figure on the left; he had been brought into the six-man junta of October 1960–January 1961, and had established himself as its main spokesman, giving it a more radical image than it would have had without him. During his period as University rector he enhanced his prestige and popularity there, and was again at the centre of the national political stage when in 1964 he visited the Soviet Union and came to an agreement whereby two Russian scientists should teach at the University of El Salvador. The government refused to grant entry visas to the two lecturers from Lomonosov University, and Colonel Sánchez Hernández, then Minister of the

Interior, appeared with Fabio Castillo on television to argue the question in a much-publicized debate. Not only were the two Russians kept out, but soon afterwards two Chileans who had been contracted by the university were also denied entry visas – presumably just to rub in the point, since neither had far left-wing views.

The result of the 1967 Presidential election gave the PAR 14.4 per cent of the national vote, against 21.6 per cent for the PDC and 54.4 per cent for the PCN; but in the Department of San Salvador the PAR led the opposition with 29 per cent as against 25 per cent for the PDC and 41 per cent for the PCN. A similar result was obtained in the department containing the second largest city, Santa Ana. In rural areas, however, the PAR was able to make very little headway, gaining, for instance, only 194 registered votes in the whole Department of Cabañas, or 1.3 per cent. Immediately after the election, the PAR was finally proscribed.

After this, the next legal party of the Left to arise was the *Movimiento Nacional Revolucionario* (MNR). It began as a small group of friends in 1964 and started public activity in 1965. Its formation was thus parallel to the battle for the control of the PAR; but the group concerned did not have the advantage of taking over an existing party and remained almost unknown to the public until after the proscription of the PAR; after this, however, it was in a position to step into the breach.

The MNR had some success in the legislative elections of 1968, the high-water mark to date in general opposition electoral strength. Two deputies were elected, alongside the nineteen of the PDC. The party lost all its representation, however, in the elections of 1970, and seems unlikely ever to achieve the degree of success attained by the PAR in its final period. The reason is that after an internal split, full control over the party was taken by a group of democratic socialist intellectuals, unwilling to adopt the somewhat populist political style apparently necessary under present circumstances for gaining mass support, and unwilling to make bargains with the leftist groups, such as the Communist Party. Such groups are beyond the pale of electoral politics except through such arrangements with legal parties, whereby organizational support is exchanged for the nomination of individuals as candidates for the Legislative Assembly. The diffusion from Europe of the ideals of democratic socialism – the socialism of Pietro Nenni in Italy or Michael Foot in Britain – has resulted in the creation of parties like the MNR in a number of countries in Latin America as well as elsewhere in the Third World;[10] but the only case in which it has borne real fruit is that of Allende's Socialist Party in Chile, of all Latin American countries the one whose political circumstances most resemble those of Europe.

The third type of opposition party for which there appears to be a natural place in the Salvadorean political system is an alternative party of the Right. Since there is not the same degree of polarization of political forces as there is, for instance, in Guatemala, the party of the Right has no prospect of taking over power as the *Movimiento de Liberación Nacional* has done in that country. The *Partido Popular Salvadoreño* (PPS) constitutes rather a ginger group, at most a minor irritant to the government, and a channel of protest against certain reforms. It also appears to act as a rallying-point for individuals among the élite who have a personal rather than a wider political quarrel with the government. The party was formed (in 1965) primarily among landowners in the west and gained its first seat in the Legislative Assembly, for the Department of Ahuachapán, in 1966. Some of the ousted old guard leadership of the PAR also entered into the formation of the party along with others who had apparently attempted to launch a *coup* against the Rivera régime some two years earlier; the *coup* was 'controlled' – discovered in the conspiracy stage and its proponents dismissed from posts in army and government. In so far as the PPS has an ideology, it is a national-ist and authoritarian one, with a considerable hint of 'national socialism': an appeal to the middle class (the party emblem is a small house); a promise of stronger measures against criminals; a hatred of communism; an almost absolute defence of property, but a mention of 'socialism' apparently in the sense of either an encourage-ment of voluntary co-operation or merely a promise of a decent life for everyone. Before the Presidential election of 1967 the party distributed an anti-communist booklet produced by the *Asociación Cívica Anticomunista de El Salvador*, and only a brief and vague state-ment of objectives. The Presidential candidate was Major Álvaro Martínez, who apart from being a military officer is a coffee-grower and had been manager of the *Compañía Salvadoreña del Café*. He gained 9.6 per cent of the total vote, and unlike the other parties the PPS did better in rural areas than in the capital, where the vote was only 5.5 per cent. Greatest success was attained in Cabañas (29 per cent); least in Morazán (4 per cent). These two departments are similar in their social characteristics, so the variation must have been due primarily to different degrees of personal influence rather than a difference in potential support for such a party.

Finally, there appears still to be room for legal parties with no defined ideological standpoint at all, with only a personalist basis of support. It seems that the politicians who organize such parties gather money from wealthy individuals and votes largely through the personal following of other individuals with whom they come to an understanding. This may be enough to gain a deputy or two and so a bargaining position strong enough to return favours to the individuals with whom such understandings have been arrived at. This may perhaps lay too much emphasis on the party as a 'business': no doubt the politicians also have grander political ambitions.

The *Partido Republicano de Evolución Nacional* (PREN) of the mid-1960s was of this type. It dissolved after having failed to achieve any notable success in the legislative elections of 1966. A considerable part of its funds came from wealthy members of the Salvadorean Palestinian community.

Later, the *Unión Democrática Nacionalista* (UDN) was formed; it has greater intellectual prestige, and takes a reformist position. The leading figure is Francisco Lima, whose maverick role might be attributed to his being an intellectual of considerable independent means. He joined Rivera's régime on the promise of the social reform programme it proposed in its early phase, and was made Vice President and ambassador to Washington. He fell out with the government publicly, however, on the question of the uses made of the American loans he negotiated. Having resigned as ambassador in November 1964, he could not be deprived of the title of Vice President; but served out his term while teaching at an American university. Another of the politicians of the UDN is Julio Ernesto Contreras, who led the 'new line' in the PAR; conceivably the UDN will move to the position occupied by the PAR when he was secretary-general of that party in 1965–67.

## Elections: how the Official Party Wins

In the elections for the Legislative Assembly and municipal councils held on 8 March 1970,[11] the PCN was credited with nearly 60 per cent of the total votes cast, while its nearest competitor, the PDC, gained 28 per cent, UDN 6 per cent, PPS 5 per cent, and MNR $1\frac{1}{2}$ per cent. The PCN won 34 of the 52 seats in the Legislative Assembly, compared with 32 in 1966 and only 27 in 1968; and won control of all but seven of the 261 municipalities; these seven went to the PDC, compared to the eighty which the Christian Democrats had won in 1968. The only cause for opposition rejoicing was the PDC's retention of control over the municipality of San Salvador.

These results, reversing the previous trend toward the progressive weakening of the official party's electoral position, are fully attributable to the victory in the war against Honduras, with the prestige it brought the army, and in general to the sentiment of solidarity with the government against the outsider. However, it is more important to explain why the rural vote is overwhelmingly in favour of the official party at all elections, despite the fact that the *campesinos* are the worst-off section of the population under the existing régime and remembering the desperate uprising of 1932. The short answer would be that in regions where educational levels are low, elections are won by the people who organize them, even if balloting is secret and there is no recourse to direct fraud.

Direct fraud appears to have been gradually reduced to what are now low levels in El Salvador, though it does seem to occur in some places even in recent elections. There has been no property or educational qualification for voting since 1883, for men over twenty-one years old;[12] but then it is precisely the persons of poorest education who still provide the greatest electoral support of *oficialismo*, and universal suffrage has normally been of advantage to the sitting government. The reasons are the weight of what the political scientists call 'political socialization': the general environment of information and ideas by which the uneducated and most of those with only a little education are surrounded; the prohibition of any form of unionization or left-wing proselytization in the countryside; and the mixture of paternalism and intimidation at election time.

First, it must be considered that the existing socio-economic and political system appears to most Salvadoreans, except those with considerable education, as natural, inevitable, and more or less immutable. The majority must see their poverty in terms of not having inherited any land or other wealth, and they would not expect to be given either. A few might know the circumstances in which land was lost by their parents or grandparents, but would probably be more inclined to blame them for lack of foresight than to consider the general concentration of landholding as a reversible social process. The terms under which they sell their labour or the goods they produce are determined by market forces, and only an individual monopoly situation would appear to them to be susceptible to correction by government. They have seen, in fact, that the minimum wage legislation has not fundamentally changed the application of market forces to the distribution of income between employer and workers. The minimum rates for coffee- and cotton-picking have been an exception, as was Martínez's prohibition against the factory production of certain types of cloth and other goods like soap. On the whole, however, government action to improve their conditions can only be seen as more being spent on local improvements in services provided by the government, such as education, hospitals, and perhaps roads. And promises to provide services are made by all parties. *Campesinos* are sceptical; but inasmuch as the existing government does provide more of these services than previous governments and is associated with the rich and powerful who can carry through such programmes, government promises are likely to carry more weight than those of the opposition parties.

Then there is propaganda and 'political socialization'. School presentation of history and civics is so much in terms of patriotism, Central Americanism, and formal legality that it is quite possible to find someone with further education – though not at the university – who carries a little copy of the constitution in his pocket, but who does not even know that there was an uprising in 1932. Some school-teachers, however, are militant radicals, and there may be some change in the grossly idealized view of politics presented at schools. Most *campesinos*, however, have not been to school or have been only for a year or two. For them, political socialization is much more directly given by the army, especially to those doing military service, and has a much more explicit anti-communist and pro-*oficialista* content. This propaganda is reinforced after military service, since ex-soldiers remain reservists and have to perform duties in the *patrullas cantonales* which patrol the villages and towns each week, helping the National Guard to maintain order. The reservists, in turn, are the intermediaries who bring other lower-class personnel into the ranks of the *oficialista* organizations, including the patrols, the PCN, and now in particular a body called *Organización Demo-crática Nacionalista* '(ORDEN='order'). ORDEN was started in semi-secrecy during 1961–65, probably 1964 or 1965, by President Rivera and General José Alberto ('Chele') Medrano, under the wing of the *Guardia Nacional*. Its purpose is anti-revolutionary activity of various kinds, particularly training, imparted by the *Guardia Nacional*, for counter-guerrilla military operations. The organization developed rapidly in the later 1960s and now embraces thousands of men[13] throughout the rural areas and even in small towns. Curiously, the dismissal of General Medrano in December 1970 led to confusion over the status of ORDEN, since the Minister of Defence, Fidel Torres, had stated in January 1970 that ORDEN was a private civil group, 'not at all official'. Military personnel were involved, however, because there was an 'obligation to educate and orient the rural population, which is constantly threatened by the preachings of Communist subversion'.[14] In December, of course, Medrano could not be allowed to remain in any way associated with ORDEN, and the same Defence Minister stated: 'ORDEN is a group for the democratic indoctrination of citizens, especially in the rural areas, whose head is (*ex-officio*) the President of the Republic'. He went on to say that the new commander of the *Guardia Nacional*, Colonel Oscar Gutiérrez, only just appointed and not yet having familiarized himself with its complex organization, did not 'yet' have any mission in ORDEN.[15]

The other side of the coin of indoctrination is the stifling of activity by opponents. Here, a delicate balance is maintained, under which a considerable degree of left-wing proselytization is permitted in the capital and other large towns. In the rural areas, however, a totally different standard applies, with what is virtually a separate legal code (the *Ley Agraria*) and a separate militarized police force (the *Guardia Nacional* as opposed to the urban *Policía Nacional*), harshly to enforce it. Any person who shows himself discontented with rates of pay, whether on a private estate or in a government work group – building roads, for instance – is liable to be immediately dismissed from his job and likely to be refused employment by any other employer in the neighbourhood, since he will be considered a 'subversive'. Co-operation exists between the landowners and the *Guardia Nacional* in the identification and intimidation of 'subversives'. Even the PDC finds it difficult to persuade local supporters in many parts of the country to undertake any form of propaganda work. for fear of losing their jobs or being arrested, and the fear is clearly well grounded. It is easier for party representatives to travel from the capital to gain supporters, since they do not fear for their jobs and their connections in the capital are likely to ensure their safety from arbitrary arrest and especially from the torture or even police murder which are widely thought to await those agitators who do not have such connections. Those with middle-class status are undoubtedly treated with greater latitude and consideration, quite apart from connections.

Such, then, is the background against which the political attitudes of *campesinos* are formed. In this situation, it is impossible for the outsider to learn what these attitudes are. He may have obtained nothing more than an impression tailored to suit him and avoid trouble. But one's impression, for what it is worth, is that the immense majority make no connection between the existing political régime and their poverty, and that the lack of any sign of rebellion, protest, or even much opposition voting since 1932 is not, as is claimed in some left-wing writings, simply a matter of fear of a repetition of the holocaust that occurred then. There is discontent, but it is vaguely focused on the rich or on landowners rather than sharply focused against the government. And many see the government and army in terms of the social services which they provide, the latter in the form of the *Acción Cívica Militar* programme of constructive action and gifts to rural localities.

A new set of influences acts precisely at election time. First, the PCN benefits from using the resources of the state for publicity: government ministries and agencies pay for advertisements in the media, and official cars are widely used by the official party for election purposes. This, in fact, is one of the strong complaints of the opposition, though it is probably much less effective than a number of other biasing elements in elections. Mobile health clinics of the Health Ministry become for the election period PCN health clinics, conspicuously marked with the party insignia, and manned by volunteer medical personnel. The official party has more funds than other parties could hope to have for giving away footballs to villages, or more obviously vests,[16] by the thousands, for adults and children, marked with the blue sign of the PCN. Such gifts do buy votes. Then there is the inscription into the party's 'membership rolls'. A party activist, not paid but hoping for a job through his *oficialista* connection, is instructed to visit each dwelling in his area and enter its adult inhabitants as members of the party in a little book, telling them when they have to go and vote, and giving them a ticket for a free meal afterwards. The opposition parties cannot afford to conduct their campaign in this way, and they cannot recruit organizers with the promise of jobs in the administration if they are not going to win. When the *campesino* arrives at the polling booth, he finds persons of authority there, and very likely soldiers or *guardias* standing around. Finally, the ballot boxes are made of transparent plastic. As the ballot papers are thin and the voter marks the party symbol with a thick black cross, another person can stand on the opposite side of the box from the voter, watch his ballot paper come down through the slit into the transparent box, and see through the thin, once-folded paper which party he has voted for. The justification usually made of these transparent boxes, and even usually accepted by opposition parties, is that it makes it much more difficult to stuff the boxes.

Finally, special difficulties are placed in the way of election campaigns even of legal parties when they take a social reformist position. Thus the PAR came under very great handicaps in the Presidential election of 1967, being denied access to news media or free movement of campaigners. Anti-communist scare tactics of a crude kind were used against the PAR, with posters claiming PAR=Communism=Death. And the initials of the party were used to form the word 'PAR . . . edón', which means the wall against which a man is executed by firing squad, or such execution itself.

An impressive array of influences favours the official party; but it is weakening, by and large, with each election, as political sophistication rises.

## The Influence of the Church

The Catholic Church is not now a particularly strong element in the maintenance of the existing order, nor is it, yet anyway, a particularly strong force for change. The main reasons for this are, I think, the lack of those strong informal controls over behaviour, exercised through gossip and public opinion in small towns and villages, through which Churches often hold much of their power – there is some of this in El Salvador but not as much as in many other Catholic countries; then, while nineteen out of twenty of the population are nominal Catholics and almost all of them accept without question the existence of God, there is a good deal of scepticism about the clergy among most sectors – a suspicion that their motives are often more mercenary than they would have people believe, and a rejection of much of the dogma and the claim to be the only true Church; Salvadoreans are not very assiduous churchgoers, the attendance at all masses held in San Salvador, on one typical Sunday in 1964 when a count was taken, being 16 per cent of the total population (20 per cent of the population aged seven or over, who are those theoretically obliged to attend); finally and perhaps most important of all, the Church is itself divided on social and political matters, like the Church in Latin America as a whole, and does not speak with one voice except as a compromise between clearly differing points of view.

Of the seven bishops, the bishop of San Vicente, Pedro Arnoldo Aparicio y Quintanilla, remains an active exponent of the ultra-conservative, anti-communist position generally held in the Church as a whole until about 1960. He is the founder and organizer of a nationwide fraternity of *Caballeros de Cristo Rey* (Knights of Christ the King), in which, as in similar *cristero* movements in other countries in Latin America in the past, *campesinos* and poorly-educated men from small towns are brought together in militant allegiance to the traditional Church and opposition to communism. As of 1963, its monthly publication had a circulation of 10,000. In a public speech in February 1967, Monsignor Aparicio referred to the participation of PAR in the March election in the following terms:

> The fatherland is in danger and asks for the generous collaboration of all, compassion, and mutual aid, so that rich and poor, worker and industrialist, extend one another their hands in generosity, nobility, and compassion, and then, compatriots, the agitators will have lost their campaign forever.

However, the collective documents issued by the Ecclesiastical Province, and the pastoral letters of Luis Chávez y González, who has been archbishop of San Salvador since 1938, have turned during the 1960s to a greater stress on deploring 'the situation of injustice in which a large part of the family of Salvadoreans finds itself forced to live'. During the Agrarian Reform Congress of 1970 (see below, p. 212), the church representatives publicly declared the firm support of the Church for an uncompromising land reform. Some priests would wish to go further than this, but so far there are no well-known apostles of the Colombian 'martyr' priest-guerrilla Camilo Torres.

Protestantism in El Salvador has little connection with politics. While about a twentieth of the population has been converted by one or other of the Churches or sects, the success has been achieved primarily not because the religion is seen as having a different, preferable, set of beliefs, but largely because it is seen by all as stronger, involving more commitment, and above all because of its greater opposition to drunkenness. A conversion to Protestantism is, for many, avowal to resist this and other temptations; for some among these it may be associated with the so-called 'Protestant ethic', the determination to improve one's economic position by hard effort; for others, particularly the very poor who provide the main part of the congregation of the *Asambleas de Dios* (Assemblies of God), the emphasis on obedience and dutiful prostration before the Lord – significantly the same concept as in *Cristo Rey* – perhaps provides a much-needed source of self-respect, in that one is at least virtuous in one's devotion to the Lord.

In the 1950s there were some occasional outbreaks of hostility between Catholics and Protestants in provincial areas, but they were never very important and seem to have died out everywhere since then.

## *The Legislative Assembly*

For a long time the Legislative Assembly had been a servile rubber-stamp for the government of the day, particularly from the mid-1930s until 1964. Since the introduction of proportional representation in that year, however, it has had a slight but significant pull upon the government in the direction of tentative reform. This is because opposition deputies have been present in sufficient numbers, between about a third[17] and just under a half of the 52 members, and have been extremely active. The attention of the PDC, in particular, has been concentrated very largely on the Assembly. The party gives its deputies detailed instruction on each of the bills proposed on any side, and plans its approach carefully. Very often this approach pays off to the extent that a number of PCN deputies are convinced by the arguments, and in a few cases measures proposed by the PDC have been passed on this basis even though the party is in a minority. More often, however, the PCN deputies simply receive and obey instructions to vote against. One revealing indication of the partial independence of the Legislative Assembly occurred when the United States intervened in the Dominican Republic in 1965. The Assembly voted for the PDC motion to condemn the intervention, but the Foreign Ministry paid no attention and gave approval by sending an observer with the Organization of American States forces.

In late 1969, however, in an atmosphere of more than the usual amount of talk of social reform after the conflict with Honduras and the return of thousands of refugees, a group of PCN deputies virtually joined the opposition, so that from 4 November 1969 until its dissolution for new elections in March 1970, the Assembly had a majority pressing for more social reforms than the government was willing to make. There was apparently some pressure from the Right for the Assembly to be suspended, but the line taken by President Sánchez Hernández was not one of confrontation. When the Assembly called a 'First National Congress of Agrarian Reform' in January 1970, the President opened it with a speech in which he said:

> The theme of Agrarian Reform can and must be discussed and analysed without fear. It is no longer a taboo subject as it was before . . . Agrarian Reform is an immediate necessity and we are going to carry it out firmly and gradually.[18]

In fact the taboo had not been complete, and even the Rivera government had mentioned agrarian reform in its five-year development plan, promising 'a law which would permit the state to acquire lands through payments spread out over a long period'.[19] Nothing had come of this, and it appears that there are periods of greater political ferment, around Presidential elections or with the return of refugee Salvadoreans from Honduras, when agrarian reform is a topic of general discussion; but at other times it becomes something of a taboo subject again, and this appeared to have happened by the end of 1970. Now the discussion was of a Law of Drainage and Irrigation, under which the state would be enabled compulsorily to purchase land for the purpose of integrated water management schemes, redistributing the land to small farmers. This measure, to be applied only to a very small percentage of the land and at first only to the Zapotitán Valley, was used in a sense as a test case. It was seen by the wealthy landowners as the thin end of the wedge of state assault on property rights, and was vigorously opposed. The vigour of the opposition was presumably taken by the government as an indication of the likely strength of opposition to a broader measure of land reform.

## *Illegal Parties*

For the right wing, such laws as that of Drainage and Irrigation are seen as socialist, and there is even substantial belief in a conspiratorial view of history according to which the military rulers of El Salvador since 1948 have been either in league with or actually members of the Communist Party.

In fact, the *Partido Comunista Salvadoreño* was, after the defeat of the 1932 rebellion, reduced to a mere shell with perhaps a dozen members, and even after May 1944 the members maintained such complete discretion that it had no noticeable effect on political life. Its influence rose, however, with a new generation of members in the 1950s, and particularly with the founding of PRAM in 1959 and the turmoil that accompanied the fall of President Lemus. It was a time of considerable polarization of political forces, but there was no call for an uprising. It appears that when the political situation returned to normal, the PCS lost a certain degree of influence. Given that certain minor victories can be won through political pressure for reforms and through trade union activity, and given that in the normal political situation neither a rural nor an urban guerrilla action would have any real hope of success, it is not surprising that the PCS has adopted a peaceful and gradualist course, pressing against the limits of toleration of leftist activity in each sphere. It might be said that there is little else the party could do in the circumstances. A more cynical view is held both on the left and on the right of the party, well stated in a semi-humorous newspaper article as follows:

> the communists [here communists in general and not just the PCS] succumb better to money than to bullets. In Guatemala the anti-guerrilla struggle costs us approximately 50 thousand dollars a day, or an annual cost of more than 18 million dollars, plus the blood. The University of El Salvador costs approximately 6 million dollars a year and there are the communists fighting among themselves. . . . When a communist earns 400 dollars a month he no longer thinks of Sierra Maestras. . . . Only dishonesty will halt the march of the peoples to the encounter with their historical destiny.[20]

There is no reason to label the attitudes of the leftist intellectuals who have positions in the university as dishonest, but it could certainly be said that university politics takes up much of their attention. The result of university elections can hardly have a very great foreseeable effect on the distribution of power or privilege in society, and cannot have any more than a long-term and gradual effect through influence on political opinions prevailing mainly in the capital. The time-scale of this influence and its effect on policy are so slow that a number of revolutionaries reject this strategy, in favour of preparing for a military action which could hope to produce a fundamental improvement for the present generation of rural and urban poor. There are two or three small organized groups of such revolutionaries, but their progress in gathering support for an armed action is slow under the present circumstances: the prospect of success seems unreal.

The *Partido Revolucionario 9 de Mayo* (PR-9M), on the other hand, is in its political complexion the successor to PRAM: a body which can operate more openly than the PCS, presumably because it does not include the word 'communist' in its title or because it includes non-communists. Unlike the PCS, it can call public meetings and maintain a public headquarters office on a street in the centre of San Salvador. Even the PCS itself, however, was permitted in late 1970 to hold in its own name a public funeral march through the capital when its secretary-general[21] died. Such an event would have been inconceivable a few years earlier. It was a public example of a certain relaxation of the curbs on the Left; a less public example would be the reduction in the police shadowing of opponents of the régime.

## University Politics

The university acts not only as the main cultural and educational centre but also as another opposition party, one which cannot be proscribed; it has even been said that it is the only real opposition. Although there are differences of opinion and emphasis within the university, as a whole it is strongly committed to radical social reforms and unanimous in its opposition to the government. Its governing authorities – particularly the rector and the deans of the faculties – are elected, the students having the vote, and the candidates' political standpoint is the most important, or at least a very important, consideration. Political activists among students and staff spend much time and effort on internal politicking, particularly over these elections. But the students also act directly on the national political scene through the meetings and publicity organized by the *Asociación General de Estudiantes Universitarios Salvadoreños* (AGEUS), which has played a very significant role in leading mass protests during turbulent periods like that of September and October 1960. At irregular intervals students also organize a 'mock parade' through the streets of the capital, using the humour of sexual obscenity as a political weapon against the President, government, top army hierarchy, ecclesiastical dignitaries, newspaper publishers, etc., both in the scenes depicted on the float, and in a sheet which is published and sold at the same time.[22] The parade uses to the maximum the factors which protect opposition activity from harassment, and hence can go further in explicit denunciation. It has only an ephemeral *ad hoc* organization for the particular event, it enjoys the special protection afforded by the university and the tradition of respect for its autonomy, its effect is necessarily confined to the capital, and it is couched in a humorous idiom. Each parade arouses much comment and has a bigger impact than the public meetings of AGEUS which are simply ignored by the press and other media.

The political impact of the university is also felt through its studies and publications; through the participation of its members in public debates such as the Congress on Agrarian Reform; and above all through informal contact and the politicization of students and even of clerical and manual staff. The internal political groupings have their own intense contacts with legal and unrecognized opposition parties outside the university, to such an extent that the university campus can be seen as the nerve centre of opposition as a whole. The internal groupings range from the *Asociación Católica de Universitarios Salvadoreños* (ACUS) to various Marxist groups; but even ACUS stands on the left of the 'social Christian' spectrum of opinion, and probably influences the PDC in that direction.

## Trade Unions

One of the ways in which the university manifests its 'solidarity with the people', a frequent theme of rhetoric, is through its links with the militant trade unionists of the *Federación Unitaria Sindical de El Salvador* (FUSS). The university has, for instance, helped FUSS to organize a school for children of the working class; and it can also help with legal advice and by finding employment for men dismissed because of their militancy.

The trade unions are divided into two antagonistic camps: on the left there is FUSS and another federation labouring under the initials FESTIAVTSCES;[23] on the right, close to the PCN and the government, is the *Confederación General de Sindicatos* (CGS). In between there are some independent unions, but the Christian Democratic-oriented attempt at union organization, the *Unión Nacional de Obreros Cristianos*, has made no real headway.

The urban workers and their organizations are in a position intermediate between intellectuals of the university, allowed a fair freedom of activity in normal times, and the rural masses who are permitted no free organization at all. The left-wing unions are in a situation of constant tension, in which the policy of the government shifts sharply toward greater or less repression according to the current political situation. The union movement picked up rapidly after Martínez's thorough repression was ended in 1944, and by 1945 there were strikes, although they were still illegal. In 1950 unions were legalized, but legality has not in fact been of very much importance, what is permitted at any time being more a matter of current government attitudes, and many leaders were jailed, exiled, or had to go underground as soon after the legalization as September 1951. At other times, strikes which do not conform to the legal prerequisites are nevertheless recognized in practice. In the years after 1951 the anti-revolutionary trade union leadership, allied to the government (and sometimes also to the employers, more or less openly), began to emerge, and although there were periods of some co-operation between the two wings of the movement, by 1957–58 the present structure had taken definite shape, with the leftist *Confederación General de Trabajadores Salvadoreños* (CGTS), embracing unions with a membership totalling some 8,000, on one side and the anti-communist CGS, with some 13,000 members, on the other. The argument of the CGS is that the leftist leaders are interested only in gaining political power, and the CGTS did spend a considerable amount of effort on the organization of opposition to the government. A change of emphasis toward the present policy of pursuing wage demands with greatest energy, in the expectation of thereby also attracting the support of most unions and their members, caused CGTS to be replaced on the left in 1965 by FUSS. The present position both of FUSS and FESTIAVTSCES can be illustrated with a quotation from a 1971 document approved by the congress of the latter:

> The bourgeoisie knows very well that if one day the unity of all the trade union movement should come about, the Salvadorean proletariat would have an irresistible force and the Republic of El Salvador would not be the same; the necessary changes in the country's institutions would occur irreversibly for the happiness of the People . . .[24]

Efforts are therefore concentrated on helping all unions, even those which are members of CGS, in their confrontations with employers, in order partly to win their support; and on appealing to CGS to join in a common front with a strongly reformist programme. Those who favoured a more direct revolutionary approach no longer have leading positions in the two federations. The greatest success of this FUSS policy was perhaps the organization in 1968 of a 'general strike' in support of the claim of one of the member unions. The strike was illegal and repression was feared, but on this occasion the

strikers won. Another big strike of 1968 was, however, broken. It was
organized by the militant teachers' association; but this profession,
like the manual workers' unions, is divided into a pro-governmental
as well as a revolutionary organization, and the dispute ended
with the victory of the government, bitterness, and some bloodshed.

The leadership of the leftist union federations is not entirely
homogeneous in its point of view. It is interesting to note, for
instance, that one response on the left to the Honduran war was a
publicity campaign urging the government to ensure that the soldiers
who had fought so valiantly for El Salvador should be able to return
to a country whose social conditions justified their sacrifice. Another,
quite different, was to say that the war was a distraction of the attention of the working class of both countries from their common
struggle – even that it was planned and intended as such.[25]

All union organization is held back to a very great extent, as are
co-operatives, by the suspicion of most Salvadoreans that the
organizers are doing it for their own personal benefit. The suspicion
probably arises largely from actual experience: numerous cases have
occurred of men who have organized unions and then run away with
the funds, and these cases are remembered and generalized. Also
apparently frequent is the case of a union within a firm which begins
to make demands after its formation; but then the employers bribe
the leaders to tone down their demands, and the union becomes
*patronal* ('of the employer'). In a country where there are no strongly
enforced sanctions against it, a union, like a political party, can be a
'business' run by an individual or group, in which the power implicit
in organization is traded for money or other advantages. It is possible
because the ordinary workers usually have little knowledge of
procedure and feel too unsure of their ground to insist publicly that
the leadership take a specific action in defence of their interests. At
a union meeting, for instance, they might be intimidated by a
recourse to formalism: 'That question is not on the agenda'.
Wherever information is a power resource – wherever one group of
people gains advantages from another group because it is more
sophisticated or knowledgeable – emphasis is laid on the kind of
knowledge which only that group commands, and which inspires
respect or awe in others. Elsewhere it may be a special religious
knowledge which is claimed; in El Salvador there is a stress on
constitutionalism and formal procedure, and this can be seen in
many cases to act against the interests of those who do not feel at
home with this procedure, since it is freely manipulated and
infringed by those who do, while it inhibits those who do not.

A union leader may be able to advance his personal interests without indulging in an actual theft or sell-out of the kind described. There are possibilities of trips abroad, or for a comfortable life not usually within the reach of a manual worker. A few union leaders sit in the Legislative Assembly as PCN deputies. Of the hundred or so CGS unionists who, up to 1966, had taken advantage of that federation's affiliation to the American-sponsored *Organización Regional Interamericana de Trabajadores* (ORIT) and had gone to Puerto Rico and the United States under its auspices for training courses, only about thirty, I was told, had remained active union leaders afterwards. The opportunities for these personal advantages are greater within CGS than in FUSS, and though a few leftist leaders have gone on trips to eastern Europe, Cuba, or Chile, it seems unlikely that many of them would have entered trade union leadership with such personal ends in view, since it is still dangerous to be a leftist union leader in El Salvador.

The suspicion which very many workers have of union leaders or would-be leaders extends, however, to all of them without distinction of their political position or which of the federations they are affiliated to. The other main, parallel, problem which union leaders face is the continuing ability of many employers to prevent the formation of unions by dismissing those who attempt to organize them, dismissing all those who join, or even in some extreme instances dismissing the entire workforce, keeping the factory closed for a while, then taking on a new selected workforce. It is possible for employers to do this because of the large number of underemployed in search of any job, and because of the relatively small size of most workplaces, which enables the owner or men in his confidence to maintain a personal relationship with a large proportion of the workers. The patron-client ties of the rural *hacienda* survive in attenuated form for the same reasons that they existed in the countryside. When one risks dismissal for joining a union, or will at least have to endure unpleasant treatment by the owner or manager or foreman, as compared with the relatively privileged position they may give to the workers who take their side against the union, one may prefer the status of the *patronal* to that of the *subversivo*. And in the absence of many large factories with more than a few dozen workers, where a tradition of workers' solidarity can grow, the sanctions which employers can bring to bear are not matched, as they were for instance in nineteenth-century Europe, by the informal social control exercised by the workers. Of course, it is not every employer who succeeds in preventing the establishment of a union or even every employer who tries. In some workplaces unions exist but are ineffective because too few join; in some the employers set up and control submissive unions; and finally, there are a number which work effectively, including those in the two or three largest enterprises in terms of numbers of workers.

The more important labour disputes quickly involve the government and become eminently political, probably because any period of public agitation is threatening to a government which relies on a delicate balance of repression and concession. In January 1967 there was a strike of the driver-conductors on the urban bus routes in San Salvador. It disrupted normal life in the capital, as most people in the city were affected; sympathy was clearly with the drivers, even the sympathy of the majority who earned considerably less than they did. In this situation the government stepped in and imposed a settlement favourable to the drivers, under which the government itself would contribute part of the pay increase. This move was probably taken because of a possible rapid rise in the political temperature of the capital and the likelihood of a crowd which might have marched on the Presidential Palace, or some similar unpredictable crisis situation. The present régime stemming from the 1961 *coup* has, in contrast to that of Lemus, been adept at avoiding such crises; but the implicit threat of crowd or 'mob' action seems to be a constant background element in the political situation. After the most recent earthquake of 3 May 1965, the government rejected a plan of the San Salvador municipality to house not only earthquake victims but also a large number of others who were living in shanty towns and insalubrious *mesones*, with the aid of $2 million given by the American government. The proposal was to buy land in a single place, where it was still cheap, to provide simple materials – wood, nails, and metal roofing – to engage engineers and put up public buildings and services, as well as model houses, but to let the people put up the dwellings for themselves with this help. According to the mayor, the government turned this plan down with the argument that it would congregate all the poor in one area, and the communists would get in to agitate. In fact the very poor in the shanty towns tend to be *oficialistas*, and certainly not good material for agitation. It may be simply that the government was afraid that this dramatic plan would lead the beneficiaries to support the party proposing it, the PDC which controlled the municipality. But it does appear to confirm that the government fears the formation of crowds or mobs.

## Municipal Government

When communications were not so good as they are now and each locality had its own separate social life, the municipal authorities had a considerable measure of real autonomy and power; in the nineteenth century, local power groups could keep their influence even in opposition to the national government, particularly in the case of the populous regional centres like Cojutepeque and San Miguel. Gradually, however, the municipalities have become impotent. Although they retain a legal autonomy, their power to collect rates and local taxes is controlled and kept low, so that most are dependent on subsidies from the Ministry of the Interior, particularly for any new buildings such as covered markets. The decline in the autonomy of municipalities is regretted, from the PPS to the PDC and the Left.[26]

The municipality which has nowadays the greatest possibilities of taking an independent policy line is that of San Salvador, and it is interesting to note that the measures associated with PDC control of this council since 1964 have been concerned almost entirely with the improvement of the services always provided by municipalities (street lighting, covered markets, cemeteries) rather than with any radical departures, and that the only assault which can be said to have been made on privilege has been a more effective and uncorrupt collection of municipal taxes.[27] On one issue in which the municipality is constantly involved in a conflict of interests between rich and poor, that of the street vendors, it has taken a vacillating and intermediate position. Street vendors abound, as a result and manifestation of underemployment, in the central area of the capital and especially in the vicinity of the market. Shopkeepers would like to see them kept off the streets, a situation that applies, effectively, in Guatemala City. They are supported by general opinion among the upper and middle classes, to judge by the press, on the grounds that it is difficult and time-consuming to drive a car through the streets near the market where the vendors tend to spill off the pavement and onto the roadway itself. On the other hand, any restriction in the freedom of the vendors to sell where they can would not only directly reduce their income but would also tend to reduce that of all the underemployed, since it would drive more people into those labour-absorbing activities which remained available, and increase the competition between them. In this situation the policy pursued by the PDC-controlled municipal council, both under Mayor Duarte and under his successor, Carlos Herrera Rebollo, has been to maintain an official prohibition of street selling but to enforce it only partially and periodically. A municipal policeman is sent to an area where vendors congregate and clears them off; they retreat into the market or around a corner as long as the policeman remains, perhaps a couple of hours, then they return. If they go into a market, disputes arise with the stallholders because they inevitably block passages, cause inconvenience, and reduce sales. Around Christmas or at other periods when street sales are particularly high, the outcry against the vendors grows greater, and then a more determined effort may be made to clear certain streets; but the situation returns to normal after the festival. In the Christmas period of 1970, Mayor Herrera Rebollo spoke of a 'lack of a policy at national level to regulate or prevent the disordered immigration from the rural to the urban sectors', but recommended that such a policy should involve the opening-up of new sources of work throughout the country, and rejected the idea of 'hiding our sad social reality' by eliminating street selling and removing this source of income from the poor.[28] It appears, however, that the municipality is under great pressure from the shopkeepers on the question, because soon afterwards the mayor did adopt a policy of partial elimination for the Christmas period.

## NOTES

[1] Except the UDN. Numerous voluntary and professional associations also adhered to the National Unity front.

[2] The best known of these is Colonel Mario Guerrero, who was strongly backed for the Presidency in the 1966 campaign within the official party (see below, p. 197).

[3] John J. Johnson: *The Military and Society in Latin America* (1964: Stanford, Stanford University Press), 107 note.

[4] The fact was reported in that year by the Prussian ambassador (quoted David Luna, *Manual de Historia Económica de El Salvador*). It is stated that when Arturo Araujo became President in 1931 there were also large-scale changes in administrative personnel in a 'spoils system'. Vicente Amado Gavidia Hidalgo: 'Equilibrio Presupuestario y Desarrollo Económico de El Salvador', *Economía Salvadoreña*, Año VI, No 15 (1957), 45. The absence of such disrupting changes of personnel today is often claimed to be an advantage of the Salvadorean political experience as compared to that of, say, Guatemala or Costa Rica, and there would be strong pressure to retain continuity of personnel even if an opposition party were allowed to take over the government of El Salvador.

[5] See above, p. 54, note 77, for a discussion of *caudillismo*.

[6] See above, p. 103. His abortive *coup* is mentioned with a few details in David Luna: 'Análisis de una dictadura fascista', 121–2.

[7] In 1960.

[8] These figures could be varied in particular circumstances by the commission charged with carrying out the reform, according to local soil fertility, etc.

[9] This quotation comes from a speech at a PAR public meeting in San Salvador during the municipal election campaign of March 1966. It was broadcast by a commercial radio station, although during this campaign PAR was already having difficulty getting on the air.

[10] Peter Worsley: *The Third World* (1964: London, Weidenfeld & Nicolson), discusses the ideas of such socialists.

[11] i.e., the most recent election at the time this chapter was written, shortly before the 1972 Presidential elections reported below, pp. 252–3.

[12] Men aged 18 to 20 could vote (1883–1950), if they were married or had a 'literary title' (a secondary-school certificate). Women's suffrage was first mentioned in the 1939 constitution, and first granted, to women aged 25 or over who had completed 3 years schooling, in 1946. Since 1950, women and persons aged 18 to 20 have had unqualified voting rights. Information culled from the constitutions and laws printed in Ricardo Gallardo: *Las Constituciones de El Salvador*.

[13] Between 50,000 and 100,000, in all probability.

[14] Quoted Stephen L. Rozman: 'The Socialization of Military Rule in El Salvador' (1970: Univ. of Nebraska; mimeo), 24.

[15] *El Mundo*, 18 Dec. 1970.

[16] More obvious, in the sense that the vests are worn with the PCN symbol conspicuously displayed, without any outer garment, particularly by boys.

[17] When the opposition has more than one-third of the members, it has a certain leverage due to the fact that any foreign loan requires constitutionally a two-thirds majority approval by the Assembly. To some extent a combined opposition can bargain in exchange for their approval of loans. In the 1968–70 Assembly, the PDC bargained their approval of some government loans for a ₡6 million loan for construction of new market buildings by the PDC-controlled municipality of San Salvador. (Information from a PDC deputy.)

[18] *Memoria del Primer Congreso Nacional de Reforma Agraria* (1970: San Salvador, Asamblea Legislativa), 37.

[19] CONAPLAN: *Plan de la Nación*, Vol. 2, 77.

[20] 'Una cena exquisita en casa de la "chica de Cipol",' *El Mundo*, 15 Dec. 1970.

[21] Raúl Castellanos Figueroa, one of the most gifted public speakers of El Salvador and a generally respected figure, who died in his prime. His death occurred in Moscow, where he was undergoing medical treatment, but his body was flown back to San Salvador.

[22] *La Jodarria*.

[23] Federación de Sindicatos de Trabajadores de la Industria del Alimento, Vestido, Textil, Similares y Conexos de El Salvador.

[24] *Documento sobre la Línea Política Sindical*, 3er Congreso Federal, 14.

[25] As stated in a resolution of the same FESTIAVTSCES congress.

[26] Under the Martínez régime and until 1952, even the formal election of municipal councils was replaced by appointment of officials. See Adams, op. cit., 468–72, where the control functions of the municipal officials are discussed at some length.

[27] This judgement is confirmed by my reading of Roland H. Ebel: 'The decision-making process in San Salvador', in F. F. Rabinovitz and F. M. Trueblood, eds., *Latin American Urban Research* (1971: Beverly Hills, Sage), 189–213, though Ebel's emphasis is different.

[28] *La Prensa Gráfica*, 4 Dec. 1970.

# Chapter 8

# Economic and Social Development:
# Policies and Realities

*Industrialization and Underemployment*

THE CASE OF THE street vendors illustrates the form which economic
development has taken in El Salvador, as in many other underdeveloped countries. There has been a growth of industry, but without any corresponding growth in the number of jobs available. The
surplus labour, denied productive employment, is forced to crowd
into the only avenues where a living of a sort can still be made, and
most of these labour-absorbing activities are in commerce and other
services, since little land is available and there are few other opportunities in the production of goods.

What is in question is not, as might be thought at first sight, a
dilemma between policies to encourage growth and policies to
promote employment. It is, much more importantly, a question of
the kind of growth and who benefits from it. It could well be argued
that what is going on should not be called growth at all: the nineteenth-century expansion of coffee which was seen at the time as the
foundation of prosperity and development would hardly be referred
to in those terms nowadays, since it is recognized that the development was lopsided and the prosperity was prosperity only for a
minority. The current development of industry is also lopsided and
it also benefits only a minority, although in this case the minority is
not so very small.

The lopsidedness can be appreciated when one examines the flow
of money between the classes, and the effect that the establishment
of modern factories has upon it. For simplicity's sake, it is best to
distinguish just two classes or sectors of the population: on the one
hand, the agriculturalists and the urban working people, and on the
other, the urban upper and middle groups, including the growers of
export crops, who live and spend mainly in the city. It was already
apparent in the discussion of coffee production that a large proportion of the product of the labour of the poor is directly appropriated
by plantation-owners; it is not necessary to accept Marx's premise

that land contributes nothing to the value of a product, and capital
no more than its depreciation cost, to agree that labour is underpaid
for the contribution it makes to the production of coffee. However,
what is also apparent about the economic system existing in El
Salvador is that the income received by the upper and middle classes
tends to be spent in such a way that it remains within this upper
sector or leaves the country altogether. A proportion does go on such
things as home-produced food and domestic service, to the lower
sector, but with the high level of incomes prevailing in much of the
upper sector and the relatively small size of this group in terms of
number of families, the proportion of income spent on food is low and
the market for home-produced food much smaller than it would be
if incomes were distributed more equally through the population.

The income received by the lower sector does tend to circulate
within that sector, as its recipients buy food and, particularly in the
rural areas, such handicraft items as hammocks and earthenware
cooking utensils. Nevertheless, a proportion of the income does
'escape' back to the upper sector, to moneylenders and in purchases
from that sector. Moneylenders, incidentally, are active not only in
rural areas but also, for instance, in urban market places, where the
rates charged work out astronomically high if calculated on an
annual basis. One type of loan, not the most extreme example,
involves the lending of, say, ₡100, to be paid back at ₡4.80 each
day for 25 days, the ₡4 being regarded as capital repayment and the
80¢ as '20 per cent interest'; it is 20 per cent interest, however, over
an average loan period of 13 days, and this, on the most conservative
interpretation (without compounding), means an annual rate of
560 per cent. If it is taken into account that the lender can relend
the money, including the interest, as it comes in, the figure reaches
fantastic proportions in the tens or hundreds of thousands per cent
per annum. One comes to realize that no moneylender in fact makes
this return and that the main constraint in his way is his inability to
place more than a certain amount of money in loans, relying as he
does on a personal relationship with his clients, collecting his
repayments himself each day, and having to be sure they will not
default. The fact remains that, even though a borrower can sometimes get away with a delay in his repayments and so a reduction
in the effective rate of interest, payments to moneylenders do constitute a substantial drain on lower-sector income.

The other main way in which money 'escapes' from circulation
within the lower sector into the upper sector is through spending on
goods which are imported or produced in factories, and on services
such as transport. When this is taken into account, it becomes clear
that the opening of a new factory usually leads people to spend

money on its products which would otherwise have been spent in the lower sector, and so causes a further transfer of income out of that sector. In other words, it increases underemployment and depresses incomes. Inasmuch as it merely diverts expenditure from imports, employs labour, and provides a new market for local raw materials, it has an effect in the other direction; in the case of certain factories, this effect is stronger, but by no means in all.

A typical case where the statistics suggest a loss of income from the lower sector is that of two factories producing tinned fruit juices.[1] They compete directly with the large number of vendors of fresh fruit juice or of the ubiquitous *refrescos*, grated fruit mixed with water and sugar. Of the ₡585,266 received by the two canning plants for the sale of their product in 1969, 15 per cent was spent on raw material bought in El Salvador and 4 per cent on wages for workers and apprentices. To this 19 per cent, which goes to the working and agricultural sections of the population, should be added a certain amount more to allow for the labour spent in constructing the factories, installing the machinery, etc. Meanwhile, 21 per cent goes abroad to pay for imported raw materials, mainly fruit concentrates, and 7 per cent goes to salaries for administrative personnel and technicians. The other 53 per cent, including the payment for machinery and all other expenses as well as profit, must – the statistics do not record its destination – almost all either go abroad or remain within the upper sector. The situation is more complex in that tinned fruit juices are also imported from Guatemala: the present pattern of industrial development is Central American in scope, and the arguments apply at that level.

There are by now something in the region of fifty food-processing factories, not counting coffee, sugar, or prawns, in El Salvador. They all compete fairly directly with food which is not processed industrially, and tend to divert income away from the lower sector. One interesting case is that of wheat flour, which has to be imported in its entirety.[2] The Spanish conquerors, presumably, introduced the taste for wheat bread and cakes, although the local word for bread, *pan francés*, suggests that it may have been a later influence originating in France. However that may be, bread is now preferred by the upper and in general the middle classes, while most of the population still eats the maize *tortillas*, but consumes large quantities of wheat pastries (*pan*). The association of wheat bread with high status and *tortillas* with low tends to bias consumption in favour of the imported and industrially processed product and so take more money out of the lower sector. This association between status and the factory product exists over a wide range of products where there is little or no difference of function between them and their handicraft equivalents; for instance, people spurn earthenware pottery and buy cheap metal pots and pans. The market left open to village potters has gradually contracted and is more and more limited to the poorer sections of the rural population. The matter of status of industrial goods merely speeds up the decline of handicrafts, it does not start such a decline. In the case of clothing, factory-made products have almost entirely replaced the artisan because he cannot compete with their cheapness; the same fate is now befalling shoe-makers, whose income is being driven down to the level prevalent among the underemployed although they still possess the special skills which in previous generations gave them an income which was high by the standards of manual workers.

It is not just a question of the competition between similar articles, one imported or made in a factory and the other hand-made. Often, the product of the upper sector replaces a very different product of the lower sector in performing a similar function. For instance, as transistor radios become common objects in the homes even of poor rural people,[3] there is less demand for live musicians to enliven dances and social occasions: again, money escapes from the lower sector. In transport, the ox-cart and mule are replaced by the lorry and bus. It is possible, in fact, that the building of a road may fail to benefit the population of the area through which or to which it goes, if the relative cheapness of the modern means of transport that can now be used accrues mainly to the advantage of the traders who come in from outside, and if the gains in income which do reach the small farmer are cancelled out by the loss to the lower sector of another source of income in local transportation, money which would have circulated in the local area.

Finally, even when the factory product does not compete with any particular artisans, it may draw expenditure away from them all. The more consumer durables available to the middle and upper classes, for instance, the less they are likely to spend on housing, which needs labour for building and maintenance, or indeed on domestic servants.

Whether one regards El Salvador's recent economic development as 'rapid'[4] or as 'fictitious'[5] depends upon how one sees and evaluates the effect of the rise of industry upon non-industrial production and lower-sector incomes. The rate of growth of value added in the industrial sector was as high as 11.7 per cent per year in the period 1962–67. The figure was so high in part because the Central American Common Market had only just come into operation, and industry was expanding fast to take advantage of the new market represented by the richest 10 per cent of the population of the isthmus as a whole. This market was largely saturated by the end of the decade, about the same time that the Common Market entered into difficulties because of the political conflict between El Salvador and Honduras; so there is no likelihood that the same rate of growth will be maintained in the future, nor indeed that it has been maintained since 1968. One suggestion made is to expand the Market to include some other small countries in the general geographical area, such as the Dominican Republic; another is to encourage American manufacturers to transfer whole plants to El Salvador, taking advantage of cheap labour and tax and tariff concessions, to make their products for the American market. This is done in some other countries and some firms have made requests to the Salvadorean government for such concessions. Others conclude that the only real solution is to increase the purchasing power of the populace at home and in the rest of Central America. There is, however, no pressure by industrialists for the agrarian and other reforms that would make this possible, because they are worried about the possibility of losing their own advantages in the process.

The expansion of industry has occurred without any corresponding increase in the number of workers employed, because the plants operate with the most modern imported machinery and use few workers. Possibly the main reason for this preference for the most modern machinery is an aspiration by the industrialists, aided by their friends in the banks and in government, to create a modern rather than a second-class economy. It seems that industrialists achieve an average yearly profit of only about 10 per cent of their capital, whereas profits as high as 40 per cent are obtainable in large-scale commerce and landowners usually make more than 10 per cent, so that embarking on industrial enterprise is itself more a question of ideology and aspiration than simple profit-seeking. It may, however, be that industrialists avoid having a large labour force in their factories in order to feel safe from the risk of strikes or political changes bringing a sudden increase in wages which would then have a substantial effect on their total costs. They prefer to have a small, relatively well-paid workforce and that the major part of their costs should be on machines, not liable to such sudden increases. There are other possible reasons, too, such as the fact that most of the training of businessmen and technicians alike is in countries, such as the United States, where the modern, capital-intensive, techniques are more appropriate, or is imparted by people trained in those countries; or that some of the factories are built under various arrangements with foreign firms requiring the use of the newest equipment.

At the time of the last industrial census, that of 1961, there were 55,361 persons employed in establishments employing five or more.[6]

However, there were 2,714 of these establishments, the majority of which were clearly not factories but small workshops. Moreover, about half of the number, 26,496, worked in the initial processing of coffee, sugar, or cotton; so they too can hardly be considered as industrial workers. These activities are seasonal. There were perhaps only just over 20,000 industrial workers and some 3,000 administrative employees in the factories. Official statistics for early 1970 still list, outside coffee-, sugar-, and cotton-processing, only 20,674 workers and 4,996 administrative employees in 611 factories ('more important manufacturing industries').[7]

The preference for modern equipment shows up also in the statistics for the percentage of the value added by the industrial process which goes as wages to the workers. Perhaps such statistical comparisons have little real validity, but the percentage for El Salvador given in a publication of the Pan-American Union, in 1963, was, at 17.3 per cent, the lowest for any country on the continent, comparing with 35.0 per cent for the United States.[8]

Until the return of refugees from Honduras in 1969 drew special attention to the question of underemployment – although in fact it increased it by little more than a drop in the ocean – the government and its planning council give no special encouragement to industrialists who proposed to employ large numbers of workers. One of the objectives of the 1965-69 Development Plan is stated as 'promoting the use of modern equipment and methods', and the objective was achieved in part by allowing the import of capital equipment free of tariff.[9] And in spite of the increased discussion of the need to find jobs, there has been no real change of policy in this regard since 1969. No spontaneous change on the part of industry itself is to be expected: each employer presumably takes into account, in deciding which techniques to use, his familiarity with the techniques, his estimate of their costs, and probably his preference for a small workforce. The employer does not have to pay the social cost of denying jobs to those he would have employed had he used labour-intensive techniques. This cost is borne by the lower sector as a whole, as those who are not offered industrial employment crowd into the labour-absorbing activities and increase the competition for the limited number of opportunities of earning money within this sector.

Another feature of the recent industrial expansion is its tendency to use imported rather than local raw materials, and so to fail to develop opportunities for the lower sector which might be developed, particularly in agriculture. In 1951, one source gives the percentage of national raw materials used in industry as 63 per cent, while in 1968 they accounted for only 39 per cent.[10] But 'raw' materials is a misnomer, since by far the greater part of the imported materials have already gone through an industrial process, and some are merely being mixed or assembled in El Salvador.

The conclusion which seems inevitable is that the form of industrialization which El Salvador has been undergoing shows no signs of leading to an improvement in the situation of a majority of the population, although it will help to elevate a small proportion of people from lower- to middle-class status. And it is this process that is also being pursued by other aspects of government policy, including the sphere where expenditure is greatest – education.

## Education

According to the radical Catholic humanist Ivan Illich,[11] the spending of vast sums of money by Latin American governments on formal education is retrogressive and absurd. Retrogressive because it concentrates resources on the tiny percentage of people who reach the upper levels of the educational system, and absurd because it insists that people acquire knowledge in a very expensive way, by going through a curriculum at a school. Moreover, the knowledge that is acquired is in any case the knowledge suitable for a way of life which the vast majority of people in the continent have no prospect of being able to afford, even if it is desirable for those who can afford it. And perhaps the main result of an education if it is only shallow and brief is to give the pupil an exaggerated respect for those whose education has been longer though not necessarily any deeper.

When one finds, in El Salvador, that a large amount of learning at school is still by rote[12] without understanding of causes and effects, and is divorced from life; and that the types of sentiment fostered – notably an awe of formality reflected in the mystification of patriotic symbols as well as, for instance, in the pride taken in the social accomplishment of 'phonomiming' (making the correct gestures with the arms while silently mouthing a song which is playing on a record-player) – probably impede the development of flexible patterns of thought or at least confine the area to which that flexibility is applied, one wonders why Illich is such a lone voice crying in the wilderness.

However, only the most reactionary section of Salvadorean opinion – those who think it pointless and dangerous to educate the rural workers – would dissent from the goal expressed by President Sánchez Hernández. He reminded school-teachers, during the period in 1968 when their militancy was a significant challenge to the government, that 'support for education' were the first words he uttered after being chosen as official candidate for the Presidency.[13]

Education absorbs the largest single slice of the national budget,

28 per cent in 1971.[14] This sum, which includes neither the expenditure in private schools nor the expenses incurred by parents in sending their children to state schools, represents about ₡1 for every ₡25 of the national product,[15] or ₡27 for every man, woman, and child in the country, or about ₡112 for every child between the ages of seven and seventeen. Private schools, mainly Catholic, provide about half the secondary-level education, but a much smaller proportion at other levels; recently a Catholic University was opened in San Salvador.

The expenditure is distributed very unequally among the children. Whereas for the payment of teachers only, the cost per pupil was ₡97 for primary education in 1965, it was ₡160 for secondary education, ₡519 for teacher-training, and ₡2,176 for university students.[16] In a country where knowledge is a scarce resource and its skilful use can bring the user a very high income relative to those who do not possess it, the state provides this differential advantage to a relatively small minority and, at the upper levels, to a select few. Ivan Illich would wish the sum to be more evenly divided among the population, and it is difficult to contest that opinion. At the same time, however, the state provision of primary education in particular represents one of the few ways in which some of the money from the upper sector of the economy does go to benefit some of the people from the lower sector.

It is difficult to say how high a proportion of the people is benefited, because the statistics differ as to the total number of children in the relevant age-groups. On the basis of census statistics and those of school registration, it is officially stated that between 90 and one hundred per cent of children receive some education,[17] and that, as of 1967, between 70 and 75 per cent of the children aged eight to twelve were registered at school.[18] However, if we take the statistics for births and deaths of young children,[19] which show about 15 per cent more children of school age than do the figures based on the census, then it appears that, even in 1969, not more than 65 per cent of the eight-year-olds were registered in school, and the proportion at every other age was less than this. Since undercounting of small children by the census is much more likely than overcounting of births, this latter estimate seems more probable than the official one. The only other possibility is that the mortality of young children is grossly under-registered, so that, for instance, well over twice as many die before reaching their first birthday as the officially registered 60–70 per thousand born.[20]

For those children who do register in school, the so-called 'wastage rate' is very high. If we look, for example, at those who registered for the first grade of primary school in 1966 (not just the six- to eight-year-olds, but also older children who were starting or restarting their schooling), we find that: 14 per cent abandoned their schooling during the year; 23 per cent were failed, receiving low marks in class tests and being refused admission to the 2nd grade; 8 per cent were passed but were unable to proceed to 2nd grade because only first grade was offered in their local school; 55 per cent were passed and were able to go on to 2nd grade.

Of the 45 per cent who could not go on to 2nd grade in 1967, about half repeated first grade; the other half were rejects who might try again later, but probably will not.

The whittling process continues in the other five grades of primary school, although it becomes less drastic as those with least determination have already been eliminated, until in 6th grade 86 per cent of the intake completes the course successfully.[21] The cumulative effect is that, in 1967, only about 20 per cent of children finished primary school. These are the people who have the best chance of finding a niche in the modern sector of the economy, and of entering the middle class, if they were not born into it. Factories commonly ask potential workers for certificates of completed primary school. Not surprisingly, the ceremonies of graduation are elaborate.[22]

One of the most conspicuous programmes of the Sánchez Hernández administration has been that of 'Educational Reform'. The general objectives of the Five-Year Plan (1968–72) are stated as being: (1) to extend education to more people; (2) to improve the quality of teaching in the sense of making it more appropriate for the needs of contemporary society; (3) to improve the efficiency of the educational system to avoid wastage or under-utilization of resources.[23] This last objective is to be achieved primarily by generalizing a standard type of rural primary school, with three classrooms, three teachers, and a double-shift system under which the teacher takes perhaps the 3rd grade in the morning and the 6th grade in the afternoon, so that the school offers all six grades. For this exhausting work the teacher gets extra, though by no means double, pay.

The extension of education is to involve increasing primary-school enrolments by 32 per cent in the five-year period (but nearly 20 per cent is needed merely to keep pace with population growth); *Plan Básico* (lower secondary level, or 7th to 9th grades) by 76 per cent; and *Bachillerato* (upper secondary) by 88 per cent. Thus perhaps 24 per cent of children will now be finishing primary school instead of 20 per cent; 12 or 13 per cent will be going to 9th grade instead of 8 per cent in 1967; and almost 7 per cent will finish secondary school instead of 4 per cent. This plan fits in well with the image of development as a gradual expansion of the modern sector of the economy and the middle class which mans it.

It is officially stated that

> the new focus which the Government of El Salvador wishes to give
> to systematic education is founded on the universally acknowl-
> edged fact that nine years of study are the minimum desirable
> basis for education and the preparation of a man for active life.[24]

The practical implication is that *Plan Básico* is to be merged with
primary schooling in a single nine-year programme of study. If, as
a result of this, 9th-grade certificates come to be regarded as necessary
qualifications for the jobs for which 6th-grade certificates now
suffice, it will mean that as the proportion of pupils completing six
grades goes up from 20 to 25 or 30 per cent, they will no longer find
that they have passed even the first effective hurdle, and the proportion passing that hurdle, at 9th grade, will be once again at around
the 20 per cent level. To the extent that certificates merely serve to
indicate to employers who has the ability and determination to get
through school, no gain will have been made.

The premise, however, is that an increased formal education will
enable its recipients to perform better in the economy, thus raising
its general level. At the moment, many of those who have formal
education qualifications, for instance in accountancy, and look for
employment for which their diplomas qualify them, find that these
jobs are already filled and they have to enter a position at a lower
level which does not call for the knowledge they have been taught.
It is presumed that during their last years in the education system
they will also have picked up ideas and ways of approaching
problems which will be valuable in any job; but this must depend on
the extent to which education provides an understanding of general
principles rather than a learning of specific procedures and facts.

It is the second aim of the Reform to make this kind of qualitative
improvement in the content of education at school. From the lofty
principles proclaimed, themselves enunciated with a considerable
degree of the formalism which they might have condemned,[25] one
can nevertheless pick out the goal 'to develop creative capacity, in
the speculative order as well as in the practical' as offering a real
promise of a change of orientation.

In contrast to the number of reports on quantitative aspects of
education in El Salvador, there is no real study of its actual content
at classroom level. In the absence of such a study, the flavour can
perhaps be illustrated by an example. Ricardo was a bright boy of
fourteen when I asked him about his schooling in 1966. Some of his
answers were quite unremarkable, but they are all included here
to give a balanced perspective.

The previous year he had attended the 6th grade of a primary school run by Spanish priests of the Marian order. There, he said, he did arithmetic, grammar, natural science, and sacred history. Now he was at one of the largest state secondary schools, in the first year. This year was divided into four classes on the basis of height. Class A were the smallest, class B – Ricardo's class – the next smallest, D the tallest. Each class had fifty or more pupils. There were five one-hour periods in the morning, Monday to Friday, while in the afternoon there were one, two, three, or no classes on the different days of the week.

Ricardo gave his views on his eleven school subjects.

*Spanish* is a continuation of what he previously knew as 'grammar': largely a matter of learning the parts of speech. When asked about essays, he said that for Independence Day they had to write something, while another time they were taken to a monument and had to copy down the epitaph and draw the scene, and could add some extra sentences if they wanted. They were not as yet taught any literature – later on in the first year he thought they would be taught something about Central American authors only.

Of *English* and *Drawing* he gave no details. (One might mention at this point that one printed textbook of English which was still generally used by state schools in 1970 had elementary errors on almost every page; an Association of Teachers of English was founded in that year, and it is to be expected that the much higher standards represented by those who formed this group will become more general in the future.)

In *Mathematics*, he had done no algebra yet. Geometry they had begun at primary school but it was now getting more complicated.

For *Geography*, at primary school they were doing such things as drawing a map of Europe – the teachers were Europeans – with all the rivers and mountains, and the capitals, but not the frontiers. Now they were studying physical geography only.

*History*, which started with evolution (Darwin's theory taught as a theory), had in eight months gone through Chinese, Indian, Middle Eastern, and Greek civilizations, and was now on the expansion of the Arabs after Mohammed. The sort of thing taught was the names of all fifteen of Mohammed's wives, which they had to learn by heart.

For *Biology* in first year they studied the plants – botany – but without any practical information on how to grow them. In the second year they would do zoology, and in the third, human anatomy.

In *Music*, one teacher had been teaching the members of the choir, of which Ricardo was one, about the human voice and its capabilities, but then he fell ill and the other teacher started off on a very different track: about Aztec music and how it was passed on from father to son, etc. Those with good voices were chosen for the choir (and could not refuse); then they had to practise twice a week – at the same time the others had either to listen or to do something equally boring – and every couple of months or so there was a ceremony at which the choir sang. The choir included only boys from first and second years, and a few tenors from third year.

Under *Manual Arts*, three separate things were taught: practical drawing (they had been doing elementary architectural drawing); woodwork – for this the pupils had to pool money to buy saws and other equipment, which they were then using to make little ornaments; perhaps they would make chairs or other large objects when they got more money together; and electricity, in which class Ricardo had learned to make electric installations and had installed a doorbell in his house.

*Morality, Urbanity, and Civics* were three subjects in one. I asked what these three subjects were, and Ricardo wrote:

Morality: manner of relating ourselves to people;

Urbanity: good treatment between people;

Civics: not to ill-treat, but to care for, public property.

What was actually taught in the class covered quite a wide range, from the physical dangers of 'deviations' (which possibly meant masturbation), to the prohibition on eating beef in India, and again to Mohammed and his wives, this time with a story about how Mohammed when dying tricked people by putting a lot of magnets in his roof and having his bed (an iron bed) untied with him in it, so that he was 'miraculously' lifted to the ceiling.

As for *Physical Education*, only the members of the football and basketball teams got any, and they were a minority. They had to buy their own gear, which discouraged those who were uncertain of getting a place.

It is proposed to improve the quality of education through 'study programmes' – books of suggestions for teachers; using school inspectors in the role of constructive helpers rather than simply to maintain control; and a large-scale programme of educational television. The television project, which has received considerable publicity, is supported by American A.I.D. funds (in 1971, a loan of $1\frac{1}{2}$ million dollars). It will serve in part to give information and suggestions to practising teachers, but its main purpose is to overcome the bottleneck of a lack of qualified teachers in the rapid expansion of the *Plan Básico* level (7th to 9th grades). The supposition is that primary-school teachers can be rapidly prepared in one-year courses to conduct classes at this higher level, if half the class time consists of a television programme and the teacher merely has to explain unclear points and elaborate on the content of the programme. Thus funds are being spent on television equipment which would otherwise necessarily have to go on a more extensive programme of teacher-training. The equipment has to be purchased from abroad so that the loaned money, or much of it, 'leaves the country twice', once in the form of payment for equipment and again as loan repayment.

Whether the projected change in the role of the school inspector will have much practical effect is somewhat doubtful, given that existing personnel are retained. The role which he sometimes, if not generally, plays at the present time can be gathered from the claim made by the Left that

> The inspection staff has been made up mainly of persons without the capacity and preparation that the position demands. Its work has been above all of a policing type and has served to keep the teacher fearful in respect of his grievances, as well as to influence him politically toward the official party. At the present time, due to the consciousness of group struggle aroused among teachers, the inspectors can no longer fulfil their improper political and repressive functions as before.[26]

It should not be omitted that inspectors are usually male, while two-thirds of rural schoolteachers are female, and that the position of power is widely said by teachers to be used for sexual advantage.

The new study programme for the first grade of primary school, the first in the series intended to improve the content of teaching, has been printed.[27] It has 167 pages full of practical suggestions for teachers. It is difficult to summarize such a carefully-prepared document without the danger of distortion, but the main impression one notes is of a tension between, on the one hand, the desire to encourage children to observe things for themselves and to relate school learning to experience outside the school, and, on the other, a continued emphasis on correct form, on propriety and neatness, and on respect for authority.

To elaborate a little: teachers are recommended frequently to take the children on outings in the neighbourhood and to places of interest from monuments to factories. The children, who are mainly aged seven, are to build up a model of their community with little houses, trees, and volcanoes on a table of sand or on the ground. Suggestions are given to teachers on how to train children in the uses of literacy: by collecting and examining letters, telegrams, news-papers, notices, and documents, and composing some of these things for themselves. But correctness of form is emphasized here, as it is even where the aim is to evoke non-verbal methods of communica-tion, for example mime and onomatopoeic sounds. The suggestion given to teachers reads: 'Orient the pupils to pronounce well, for example, the sound of the wind and of the rain . . . make the necessary corrections'. Then teachers are throughout reminded constantly to evaluate (an evaluation which apparently counts in whether or not the child will be admitted to the next grade at the end of the year) how much progress each child is making in the development of orderly habits and attitudes of respect. Respect is to be encouraged toward the teacher himself, to parents, 'distinguished persons in the community', the security forces, and of course the patriotic symbols, which are to be 'venerated'. It should also be mentioned that many rural schools are located on *haciendas* or *fincas*, whose owners have traditionally paid the teacher's salary under a legal obligation dating back to the early *encomienda*, and that the atmosphere at the school depends very much on the attitude of the local landowner and his relations with the school-teacher. But it should also be mentioned that a number of rural school-teachers do much more than merely give classes to the children: they try to foster the progress of the community in many other ways. They could constitute the basis of a rural organization for self-development at grass-roots level; but this depends on a favourable national political situation and local distribution of power. They can do little at present, especially where landowners are antagonistic.

In the second half of the 1960s there was a considerable growth of militancy among many teachers in a demand for general social reforms as well as improvements for teachers themselves, and the profession was divided between a pro-government association and the revolutionary *Asociación Nacional de Educadores Salvadoreños* (ANDES: 'walk'). The government emerged victorious from its confrontation with ANDES in 1968, but the organization survived as one of the few organs of opposition penetrating into the rural areas.

The line of criticism taken by ANDES on the government's Educational Reform is that it is a mere publicity effort, that the reality is a closing of teacher-training colleges, which will reduce the number of new teachers and hence increase the average class size, and that, in general, the human factor is given no importance in the reform plans, neither in giving adequate preparation to teachers at any level, nor in paying them adequately or giving them reasonable living conditions.[28]

A more fundamental objection, perhaps, is that the system remains one of treating knowledge and information as a scarce resource which individuals possess and use for their own advantage, only imparting it to others in small doses and in return for rewards in money and status. Whereas in commerce people do best for themselves by monopolizing information itself, in other fields including teaching people do best by monopolizing at least the right to exchange the information for a reward, through paper certificates of schooling completed, and through the encouragement of a mystique of the teacher which finds one of its expressions in the respect for the correct form and the flowery written language which he masters.

Knowledge and information are not intrinsically a scarce resource: they can be imparted and multiplied indefinitely without diminishing their value in use to their possessor, except their monopoly value. But very frequently the value of knowledge to its possessor consists precisely in the fact that comparatively few other people possess it. This is one of the basic reasons why many educational systems, including the Salvadorean, are constructed as they are. If it were not for this, there would be no reason to carry out testing to limit the number of people going on to the next educational stage. Nobody would attend a class at a higher level than his understanding warranted if he did not get a certificate at the end, if his motivation were the acquisition of the knowledge for its own sake or for the sake of the use he could make of the knowledge itself as opposed to the piece of paper proclaiming his possession of it. And in that case, there would be more demand for the kind of knowledge that is valuable in itself or relevant to the needs of the milieu, in contrast to the pursuit, as is largely the case at present, of that knowledge which the teachers want to test.

The present position is similar in all countries where people are paid according to qualifications – radical departures appear to have been made in China particularly since the Cultural Revolution – but it is in those underdeveloped countries like El Salvador where the rewards for those with educational qualifications are many times the income of those without, and where knowledge is particularly scarce and monopolized, that most effort is put into gaining formal qualifications by learning the correct bits of knowledge, and that correspondingly less effort is put into the acquisition of the ability to think of new solutions to problems.

## University Education

University education is not under the control of the Ministry of Education at all, nor under that of the government except in the last resort, through denial of funds or physical occupation. The University of El Salvador has undergone a process of modernization and reform beginning in 1950, when militant student activity at the time of the drawing-up of the country's constitution of that year led to the establishment of a degree of student power within it: since 1951 the deans of faculties and the rector, who serve four-year terms, have been elected by an assembly consisting of two representatives elected by the academic staff of each faculty, two by the graduates' associations of each faculty, and two by the students of each faculty; there is no re-election for a second term.

The reform gathered momentum slowly in the 1950s. Most faculties still suffered from the rather poor standard of much of the teaching, and the lack of research, that resulted from the situation whereby almost all staff and many students were only part-time, and the staff often gave more attention to their more lucrative professional activities outside the university. Two early achievements of the reform, however, were the founding in 1950 of a research institute, the *Instituto Tropical de Investigaciones Científicas*, whose valuable work (in the 1950s and early 1960s), mostly done by visiting German scientists, was published in its journal *Comunicaciones*, and about 1954 the overhaul of the Medical Faculty, largely with American funds and advice, making it efficient and highly respected.

From the period of Fabio Castillo's rectorship, 1963–67, there has been a re-emphasis both on thorough reform and on finding Salvadorean solutions rather than depending on foreign expertise. By 1966 the majority of the teaching staff were employed full time, and most of the faculties had moved to a new campus site or *Ciudad Universitaria*: the atmosphere had been transformed. By 1971 almost all the teaching was being done and some residential accommodation was provided in new buildings on the campus. The standards of teaching are undoubtedly much improved, although not surprisingly there have been accusations that dismissals and appointments have been made on political and personal grounds rather than purely for quality of teaching. To solve the problem that many students must also work for a living, a flexible system has been introduced whereby it is possible for some to accumulate 'course credits' slowly and to attend classes held in the evening, while others proceed faster and full-time. The former preponderance of 'traditional' subjects – law, medicine (with dentistry and pharmacology), and engineering – has been complemented and balanced by fast-growing faculties of Economics (founded in 1946) and Humanities (founded in 1948 and including such departments as psychology, journalism, and education). Branches of the university have been opened in Santa Ana and San Miguel to teach some of the subjects especially at initial levels.

Largely because of disquiet among some sectors of the economic élite and of the Church over the 'Marxist bias' of the university, a private Catholic University was opened in 1966, also in San Salvador, under the name *Universidad Centroamericana José Simeón Cañas*. (Cañas moved the decree abolishing slavery in 1824.) It has begun with three faculties: Economics, Industrial Engineering, and 'Sciences of Man and Nature'.

## Health

El Salvador suffers from all the health problems of a hot and fairly humid country where all living organisms multiply fast and the consciousness of the need for combating flies and other sources of infection is, in general, very low. In rural areas, malnutrition and intestinal parasites are the normal condition. This state of affairs is closely linked to the prevailing poverty and inequality of wealth and income.

There are five broad classes of medical provision, each corresponding to a level on the elongated scale of inequality.

At the top, unless one counts separately the visits which the wealthy make to the United States for treatment, is the private practice of doctors, dentists, and qualified nurses within the country. This level is for those who can afford the scale of fees ranging up from the typical ₡25 for a consultation with a doctor. The treatment is usually very good; many of the doctors have gone abroad for specialization, and they have an economic interest in retaining their paying clients, and establishing a reputation. Private health insurance schemes are not highly developed.

Second, there is treatment through the social security institution ISSS; this was created in 1954 to cater for the growing 'new middle class', particularly in San Salvador, of those who were regularly employed in white-collar or well-paying manual jobs, and who found the treatment offered to all by the Ministry of Health inadequate, but could hardly afford private fees.[29] It now covers about 100,000 employees and their families.[30] With a contribution from the employer[31] as well as from the employee, and additional subsidy from the state, the funds available to the ISSS per person under its coverage, and hence the quality of attention offered, are roughly equivalent to the British National Health Service.[32] Alongside the ISSS there are now the beginnings of a parallel service for government employees, with the building of the *Administración Nacional de Telecomunicaciones* (ANTEL) hospital in 1969–70, catering for the personnel of the telephone and telegraph service and of the Ministry of Education.

The third level, at which most attention is concentrated in practically all discussions of medical provision in El Salvador, is that

of the Ministry of Health. Its network of services is free to all: it has
evolved historically from the free charity hospitals for the poor which
existed as early as the sixteenth century.[33] Free as it is, the service
suffers from lack of resources. As of 1962, ₡10 per inhabitant were
spent in the central region around the capital; but only ₡6 in the
western region around Santa Ana; ₡1.50 in the region centred on
San Vicente, and ₡2 in the eastern region of San Miguel.[34] By 1971
the national average had reached the ₡10 figure,[35] in comparison
with ₡5.50 in 1962, but regional disparities were still very much in
evidence.

The lack of resources is translated into long queues for treatment
at out-patients clinics, and consequently extremely brief and superficial consultations with doctors. In 1965, there were only 650 doctors,
175 dentists, and about 750 qualified nurses in the country. About
eighty doctors per year are prepared by the medical faculty of the
university, while some others receive their first degrees abroad. In
1965, only 209 of the 650 doctors had a full-time post in the national
system, while many others served part-time.[36] Despite these small
numbers, the Ministry of Health revolves around the doctors. The
preparation of para-medical personnel, capable of carrying a reasonable standard of treatment into the rural areas and able to devote
more time to each case because of their larger numbers, is not undertaken on any significant scale while resources continue to be chan-
nelled into the expensive training of a comparatively small number of
doctors. Use is, however, made of the medical students before they
are given their doctorate. They have to serve in the public system for
a year.

The body of doctors undoubtedly acts on the whole as a conservative force hindering the development of innovations such as the
training of para-medical workers. This conservatism has its greatest
effect at the level of the fourteen hospitals which take the main part
of the funds allocated by the state to health. It is the conservatism of
an entrenched hierarchy which is comfortable operating in the old
ways. The hospitals are autonomous, and jealous of their autonomy:
the director of each hospital appears to be under more influence or
pressure from the other doctors than from the Ministry of Health.
The great power of doctors within the hospitals tends to lead to
inefficiency and time-wasting. They frequently arrive late without
rebuke, least of all from the long uncomplaining queue of poor out-
patients, and there is a chain-reaction of ill-organized work which
affects the medical students, nurses, and other personnel.[37] It could
even be said more generally that it is the elevated position of doctors
which prevents a more adequate treatment of illness, at least among
the poor. Where the patient has no social position giving him a

countervailing power to expect or demand adequate treatment, the degree of care and attention given by the doctor depends only on his own conscience; and while this may be admirable in many cases, it is no substitute. Moreover, as elsewhere, doctors press for the spending of money on expensive training, equipment, and luxuriously appointed new hospitals, all of which are appropriate for a wealthier country, but are not the allocation of funds which can make the greatest impression on the population's general level of health for which the Salvadorean Ministry of Health caters.

So there are many for whom the Ministry caters only partially. Some additional provision at the level of formally trained medical personnel is provided by charitable organizations – run in the main by nuns or by ladies of the upper social strata. The Society of Doctors' Wives, for instance, has built a modern clinic and nutrition centre for poor children in a mainly shanty area of San Salvador. Nuns have a thriving dental clinic in another part of the capital.

However, this is a relatively small contribution in comparison with the need, and it does little to correct the overwhelming concentration of medical services in one or two large towns; at the 1961 census, no less than two-thirds of the doctors lived in the capital alone, three-quarters either in San Salvador or the second city, Santa Ana. At the other extreme, the whole Department of Morazán registered only one doctor. The fourth general level of treatment goes some way toward redressing this balance: the treatment provided privately by the number of people who have had some contact with formal medicine, but who have not completed any formal training. Large numbers of people have some medical knowledge, and they use it freely – there is a demand for it. Assistants in chemists' shops, for example, only a minority of whom have formal training, nevertheless are generally expected to give medical advice, and appear typically to acquire considerable skill in doing so. There are far more untrained nurses practising than there are trained ones: they are much in demand particularly for the giving of injections. One of the most frequent notices seen in neighbourhoods of almost every type of housing is 'Injections given here'. There is a strong belief, not only among the uneducated, in the efficacy of injections, and they are given for almost any complaint including the common cold. They are said by some to 'go directly to the blood', and in any case partake of the prestige of anything modern.

In earlier years, before the 1960s, it was common throughout Central America for entrance into the medical schools of the universities to be unrestricted except for the requirement of the secondary-school certificate – and this, it is clear, could frequently be obtained, as is still sometimes the case today, by keeping on the right side of the

Catholic fathers who run about half the schools, by keeping the
religious observances and contributing financially to the many small
funds for which contributions are requested. In this situation, the
drop-out rate in the medical schools was very high, only about 15 per
cent of the entrants eventually completing their degree.[38] The drop-
outs, who may have given up their studies through lack of application, of funds to keep them while studying, or of ability, form a large
group of partly trained people, many of whom are today practising
medicine at this fourth, 'sub-official', level. In dentistry, parallel to
the 'official' training at the Odontological Faculty of the university,
there is still a quite separate apprenticeship into the trade of practical
dentistry, following similar lines to apprenticeship into skilled
manual crafts such as carpentry – possibly surviving better in the
current situation of decline of such apprenticeships. It will give an
idea of the importance of these dental practitioners that in the
Department of San Vicente no dentist was registered by the 1961
census; only those with the 'official' training and higher status could
be entered as dentists in the census. In 1970–71 there were, I was told,
four 'sub-official' dental practitioners in the departmental capital of
San Vicente alone, and others in the more important other towns of
the department. The practitioner who gave me this information (not
himself practising in San Vicente) also remarked quite revealingly
about the relationship between medical man and client which can
exist at this fourth level. He has periodic bouts of drunkenness, a
failing extremely frequent in El Salvador, and it was in tacit reference
to his alcoholism that he said that he was not very reliable. For
instance, he might not have a set of dentures ready the day he had
promised. The patients, who often came from villages several miles
distant, knew him well and did not object, but simply returned
another day, because they liked his work.

    The fifth and last level of medical provision is that of the folk
healers, who undoubtedly account for a very high proportion of all
treatment in the rural areas, but whose practice is difficult to
investigate because laws last renewed in 1895 and still in force pro-
hibit the exercise of medicine without a title, except that where there
is no doctor a chemist 'or other honourable person' can hold consultations and make prescriptions. This law is applied against the
healers, whom the doctors generally regard as harmful enemies
rather than as potential colleagues in the fight against disease, who
could be taught some modern specific treatments, and who may
already be at least as effective in the curing of psychosomatic
complaints.

    Healers can be roughly divided[39] – though each one has his own
combination of skills and there are undoubtedly local variations

which have not been studied – into five categories. First are the curers (*curanderos*), the 'general practitioners' who are experts in the traditional folk medicine of the region, and who use as remedies various substances of animal, vegetable, and mineral origin. Secondly, the 'suckers' (*sobadores*), who treat mainly by massage such ills as stiff neck, bones out of joint, fractures, and inflammations. Thirdly, the 'patchers' (*parcheros*), who treat wounds or other specific parts of the body which are afflicted, using balms and ointments. Fourthly, the herbalists (*especieros*), who operate more openly and without persecution, displaying their wares at markets, including those in the capital; most customers ask which of the dozens of herbs on display is best for treating their symptoms. The herbs, a few of which come from as far afield as other continents, range in price per item from about 5¢ to 75¢, so this cure is often the cheapest of all. Fifthly, the witch-doctors (*hechiceros*), who invoke supernatural spirits, and who are the most elusive of all, apparently preferring to live outside the villages in order to encourage an air of mystery and awe for their powers. No doubt a study would reveal further separate types of healer using supernatural or magical methods, to judge at least from the variety of words used for them; but it can be said without doubt that witchcraft and the beliefs associated with it have none of the importance that they have in Africa, for instance, or even in some parts of the Americas.

The poor rural population is very ready to try both folk healers and treatment at the higher levels of medical provision if they can obtain it. Indeed, in general it can be said that people will go as high up the scale of levels of treatment as they can afford although some do prefer the folk healers with whom they feel at ease. There is some competition between the 'official' levels of formally trained personnel and the practitioners at the lower levels, and this means, for instance, that a chemist in a provincial town may oppose the establishment of a Ministry of Health clinic. The folk healers have no means of expressing any antagonism they feel towards the doctors effectively.[40]

## Housing and the Family

Apart from education, health, and social security, the only other major areas in which the government promotes 'social progress', as understood in distinction from 'economic progress' in the 1968–72 development plan, are the provision of housing and of piped water and sewage disposal.

There is little to say about the latter, beyond quoting the official statement that as of 1967, four-fifths of the 'urban' population and one-fifth of the rural had piped water and sewage facilities,[41] but with the reservation that what is counted as provision may be as little as having a tap somewhere in the neighbourhood. Where one of the most typical forms of urban housing, the *mesón*, consists by definition of a number of rooms – at least five – each let to a different family but without individual taps or toilets in the rooms, it is clear that many of those who are reported in the statistics as being supplied with piped water and sanitary facilities are, in reality, worse off than many a person who draws water, say, from his own well and has built himself a toilet over a hole in the ground.

The government's aim is to extend the provision of water to rural and urban populations, and of sewage facilities to all urban centres, through its national agency, *Administración Nacional de Acueductos y Alcantarillados* (ANDA). The one case where ANDA is clearly reluctant to provide facilities is that of the shanty neighbourhoods. Government policy with regard to these squatter settlements and areas of land where private landowners have allowed poor people to put up their own shacks but charge a land rent of ₡5 or ₡10 per month, is that it would be desirable to eradicate them. The corollary is that it would be a mistake to provide services such as water since this would encourage the squatters to stay and to make their dwellings permanent. The policy is successful: the huts are usually not much improved, the inhabitants never feel secure even after ten or more years on the site, and it remains quite easy to move them off. For instance, the landowner had no need to use force when he wished to clear a population of over 2,000 from 'Colonia Tutunichapa', a squatment which occupied a central position in San Salvador until it was removed in the late 1960s. The people were merely told they would have to go, and they went.

The government has not as yet cleared any settlements of comparable size on national (publicly owned) land; but neither has security of tenure been given. If it were, it is likely that the condition of the shacks would be improved in such a way as to transform the slums gradually into neighbourhoods as solid as many others, though perhaps remaining more crowded.

The shanty settlements began to make their appearance as more than just isolated shacks around 1948–50, though poor people have always put up straw huts to live in, usually at the edge of towns where land was available. Nowadays, usually, they are crudely made of *bahareque* (mud held together by canes) walls and tiled roofs, though materials which are even less adequate, such as flattened tins and even cardboard, are also much in evidence. They are found principally in San Salvador and its suburbs, but also in other towns such as Santa Ana and Santa Tecla. Many of the inhabitants have moved there from *mesones*. In going from a *mesón* room to a shack one builds for oneself or buys for about $24 (£10) to $120 (£50), one is not necessarily going to a less hygienic environment. Some *mesón* rooms are windowless hovels with mud floors, although at the other extreme there are some which are clean, well-furnished, and quite attractive. One is probably going to a place where one will feel less constricted in space and less bound by the petty restrictions of the *mesón*-owners over, for instance, the use of 'their' water or electricity for lighting. For those with larger families, the greater amount of room usually available in the shanty neighbourhoods is likely to make life a little easier; and it may be the only possible solution to their housing problem, since in recent years with the demand high, many *mesón*-owners will not let rooms to large families, and other accommodation is too expensive. In particular, those who want to live in various larger family groups – perhaps two sisters and their children, or three-generation families of any kind – tend to gravitate to the shanty neighbourhoods where they can build their dwellings together or in the way that suits them; often in such cases it is impossible to decide whether a structure constitutes a separate 'house' or not.

So there is a close correspondence between the types of housing in the city and patterns of family life. Government housing is mainly for households consisting only of a couple and their children, with perhaps an old parent. Only the Church is very much concerned to foster formal marriage ceremonies, but the government and 'polite society' show a great concern that unions, whether formalized or not, should be stable and 'regular', and this concern is frequently translated into penalizing those who do not adopt this pattern. One result is that the proportion of simple 'nuclear' households on government housing estates is much higher than elsewhere. In the *mesón* there are also a number of regular stable families, but there are more households which reflect the fact that in El Salvador as a whole, both in town and country, the ties that bind the partners to each other are not very strong.[42]

The weakness of the marital bond is probably because there is, among the great majority who have no property to inherit, no particular reason for people who no longer get along with one another to stay together. There is no effective pressure from their families or from public opinion in any community or group to which they belong. That is not to say that the very frequent separations are all by mutual agreement; it is rather that there is nothing to prevent a man from leaving a woman, nor a woman from leaving a man, if they wish to. A woman can earn a living for herself, even if encumbered by children, not much poorer than a husband can give her, unless he has a regular job; and the independence which this position gives them is valued by some women who do not want to form permanent unions. Men are even less tied. At the same time, the social spheres of working-class men and women remain, for most couples, quite widely separated, so that the conjugal relationship does not often have the strongly companionate quality which tends to draw the partners to remain together by choice.

Although formal, legal marriages do sometimes break up, while unformalized unions are often stable and permanent, the percentage of marriages formalized by a civil ceremony is, for any social group or category of people in society, a good index of the stability of unions in that group, compared with the rest of society. In the country as a whole, about half the marriages are legal, while there is a tendency for some people to enter free unions first but to get married later, so that below the age of thirty there is a predominance of free unions, whereas after that age there is a majority of marriages. The only geographical region where the pattern is strikingly different is that comprising the Departments of Chalatenango, Cabañas, and Cuscatlán, where legal marriages outnumber free unions by about 4 to 1.[43] This area is also one where there are relatively more independent landholding peasants, and it is likely that the inheritance of property makes marriage there more of a contractual relationship, gives parents more control over their children, and provides an incentive for families to stay together.

The city of San Salvador also has about equal numbers of free unions and marriages. Here, the percentage of free unions rises from virtually none among the professional groups (though there are divorces and there are mistresses) to about 30 per cent among white-collar workers, 40 per cent among sales employees, 60 per cent among skilled workers, and 70 per cent among unskilled workers.[44]

Not surprisingly then, the *mesones* contain large numbers of women bringing up their children, at least for the time being, without help, or with limited help from a man who only comes to visit. With underemployment and widespread alcoholism, many of the men who do live together with their wives are more of a hindrance than a help. Then there are the very many cases where a couple living together are bringing up not only the children they have had together but also children that one or both partners – most often the women – have had by a previous union.

Frequently, though, several people who have grown up together, perhaps sisters, prefer to stay together to bring up their children, with or without their own marital partners. These larger family groups cannot easily be accommodated in *mesones*, and if they cannot afford their own house, then they are likely to turn to the shanty squatment. These neighbourhoods are by no means the dens of criminals and prostitutes they are sometimes thought to be. Indeed, such groups prefer to remain closer to the city centre where the action is; not that the incidence of crime for gain is very great, nor any part of the city dangerous.[45]

The government's response to the housing situation has been, first of all, fully to acknowledge its gravity. The Development Plan document for 1965–69, for instance, contains a thorough indictment of a state of affairs which has not changed in any fundamental respect since it was written:

> The housing situation of El Salvador is worsening annually through the growth of population, the gradual deterioration of existing dwellings, the low purchasing power of the population, and the lack of adequate finance to build new houses in sufficient quantities. In the urban areas, 28 new dwellings per day are needed on the basis of population growth and rebuilding alone, but only 8 are built. The overcrowding is so alarming that of every hundred families about 60 cook, eat, and sleep in a single room per family. . . . A great majority of rural dwellings consists of huts of deficient construction, lacking facilities for drinking water or elimination of excreta, comprising a single room of approximately 30 square metres characterized by lack of light and ventilation and serving for all the needs of the family. The roof is of tile or straw, the walls of *adobe* or straw or very rarely of *bahareque*; they lack a flat ceiling and the floor is of earth. The insalubrity and over-crowding are well known. A great part of the deficiencies noted are due to the fact that our *campesinos*, because of their low educational level and low economic level, resign themselves to living in such traditional huts.[46]

Having acknowledged the problem, the next stage in the government's response is to give it spuriously exact statistical treatment. Thus it is stated, on arbitrary and even illogical assumptions, that the housing deficit in urban areas was 132,000 at the time of the 1961 census and grew to 173,000 in 1967; that 41 per cent of urban houses are in no condition to be lived in, while 80 per cent of rural dwellings are deficient, etc. The use of these exact figures seems to make it easier for the government to turn to sponsoring the building of housing for the middle classes rather than the poorer sections of the population which are really those in need. The pursuit of distant numerical goals is postponed to a period beyond the immediate Five-Year Plan or Presidential term, and the immediate task becomes merely an expansion of existing government-subsidized construction, which is overwhelmingly for the middle classes, especially if the middle classes are taken to include that minority of manual workers who have regular, high-paid jobs.

Up to 1964, the government's housing agency (IVU) had built only some 8,000 dwellings since its minuscule beginning in the 1930s. It was then hoped that 11,700[47] would be added in the next three years, but the reality was 4,200.[48] Most of the occupants of these houses and apartments are office workers, office messengers, teachers, etc., but there are also accountants, professionals, even army officers on the one hand, and skilled mechanics and railway-workers on the other. The average rent or hire-purchase instalment is ₡35 per month, with a range from ₡17 to ₡150 or so. The average family income of the occupants is in the region of ₡250 a month. Most of the new housing built by IVU is in the upper part of this price range. Hence the occupants tend to have high incomes. Indeed the absurd position was reached with one large development erected on the outskirts of the capital in 1967–69, Colonia Zacamil, that many apartments remained empty because those who could afford to pay the rent had other more desirable alternatives in private housing.

There are a number of voices raised in favour of building for the poorest sections of the population. In the mid-1960s the Legislative Assembly passed a resolution recommending IVU to build apartment blocks for the inhabitants of the shanties, but the recommendation was dismissed as unrealistic by the institution. However, there have been some moves towards putting up 'minimal housing' for the poor, beginning with 'temporary' housing constructed by IVU for some of the victims of the 1965 earthquake, which became permanent in fact since they were far superior houses to the shanties or the *mesones*. Later, a pilot plan was carried to completion to house some other shanty-dwellers, and a charitable association has been founded with this aim. As yet, however, this activity is far from keeping pace with the growth of that section of San Salvador's population which is too poor to pay for anything better. Meanwhile, catering for those who can afford something much better, a government subsidy is being given for private house-building, through a national housing finance corporation (the *Financiera Nacional de la Vivienda* or FNV), for houses costing up to ₡25,000.[49]

In summary, one can say that El Salvador is at the moment following a development policy which, by encouraging the building of modern factories with expensive imported equipment (rather than a progressive mechanization of existing processes using existing skills and personnel), tends to impoverish rather than enrich the majority of the population, but enriches the top 5 to 10 per cent and draws a certain proportion of others up from the masses to form a 'new middle class' of people whose relatively scarce skills (or whose connections or luck in landing a regular job) enable them to earn an income of more than about ₡200 a month. Less than 40 per cent of the urban population earns this amount: almost certainly less than 20 per cent of the total population of El Salvador, since the new middle class is an almost exclusively urban phenomenon. For the rest, the prevailing wage-rate in the capital for unskilled work is ₡3 a day; so that a man who can find work can earn about ₡90 a month; but some will take work at ₡60 a month if it is regular.

This is the effect of the kind of economic development being pursued by the government, and it is reinforced by its social policies. They tend to serve the middle class as already formed, as in the case of the housing provision, or help to select which individuals or families from the mass of the population are to be drawn up into the middle class.

## NOTES

[1] The data in this paragraph are calculated from *Boletín Estadístico* No 84 for Oct.–Dec. 1969. It would have been preferable to compare aggregate figures for various types of factories, but this was impossible because some of the data are missing from each of the compilations of statistics, so an example has to suffice.

[2] In 1970 the bakery workers' union, with the backing of FUSS, organized a strike as a result of which they succeeded in gaining a minimum wage of ₡3.20; the strike was, however, directed not so much against the immediate employers, themselves in the main not very well-off artisans, but mainly against the price charged for imported Canadian wheat. It appears that they succeeded in getting the government to negotiate a lower price.

[3] A commercial radio station, in early 1971, broadcast the information that there were 900,500 (*sic*) radio sets in El Salvador, each listened to by an average of two and a half persons each day (*Radio Sonora*, advertising claim).

[4] Like David Raynolds: op. cit.

[5] Miguel S. Wionczek calls it 'in large part fictitious' in 'La Inversión Privada Norteamericana y el Desarrollo de Mesoamérica', *Comercio Exterior*, Vol. XVIII, No 8 (Mexico, Banco Nacional de Comercio Exterior, Aug. 1968), 675, quoted André Gunder Frank: 'The Underdevelopment Policy of the United Nations in Latin America', NACLA Newsletter, Vol. III, No 8 (New York, North American Congress on Latin America, Dec. 1969), 9. Perhaps Jacobo Waiselfisz is wisest to offer two alternative apt names when he characterizes the process as a 'pseudo-industrialization or dependent industrialization' (op. cit.), 76.

[6] *Tercer Censo Industrial 1961* (Aug. 1966: San Salvador, Min. de Economía), 126ff. The figure includes administrative employees.

[7] *Boletín Estadístico*, No 85 for Jan.–Mar. 1970.

[8] *América en Cifras*, Vol. 2 (1963: Washington, Pan-American Union).

[9] Also by the activities of the government development agency *Instituto Salvadoreño de Fomento Industrial* (INSAFI), which lends at favourable rates for the purchase of machinery, etc. *El Crédito Agrícola*, Vol. I, 334. INSAFI has a wider role in industrial promotion, but the report cited charges it with insufficient dynamism and with having neglected these other activities. ibid., 346.

[10] Waiselfisz, op. cit., 73, 22, quoting government statistics.

[11] See, for instance, his *Celebration of Awareness* (1971: Doubleday, Garden City, N.Y.).

[12] Mélida Anaya Montes: 'Problemas de la Enseñanza de la Historia', *Educación*, Vol. 1, No 1 (1964: Univ. of El Salvador), 59–63.

[13] *Mensaje al magisterio nacional el 20 de septiembre de 1968*, in *Discursos del Señor Presidente de la República General Fidel Sánchez Hernández*, Tomo II, 56 (1969: San Salvador, Casa Presidencial).

[14] Budget figures in *Diario Oficial*, 23 Dec. 1970: total budget ₡351 million; to Education, ₡97 million.

[15] GNP at market prices estimated as ₡2,283 million in 1968, and provisionally as ₡2,382 million in 1969. CONAPLAN: *Indicadores*, 44.

[16] Ovidio Soto Blanco: *La Educación en Centroamérica* (Nov. 1968: San Salvador, ODECA), 108, Cuadro 30.

[17] Ministerio de Educación: 'Diagnóstico Estadístico y Proyecciones de la Educación Primaria en El Salvador', *Documentos de la Reforma Educativa*, No 1 (1970), 19.

[18] ibid., Cuadro H-3, following p. 42.

[19] From *Anuario Estadístico 1964*, showing figures for births in the year (1961) in which the census was taken, and age-specific mortality figures for 1964, which can be taken as representative of the years 1961–67.

[20] This may certainly be the main explanation of the discrepancy; but only if it happens in about half the cases of infant mortality that the birth of the child has been registered, but its death at an early age is not.

[21] 'Diagnóstico Estadístico', Anexo II, following p. 72.

[22] Rather like university degree ceremonies in Britain.

[23] Ministerio de Educación: 'Plan Quinquenal de Educación, Julio 1967–Junio 1972', *Documentos de la Reforma Educativa*, No 2 (1970), Cuadros resumenes, following p. 61.

[24] ibid., 34.

[25] See particularly the discussion of the 'ends, objectives, and goals' of the reform, in Min. de Educación: 'El Sistema Educativo', *Documentos de la Reforma Educativa*, No 3 (1970), 15–24. The quotation is from p. 22.

[26] José Mario López: 'Situación actual del maestro en la educación de El Salvador', *La Universidad*, Año 94, No 3–4 (May–Aug. 1969), 225.

[27] Ministerio de Educación: 'Programas de Estudio del Primer Grado de Educación Básica', *Documentos de la Reforma Educativa*, No 4 (1970).

[28] López, op. cit.

[29] Allwood Paredes, op. cit., 62.

[30] *Diario Oficial*, 23 Dec. 1970, 15230, 15234. ISSS = Instituto Salvadoreño del Seguro Social.

[31] In this connection, I was told by a shoemaker in 1966:

I had a workshop but what broke us small producers [i.e., finally, following the establishment of a large shoe factory] were the social security laws. I had 10 workers who earned ₡100 [per month]. Then I had to pay 5 per cent for social security, that is, ₡50 for the 10. And that's what bankrupted me, about 4 years ago. These expenditures can't be recovered in production. You don't have enough to pay the social security, and if you don't pay it they put you in jail. You should see how many workshops have been ruined like that. There were protests in the trade unions but the capitalists and the government got their way Osorio said the country had to industrialize.

[32] Allwood Paredes, op. cit., 56, 65, 151.

[33] In 1594 an earthquake destroyed the charity hospital of Santa Bárbara in San Salvador, and the crown was petitioned to grant an *encomienda* in perpetuity so that the tribute could be used to re-establish and maintain it. Document of 1595 printed in Barón Castro, *La Población de El Salvador*, 591.

[34] CONAPLAN: *Plan de la Nación*, Vol. II, 690.

[35] Budget allocations ₡39,105,130. *Diario Oficial*, 23 Dec. 1970, 14939.

[36] *Salud en El Salvador*, Año 1, No 10 (Jan. 1966).

[37] Arístides Palacios: 'Apreciaciones sobre organización en nuestros hospitales' *La Universidad*, Año 83 (1958), 313–18.

[38] Allwood Paredes, op. cit., 38–9.

[39] The account of healers draws heavily on the description of the situation in northern San Miguel department in Menandro Alcibíades Canelo: *Los Servicios Médicos Rurales y la Medicina Popular* (Dec. 1964: doctoral thesis in medicine, Univ. de El Salvador). Richard N. Adams, in *Cultural Surveys of Panama – Nicaragua – Guatemala – El Salvador – Honduras* (Dec. 1957: Washington, Pan American Sanitary

Bureau), 479–80, makes a somewhat different classification of curers; see also Edwin James: 'Concepts of sickness and practices of curing in the Cantón of El Jícaro, San Matías: a series of cases', in Adams, op. cit., 515–22.

[40] In his autobiographical work *Memoria en Dos Geografías* (1964: Mexico, Costa-Amic), 311–16, the Guatemalan writer Carlos Manuel Pellecer recounts an incident in which he humbles a folk healer by demonstrating to the whole village the superiority of modern medicine and the trickery of magic practices. Here, the reaction of the healer is to doubt his own powers, borrow from Pellecer a book on mechanics, and go off to become a tractor-driver. Probably, most folk healers respond to organized medicine with a mixture of hostility and feelings of inferiority.

[41] CONAPLAN: *Plan de Desarrollo Económico y Social 1968–1972*, Parte general, 74.

[42] I discuss these questions in ch. 6, 'Family Structure', of my Ph.D. dissertation.

[43] *Tercer Censo Nacional de Población 1961* (June 1965: San Salvador, Min. de Economía), Table 5, 54–66.

[44] Alastair White, op. cit., using a 10 per cent sample of 1961 census cards for San Salvador.

[45] There is, however, a much higher incidence of 'crimes of passion', often connected with drunkenness. Thus, there are more than five times as many arrests for homicide (1,313 in 1969, whole country) as there are deaths from traffic accidents (243); and more are arrested for causing bodily harm (5,760) than for all crimes against property (4,199). *Anuario Estadístico 1969*, Vol. V, 202, 205, 224.

[46] CONAPLAN: *Plan de la Nación*, Vol. II, 544, 553–4.

[47] ibid., 565, Cuadro XXII–10.

[48] CONAPLAN, *Plan de Desarrollo*, 74. IVU = Instituto de Vivienda Urbana (Urban Housing Institute). As for rural housing, the only government projects have been pilot projects carried out by the Rural Colonization Institute on its estates, which cover only about 3 per cent of the agricultural land.

[49] The approximate cost of various types of housing, including land, service roads, etc., is: for 'minimal housing', ₡2,000 or less; for single-family IVU housing ₡6,000; and for apartments ₡6,500. The FNV programme, intended to cover housing of 'medium' cost, i.e. between this last figure and ₡25,000, is largely financed by the United States A.I.D.

# Chapter 9

# The Outlook

---

IN THE PRESIDENTIAL ELECTION of 20 February 1972[1] the official party candidate won by only the narrowest of margins. Colonel Arturo Armando Molina, the chosen successor of General Fidel Sánchez Hernández, obtained, according to the final figures issued by the Electoral Council, a total of 334,600 votes as against the 324,756 accorded to the Christian Democrat opposition candidate, Napoleón Duarte. The difference, 9,844 votes or 1.3 per cent of those cast, was so small that it is very reasonable to suppose that the amount of direct electoral fraud carried out in provincial areas on behalf of the official candidate could have been decisive in assuring his victory. It was natural, anyway, that the opposition should feel cheated of power, since the early results from the capital gave Duarte a lead of no less than 62,000.

A few weeks were spent by the opposition in contesting the result and claiming fraud; then, at dawn on 25 March, the commander of a garrison in the capital, Colonel Benjamín Mejía, led an attempted *coup* on behalf of Duarte. President Sánchez Hernández was taken prisoner for a few hours, and Duarte announced the formation of a triumvirate to rule provisionally. However, the air force and other garrisons in the provinces remained on the side of *oficialismo*, and by the end of the day had restored the *status quo* in an action costing an estimated hundred lives, with a thousand wounded. It was announced in the next few days that seventy-eight persons were arrested[2] for participation in the plot: 46 members of the municipal police force of San Salvador, 7 other officers, and 25 civilians. The predominance of municipal policemen among the accused is of interest, given the dual subordination of the municipal police both to the mayor and to the Minister of Defence. (The new mayor, Duarte's successor, Carlos Herrera Rebollo, was abroad at the time of the abortive *coup*.)

At the time of writing, Colonel Molina has not yet taken office as the new President. He was Sánchez Hernández's secretary and had no personal political base. His programme was summed up in his statement issued after being declared the winner of the election: 'I shall continue the policies of Fidel Sánchez. No communist will participate in my government. There will be no Soviet embassy under my Presidency'.

But things can never be quite the same after this election. The basis of the régime was that voting in the provinces could be kept sufficiently massively behind the official party to outweigh the far greater popularity of the opposition in the capital; and the massive rural vote for the government was only possible because of massive interference with political communication. At the 1972 election, the opposition showed that it had already all but overcome this huge obstacle. The process was bound to continue. How it has changed after the *coup* remains to be seen. It is true that the opposition was in a particularly favourable position for this election. The PDC, MNR and UDN came together in a United Opposition Front behind the popular candidature of Duarte, while the official party was suffering the electoral consequence of the decision to dismiss General Medrano.[3] An *ad hoc* right-wing organization was formed to advance his candidature for the Presidency, the *Frente Unido Democrático Independiente*, and polled 10 per cent of the votes. In addition, the PPS, with its own right-wing candidate, took 3 per cent. If Medrano had been able to muster a somewhat higher percentage of the vote, the split between the government and the authoritarian Right might have allowed the liberal opposition to obtain the highest number of votes. This might not have been enough to assure Duarte of office, however. In the event of no candidate gaining an absolute majority, the election passes to the Legislative Assembly, and here the PCN still held a comfortable majority, 36 seats to 16. In the event, this majority was used to endorse the election of Molina. If, however, Duarte had been ahead of Molina on the recorded popular vote, the situation would have been one of crisis in which there would have been a strong public demand for the deputies to confirm the people's choice.

Such a situation would have been without precedent in El Salvador. In Guatemala, where similar electoral rules apply, Julio César Méndez Montenegro won the 1966 election against two colonels, because there was a split between the government party and the extreme Right, while the liberal and left opposition united behind Méndez. However, the parallel is not exact, because in addition to winning the most popular votes in the direct balloting for President, the party of Méndez also won, in the concurrent legislative elections, an absolute majority of the seats. Even then, he was allowed to take office only after the Guatemalan military had assured themselves that he would not make any fundamental change in the political and economic organization of the country nor inhibit their pursuit of the Guatemalan guerrillas. He was, in effect, hamstrung by a virtual military veto on his actions as President.

It is worth mentioning this Guatemalan precedent because it provides a possible model for the transition of the Salvadorean political system. A civilian reformist régime closely constrained by the ever-present threat of a *coup* from the military establishment would not be anyone's ideal form of government in El Salvador, but it might be accepted as a compromise, and it might allow a progressively greater freedom of manoeuvre to a government trying to move in the direction of reducing inequality. As time went on it would be likely that the strength of demands for more radical reforms would grow, while the electoral support for the party based on the military and the entrenched élite could be expected to crumble even in the rural areas. In these circumstances, the military veto would become less effective, since a military *coup* could not easily result in a restoration of the present position, but only in an authoritarian régime operating within a polarization of political forces, as in Guatemala. Such an outcome would not be welcome to many, even within the military and civilian élite circles, except in preference to a government which took on a strongly social revolutionary rather than reformist character. In other words, even under the threat of a *coup* from the military command, as public opinion moved more strongly to the left, it would be reflected in a real rise in the power of a reformist government to move cautiously in a left direction. The test for such a gradual transition might come at the point when a party further to the left than the Christian Democrats either won or appeared likely to win an election. Then, it is likely that there would be renewed support for a preventive *coup* which would inaugurate another period of military authoritarianism.

The most unpredictable factor here, perhaps, is the strength of reformist opinion within the army officer corps itself. The attempted *coup* of 1972 gave some indication: it exists, it is strong enough for its exponents to consider they had a chance of succeeding with a *coup* at a time when conditions were favourable, but it is too weak for them actually to succeed. It is impossible to know what weight the particular circumstances of the attempted *coup* may have had. In particular, the possible weight of 'constitutional' arguments suggesting, on the one hand, that the election results had been a fraud, or, on the other, that the results announced should be respected.

For this reason, one cannot argue directly from the outcome of the attempted *coup* that a 'Peruvian' solution is impossible in El Salvador: a military *putsch* with a vigorous nationalist and reformist programme. But it does seem that opinion within the Salvadorean military is still far from the sophisticated ideology of the Peruvian officers. The policy of the military government in Peru can be seen as one of maximizing the possibilities for reform – even 'revolution from above'

– by adopting highly authoritarian, even repressive, political measures to ensure that the process does not pass out of their control into popular ferment and revolution from below, and so providing sufficient reassurance to the conservative forces. Conversely, it can be seen as one of maximizing the possibilities of authoritarian control by conceding to the radical Left many of the points of their programme, such as agrarian reform and a more neutralist international stance.[4]

This policy appears to be a viable one for the military of El Salvador too, but one which does not at the moment command sufficient support among the military. It seems much more likely in El Salvador that any concessions to the Left will be made in the form of political liberalization rather than by relaxing directly the economic repression against the majority of the population which the existing economic structure entails.

Another model whose applicability to El Salvador should obviously be discussed is that of Cuba. The prospects for rural guerrilla warfare in El Salvador are, as things now stand, very slim. No such movement could get off the ground, because the whole country is densely populated and the Salvadorean military has effectively incorporated a large proportion of the rural population throughout the country under its direct authority: to the extent that former soldiers always remain active reservists subject to the local army commanders, the rural population is in effect semi-militarized. Furthermore, the anti-communist ORDEN organization has been set up to incorporate large numbers of others on a voluntary basis. Probably, however, ORDEN is superfluous to this purpose. Even without it, the army would have little trouble in stamping out any incipient guerrilla movement. Even the small left factions which reject the economism[5] of the Salvadorean Communist Party for a revolutionary stance recognize that it is impossible to start a guerrilla campaign on the Cuban pattern now. There would have to be some disintegration of the military apparatus or else a powerful movement in neighbouring countries first. El Salvador could perhaps provide strong support in the latter stages of a general Central American revolutionary war which had first established strong bases in Guatemala and Honduras, but even such a scenario assumes a degree of international solidarity which might fail to materialize, judging by the popular reaction to the recent stresses between the countries: the Central Americanist spirit is, at least at the moment, strongest at the upper levels of Salvadorean society and weakest among the populace.

As for an urban guerrilla movement on the lines of the Uruguayan *tupamaros*, the present position is that there are almost certainly too few potential participants or active supporters to give such a movement a chance of success. It can be argued that a revolutionary consciousness is formed in struggle, particularly among the urban masses, but even the revolutionaries are now attempting to make converts first for the purpose of launching action later, and this does indeed seem the only course open to them, however ardently they agree that 'the duty of every revolutionary is to make the revolution'. The position would change if the balance of the present political system broke down and it became as polarized as in Guatemala.

There is little doubt that the balance of opinion at the upper – though not uppermost – levels of society is shifting somewhat toward the Left. Apart from international influences, and the growing realization that industrialization of the present type cannot eradicate poverty, the shift is probably due mainly to the sheer growth in the numbers of professionals and new members of the educated middle class connected with the university and with the government ministries. The growth of business has fostered also the formation of an unpoliticized, non-intellectual middle class concerned, as elsewhere, with maintaining outward signs of status on an income which is never quite enough; but at present the main political effect of the growth of the middle class seems to have been a radicalizing one.

Thus, although it is improbable that there will be a successful revolution in the near future, giving the leaders of the Left full freedom of governmental action, it does seem likely that more and more of the ideas they advocate will be put into effect sooner or later.

The first and most obvious reform of a fundamental nature would be a redistribution of land. However, there is not enough land to allow adequate family-sized plots for the whole rural population; similarly, minimum-wage legislation could only benefit a part of the population, those lucky enough to be employed. It is doubtful whether the extent of redistribution of income toward the working classes, even from quite substantial reforms, would be enough to expand demand for locally-made goods and services to the degree required to absorb the great numbers of underemployed into productive employment. It might well be found that the reforms of which so much had been hoped had in fact left the size and the distribution of the national income comparatively unchanged.

At this point more efficacious measures, such as direct government creation of employment by the foundation of state enterprises throughout the country, might well be seriously considered. At present, the need for the government to generate employment, and to do so in provincial towns as well as in the capital, is mentioned vaguely, but in the context only of public works programmes, and these could not be expected to absorb all the labour now underemployed unless they descended to unnecessary and hence essentially unproductive schemes.

Considerable opposition would be encountered against any proposals for state enterprise, but it does seem at least possible that El Salvador could pass peacefully to a social system in which private enterprise is controlled in the interest of a very much more equal distribution of income and is complemented by national and perhaps also municipal enterprise – which could restore an important place to the municipalities now that they have lost their real autonomy. It would not be necessary for the state to absorb directly the whole of the present pool of underemployment; with other redistributive measures, the income that some such employment would put into the hands of the populace would be enough to raise their demand sufficiently to provide for the expansion of agricultural and artisan production and services, and so reach full employment. Once that position had been reached, the basis would exist for further rapid growth by the application of intermediate technology to increase the productivity of the small enterprises and artisans – improvements in technology that would be easy to introduce if full employment were guaranteed. Intermediate technology has up to now received virtually no attention in El Salvador – indeed, it appears that the industrialists have had the enthusiastic help of the government in going out of their way to adopt the most advanced labour-saving methods. But if the government were to be brought to consider setting up state enterprises to absorb labour, it would necessarily have to ask itself what industrial processes were most appropriate to the abundance of labour and the relative shortage of other resources: to examine intermediate technology.

It will be noted that this prognostication has more in common with the Chilean political experience, and even with Chinese economic practice, than it has with geographically closer precedents such as Mexico or Cuba. It is based on the belief that a guerrilla campaign such as the one which completely demolished all opposing power in Cuba could not be successful in El Salvador, and the expectation that the labour-using methods struck upon by the Chinese will come to be recognized as the only ones appropriate for a country with a very great endowment of people but relatively few other resources.

The prognostication is dependent, however, on a realization among the hitherto ruling classes that their power is waning as enlightenment spreads among the population, and on their acceptance of compromise solutions in the political and economic spheres reflecting the change in the strength of political forces. If they attempt to preserve the *status quo* unmodified, then tensions are bound to grow and to lead to a long period of strife, such as has occurred in neighbouring Guatemala. One possibility which might then come up over the horizon is Salvadorean participation in a loosely-combined Central American liberation struggle,[6] involving both rural and urban guerrilla warfare in several of the countries at the same time.[7]

## NOTES

[1] I last visited El Salvador in 1970–71, and have had to rely on newspaper accounts for the details of this election and the subsequent attempted *coup*.

[2] Many of the leading participants in the *coup*, or those who joined them during the day it took place, found refuge in diplomatic missions, in accordance with the Latin American practice whereby such refugees are given safe-conducts out of the country. Thus Mejía with 3 others gained asylum in the Papal Nunciature. Napoleón Duarte, however, sought asylum in the residence of the first secretary of the Venezuelan embassy, not at the embassy itself. He was arrested there, and Venezuela issued a strong protest. According to Duarte's account, he was forcibly taken from the house, bundled into a car, blindfolded, and struck repeatedly with revolver butts; then taken for interrogation by a military officer, with interruptions during which he was again struck (*L'Information Latine*, Paris, 6 April 1972). However, he was then deposited in Guatemala on 28 March and was able to go to Venezuela on 4 April (then to Costa Rica in August). After the inauguration of President Molina in July the decision appears to have been taken not to punish the leaders of the *coup* but rather to strike against the centre of the opposition, the university (see below, note 7). On 19 July a military judge ordered the freeing of all those imprisoned for implication in the *coup*, and although this decision was appealed and a military court did meet to judge the case on 29 November 1972, only half a dozen of the accused were still prisoners in El Salvador, and these were all acquitted. So too, in their absence, were Duarte and Herrera Rebollo – the latter had been accused of implication in the *coup* by Sánchez Hernández and had not been allowed to return to El Salvador. Only two men were found guilty, and they had both reached asylum in Argentina: Colonels Mejía and Manuel Rafael Reyes, sentenced in their absence to 25 and 15 years' imprisonment respectively. One participant, however, Lieutenant Héctor Padilla, had been reported on 30 March as killed within the barracks of Sonsonate in the first days following the *coup*.

[3] See above, p. 108. General Medrano was arrested on a murder charge a few months after his dismissal, and it appeared that an attempt was being made to prevent him from presenting his candidacy; but he was released, found to have acted in self-defence in the incident in question. It is of interest that Medrano, who had always been identified with the extreme Right, adopted a nationalist and neutralist standpoint, praising for instance the régime of President Torres in Bolivia, when shortly after his dismissal he announced his intention to seek the Presidency. Interview in *El Independiente*, 22 Dec. 1970.

[4] This interpretation of the Peruvian régime is based mainly on the reports of events in that country in 1969–70 by James Petras (with Nelson Rimensnyder) in Petras: *Politics and Social Structure in Latin America* (1971: New York, MR Press) and Aníbal Quijano: 'Nationalism and capitalism in Peru: a study in neo-imperialism', *Monthly Review*, Vol. 23, No. 3 (New York, July–Aug. 1971); whole issue.

[5] i.e. the pursuit of economic gains for the working class within the capitalist system, as the main activity in which the party engages on a day-to-day basis. The groups to the left of the PCS argue that if the party members concentrate on trade union activity to win wage increases, then they are bound to lose sight of their revolutionary goals or have already done so.

[6] Roque Dalton: '*Revolución en la Revolución*' *y la Crítica de Derecha* (1970: Havana, Casa de la Américas), 83, 200.

[7] Although at his inauguration on 1 July 1972 President Molina announced that his policy would support the hitherto least favoured sections of the population, events soon afterward appeared to follow the path of increasing polarization, with the physical occupation of the university by the army and the first actions of a new

urban guerrilla organization. The Supreme Court had declared the election of the university authorities unconstitutional (the new rector was Rafael Menjívar, ex-dean of the Faculty of Economics and an authority on land reform programmes in Latin America, a former member of PAR, and advocate of the kind of reforms which formed that party's electoral platform in 1967: see above, p. 201). On 19 July the new Legislative Assembly, which had been elected in March during the turmoil following the Presidential election and whose composition is PCN 37, UNO (PDC, MNR, and UDN) 8, PPS 6, FUDI 1, an overwhelming right-wing majority, issued a decree reforming the governing statutes of the university. The same day the campus was occupied. Rafael Menjívar, Fabio Castillo, and 13 other university figures were expelled – to Nicaragua at first, but most later went to Costa Rica. Teaching and all university activity was suspended and, although Molina at first envisaged its reopening in 60 days under new management 'not as a refuge of communists or mediocre professionals', in August the government-appointed committee of professionals who were to bring this about announced that it would remain closed at least until the end of 1972. In September, the Ministry of Labour dissolved the trade union of university employees (a member union of FUSS) and 9 new exiles – university teachers and trade unionists – arrived in Nicaragua. Meanwhile, in July, the 'People's Liberation Army' carried out its first raids on commercial establishments and a radio station.

# Glossary of Spanish Terms

PAGE NUMBERS refer to pages in the text where the word is discussed at greater length.

| | |
|---|---|
| *adobe* | = large mud bricks, not fired, a building material |
| *beneficio* | = works for initial processing of coffee, cotton, etc. |
| *cacique* | = Indian chief or headman; local boss. p. 40. |
| *campesino* | = peasant or agricultural worker or poor rural person |
| *cantón* | = smallest rural administrative division, with a few hundred inhabitants |
| *caudillo* | = leader. p. 42, and p. 54, note 77. |
| *chele* | = light-skinned |
| *colono* | = agricultural worker living on the estate. pp. 117–18. |
| *colorado* | = red; political connotation Liberal, as opposed to *rojo*, also red, with proletarian or socialist connotation |
| *criollo* | = Spanish person born in colonies |
| *encomienda* | = right to receive tribute from Indians of a certain village. pp. 29–33 |
| *encomendero* | = holder of an *encomienda* |
| *finca* | = cash-crop farm smaller than 100 hectares; coffee plantation of any size |
| *gobiernista* | = supporter of the government, often just because it is the government |
| *hacienda* | = estate of over 100 hectares, not under coffee. p. 32, 138–9 |
| *hacendado* }<br>*hacendero* } | = owner of an *hacienda* |
| *ladino* | = member of the Spanish-American rather than Indian ethnic or cultural community, irrespective of ancestry. pp. 35–6 |
| *mancha brava* | = 'savage stain' – a Honduran political gang |
| *manzana* | = 1.73 acres or 0.7 hectares. City blocks in Spanish American citie sare generally exactly this size, 100 *varas* square, and the word also refers to a block |

| | |
|---|---|
| *mesón* | = a set of at least 5 rooms, each occupied by a different family, without cooking or washing facilities in the rooms; almost always the rooms are all at ground level, often around a courtyard; but *mesones* vary greatly in construction standard, space available per family, and overall size – up to over 100 rooms. pp. 118, 244–6 |
| *mestizo* | = person of mixed Spanish and Indian ancestry |
| *milpa* | = a field or plot for cultivation of maize, typically, or of sorghum or beans; such cultivation, by traditional methods using hoe and digging-stick, and ideally allowing the land to recover (shifting, slash-and-burn, or swidden agriculture); the first and main crop harvested in August–October. p. 142. |
| *oficialista* | = supporter of the official party, *gobiernista* |
| *patrón* | = owner, regarded as being by virtue of proprietorship at the head of the chain of command |
| *peñol* | = hill with steep sides; fortified hill, village |
| *peón* | = ordinary worker, regarded as at the bottom of the chain of command and of status, particularly on *fincas* and *haciendas* |
| *quintal* | = 100 *libras*, approx. = 100 lb. |
| *repartimiento* | = distribution of Indians among Spanish colonists, to work for a period on their properties. p. 33 |
| *sindicato* | = trade union |
| *tortilla* | = the basic food item: maize dough shaped to disc about 10 cm. in diameter and 5–8 mm. thick, then cooked on a flat pan over the fire, without oil. Often eaten with beans |
| *trapiche* | = sugar-cane press |

# Figures

---

## Currency

1 *colón* (₡1) = 100 *centavos* (100¢)

Since 1934, 1 *colón* = $0.40, i.e., ₡2.50 = 1 U.S. dollar

Thus, with the dollar at $2.80 to the £, ₡7 = £1

with the dollar at $2.60 to the £, ₡6.50 = £1

with the dollar at $2.40 to the £, ₡6 = £1

*Popular names for small amounts of money* (carried over from colonial Spanish currency)

3¢ = *cuis, cuartillo*
6¢ = *medio*
12¢ = *real* (12.5¢ when in multiples)
25¢ = *peseta, cuarto, 2 reales*
50¢ = *tostón*
₡1 = *peso*

## Distribution of family incomes, urban population

*As of 1963*
*Per month*

| | | | |
|---|---|---|---|
| Up to ₡120 (£17.14) | 38.9% | Up to ₡120 | 38.9% |
| ₡121 – 180 (£25.71) | 21.0% | Up to ₡180 | 59.9% |
| ₡181 – 240 (£34.29) | 10.9% | Up to ₡240 | 70.8% |
| ₡241 – 320 (£45.71) | 8.0% | Up to ₡320 | 78.8% |
| ₡321 – 400 (£57.14) | 5.7% | Up to ₡400 | 84.5% |
| ₡401 – 600 (£85.71) | 6.2% | Up to ₡600 | 90.7% |

More than ₡600 (£85.71) 9.3%

Source: CONAPLAN: *Plan de la Nación para el Desarrollo Económico y Social*, Vol. II, Cuadro XXII–11, 566.

## Minimum wage for agricultural work

Prevailing except during coffee- and cotton-picking season, Dec.–Feb.

Men: ₡2.25 per day (₡68.43 or £11.40 per month if continuously employed)

Women: ₡1.75 per day when employed.

## Population
Official estimate for 1972: 3,685,000
San Salvador: The population of San Salvador at the 1961 census
was 349,320, including 4 suburban municipalities. The growth-rate
of the capital between 1950 and 1961 was at 4.8 per cent per annum;
assuming this rate was maintained, the population estimate for 1972
would be 585,000.

## Weights and measures
Three systems are in use: the metric, which is the official one; the old
Spanish system; and more local measures.

*The Spanish system of weights*
1 *tonelada* = 20 *quintales* = 10 *cargas*
    1 *quintal* = 4 *arrobas* = 100 *libras* = 46 kilograms
        1 *arroba* = 25 *libras*
            1 *libra* = 16 *onzas*
                1 *onza* = 16 *adarmas*

*Local system of weights*
Grain: 1 *fanega* = 24 *medios* (for maize; varies a little regionally and
                for other crops, e.g., 22 *medios* for
                sorghum)
        1 *medio* = 2 *cuartillos*
1 *medio* of maize = 16.875 lb.
1 *medio* of beans = 16 lb.
(*medio* = *medio almud*, but 'almud' is seldom used)
        1 *fanega* = 4 *quintales* = 400 *libras*, most commonly
             or elsewhere = 360 *libras*

*Spanish measures of distance*
1 *legua* = 3 *millas* = 6,660 *varas* and 2 *pies*
        1 *vara* = 3 *pies* = 0.854 metres
    1 *cuadra* = 100 *varas* (the length of a city block)

*Local measures of distance*
1 *brazada* = about two yards, sometimes locally standardized but
           basically the distance between tips of outstretched arms
1 *cuarta*   = distance between the tips of the outstretched little finger
           and the outstretched thumb of one hand

*Spanish measures of area*
1 *caballería* = 64 *manzanas*
        1 *manzana* = 1 *cuadra* × 1 *cuadra* = 10,000 sq. *varas*
1 *manzana* = 1.73 acres = 0.7 hectare approx.

*Local measure of area*
1 *tarea* = variable, e.g. 1/16 *manzana*; 1/8 *manzana*; 13 *brazadas* × 13
*cuartas*

# Wars Involving Salvadorean Forces since Independence from Spain in 1821

| Date | One side | Other side | Result |
|---|---|---|---|
| March–June 1822 | Most Salvadoreans, opponents of adhesion to Mexican empire | Guatemalans, proponents of adhesion | Guatemalan attack on San Salvador repulsed |
| July 1822–Feb. 1823 | As above (led by Arce, Delgado) | As above, and Mexican army (Filísola) | Victory of Mexican-Guatemalan force |
| Jan. 1825 | Salvadorean expedition, some Nicaraguans (Granada, León) (led by Arce) | Nicaraguans (esp. cities of Managua, Rivas) | Victory of the Salvadorean force and establishment of Federal authority |
| March–Dec. 1827 | El Salvador (liberals) (led by Delgado) | Guatemala and Federal govt. (conservatives) (led by Arce) | Stalemate |
| Jan.–Oct. 1828 | El Salvador and Honduras (liberals) (led by Morazán) | As above (now led by Aycinena) | Siege of San Salvador lifted: victory of liberals in El Salvador |
| Jan.–Apr. 1829 | As above | As above | Victory of liberals in Guatemala and over Federal govt. |
| March 1832 | Federal govt., Honduras, Guatemala, Nicaragua (liberals) (led by Morazán) | El Salvador (conservatives) (led by Cornejo) | Victory of Federal govt.: capture of San Salvador |
| May–June 1832 | Federal govt., San Salvador | San Miguel (Joaquín de San Martín) | Victory of Federal govt. |
| Oct.–Dec. 1832 | Various small insurrections (incl. San Miguel again) | govt. | Put down but govt. weakened |

| Date | One side | Other side | Result |
|------|----------|------------|--------|
| Jan.–<br>Feb. 1833 | Population of Los Nonualcos, esp. Indians (Anastasio Aquino) | govt. | Rebellion put down with difficulty |
| Jan.–<br>March 1833 | Further insurrections | govt. | San Martín assumes govt. (more conservative) |
| June 1834 | Federal govt. (liberals) (Morazán) | El Salvador (San Martín) | Victory of Federal govt. Its seat is transferred to San Salvador |
| May 1837–<br>Apr. 1839 | Federal govt. and state govts. (liberals) (Morazán) | Insurrections esp. in Guatemala (Carrera, joined by some conservatives) | Victory of Carrera and breakdown of Federal authority except in El Salvador |
| March–<br>Apr. 1839 | El Salvador (liberals) (Morazán) | Honduras, Nicaragua (conservatives) | Honduran-Nicaraguan force driven out of El Salvador |
| July–<br>Aug. 1839 | As above | Guatemala (conservatives) (Carrera) | Guatemalan force driven out of El Salvador |
| Sept. 1839 | As above, some Hondurans (liberals) | Honduras, Nicaragua, some Salvadoreans (conservatives) | Stalemate |
| March–<br>May 1840 | As above (Morazán) | Guatemala (Carrera) (conservatives) | Victory of Carrera; liberals flee aboard ship |
| Feb.–<br>Sept. 1842 | Salvadorean liberals (c. 500, recruited by Morazán) | Costa Rican conservatives | Morazán briefly captures Costa Rica but is then defeated and executed |
| Feb.–<br>Aug. 1844 | Some Salvadoreans (led by Arce), Guatemala (Carrera) | Govt. of El Salvador (Malespín) (conservative) | Stalemate |
| Sept. 1844–<br>Jan. 1845 | Some Salvadoreans (liberals, with others from Honduras) (led by Barrios and Cabañas); govt. of Nicaragua | Govts. of El Salvador and Honduras (conservatives) (Malespín) | Victory of conservatives |

| Date | One side | Other side | Result |
|---|---|---|---|
| Feb.–<br>Aug. 1845 | New Salvadorean govt. (liberals) | Salvadorean conservatives (Malespín); Honduras | Stalemate |
| Nov. 1846 | Govt. (liberals) | Malespín, conservatives | Defeat and death of Malespín |
| Nov. 1850–<br>Feb. 1851 | Guatemalan liberals, El Salvador, Honduras | Guatemalan govt. (Carrera) | Victory of Carrera |
| May 1856–<br>May 1857 | Some Nicaraguans; El Salvador, Costa Rica, Guatemala, Honduras | U.S. adventurers, some Nicaraguans (William Walker) | Defeat of Walker |
| Feb.–<br>Apr. 1863 | El Salvador (liberals) (Barrios) | Guatemala (Carrera) | Stalemate; widening of war |
| Apr.–<br>Oct. 1863 | El Salvador, Honduras (liberals) (Barrios) | Guatemala, Nicaragua (Carrera) | Victory of Carrera; Barrios flees on ship |
| May 1865 | Salvadorean liberals (Cabañas) | Govt. (conservative) | Victory of govt.; Barrios captured and executed |
| March–<br>Apr. 1871 | Salvadorean liberals, Honduran govt. | Salvadorean govt. (Dueñas, conservative) | Liberal victory |
| May–<br>July 1872 | El Salvador, Guatemala (liberals) | Honduras (Medina) | Salvadorean–Guatemalan victory; Honduran govt. changed |
| Nov.–<br>Dec. 1873 | As above | Honduras (Arias) | As above (they change their nominee) |
| March–<br>Apr. 1876 | El Salvador | Guatemala | Guatemalan victory |
| March–<br>Apr. 1885 | Guatemala (Justo Rufino Barrios) | El Salvador | Guatemalan invasion force defeated; death of J. R. Barrios |
| May–<br>June 1885 | Revolt (Menéndez, with support of new Guatemalan govt.) | Govt. of Zaldívar then of Figueroa | Francisco Menéndez occupies Presidency |
| July 1890 | Guatemala; some Salvadoreans (Rivas) | El Salvador (govt. of Ezeta) | Ezeta brothers keep control of El Salvador |
| Apr.–<br>June 1894 | Revolt (Gutiérrez) | Govt. of Ezeta | Success of revolt |

| Date | One side | Other side | Result |
|------|----------|------------|--------|
| Nov. 1898 | Revolt (Regalado) | Govt. of Gutiérrez (Alfaro, Villavicencio) | Success of revolt |
| July 1906 | El Salvador (Regalado), some Guatemalans | Guatemalan govt. (Estrada Cabrera) | Stalemate; peace signed with pressure of U.S.A. and Mexico; Death of Regalado |
| March 1907 | Some Hondurans, Nicaraguan govt. (Zelaya), some Salvadoreans (Rivas and Alfaro) | Govt of Honduras (Bonilla); govt. of El Salvador (Figueroa) | Stalemate; third party (Dávila) made President of Honduras |
| June 1907 | Revolt (Rivas and Alfaro) | Govt. of Figueroa | Failure of revolt |
| Jan. 1932 | Poor people of small towns and countryside, western El Salvador (Communist leaders) | Govt. of Hernández Martínez | Failure of uprising; massacre of suspected participants |
| Dec. 1944 | Revolt (Romero) (Jornada de Ahuachapán) | Govt. of Aguirre y Salinas | Failure of revolt |
| July 1969 | El Salvador | Honduras | Advance of Salvadorean forces into Honduras halted after 5 days through diplomatic pressure; then troops withdrawn |

Note: Many of the entries are simplified for the sake of brevity. *Coups d'état* are not included even if there was some fighting within the capital; the 'revolts' mentioned involved fighting outside the capital. Many nineteenth-century revolts and minor insurrections which ended in failure are not included; they appear to have been particularly frequent in the years 1829–35, 1840–46, 1858–62, 1875–79, 1886–90.
   Main source of information: Coronel Gregorio Bustamante Maceo: *Historia Militar de El Salvador*, 2a. edición (1951: San Salvador, Ministerio del Interior).

# Bibliography

Two studies devoted to El Salvador in English can be recommended:
Browning, David: *El Salvador, Landscape and Society* (1971: Oxford,
Clarendon Press). Though meticulous in its scholarship, being
originally written as a doctoral dissertation in (historical) geography for Oxford University, this book is fully accessible and
interesting to the non-geographer.
Anderson, Thomas P.: *Matanza, El Salvador's Communist Revolt of 1932*
(1971: Lincoln, Nebraska, Univ. of Nebraska Press).

In Spanish, the most vivid impression of life in El Salvador during
the twentieth century is given in:
Dalton, Roque: *Miguel Mármol, Testimonio Político-Autobiográfico.* This
work, written by a gifted Salvadorean writer now resident in Cuba,
is in the form of a shadow autobiography of the old working-class
militant Mármol, who survived the bullets of a firing squad in the
mass executions of 1932 and is still living. It is, I understand, to be
published in Cuba and also in translation in Italy.

Of earlier works in English, the most interesting is:
Martin, Percy F.: *Salvador of the Twentieth Century* (1911: London,
Edward Arnold). Martin's interest centred on economic and commercial matters; he also covers military and political affairs and
gives a description of each town.

For ethnography, see the section devoted to El Salvador in:
Adams, Richard N.: *Cultural surveys of Panama – Nicaragua – Guatemala
– El Salvador – Honduras* (1957: Washington, Pan American
Sanitary Bureau).

and in Spanish:
Marroquín, Alejandro Dagoberto: *Panchimalco, Investigación Sociológica*
(1959: San Salvador, Editorial Universitaria).

For economics, a very different view from mine can be found in:
Raynolds, David R.: *Rapid Development in Small Economies, the example
of El Salvador* (1967: New York, Praeger).

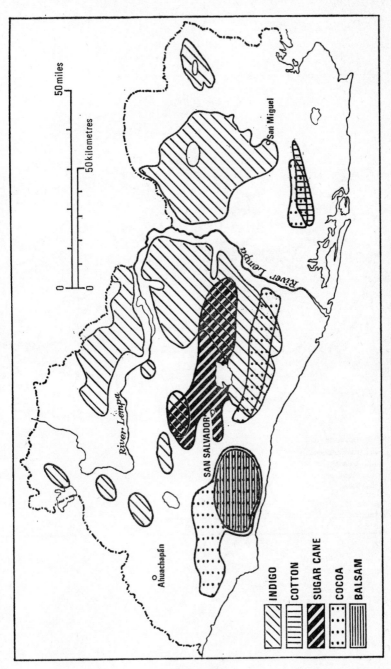

El Salvador—main resources *c.* 1770

INDIGO

COTTON

SUGAR CANE

COCOA

BALSAM

San Miguel

San Salvador

Ahuachapán

River Lempa

River Lempa

50 miles

50 kilometres

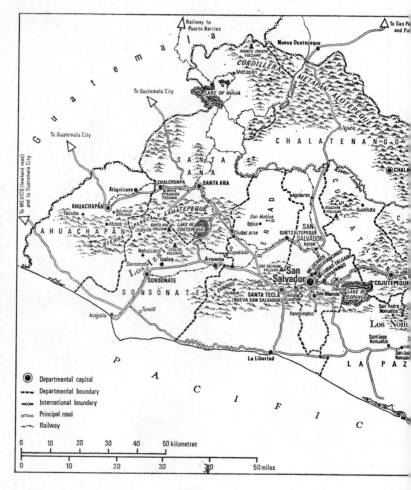

El Salvad

al map

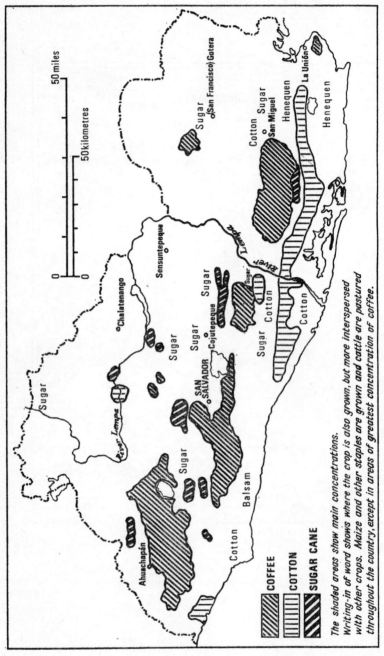

The shaded areas show main concentrations.
Writing-in of word shows where the crop is also grown, but more interspersed
with other crops. Maize and other staples are grown and cattle are pastured
throughout the country, except in areas of greatest concentration of coffee.

COFFEE

COTTON

SUGAR CANE

El Salvador—main resources late twentieth century

# Index

Printed in Great Britain
by W & J Mackay Limited, Chatham